INCLUSIVE TEACHIN
CHILDHOOD SCIENCE CLASSROOM

Focused on engaging all students, *Inclusive Teaching in the Early Childhood Science Classroom* walks readers through the process of planning, developing, and implementing science instruction for early learners. Drawing on a range of pedagogical processes and approaches, this comprehensive text links science to other disciplines and explores how we develop language, social-emotional, and content learning through early childhood science. Each chapter is framed around an essential question and features success criteria and reflection tasks to guide readers through the content. Aligned with the Next Generation Science Standards and addressing the Interstate New Teacher Assessment and Support Consortium Model Core Teaching Standards, this textbook is critical reading for preservice teacher education students enrolled in an inclusive early childhood or early childhood science methods course.

John T. Almarode is Associate Professor of Education at James Madison University, USA.

INCLUSIVE TEACHING IN THE EARLY CHILDHOOD SCIENCE CLASSROOM

John T. Almarode
with Katy Campbell and Cheryl Lamb

NEW YORK AND LONDON

First published 2021
by Routledge
52 Vanderbilt Avenue, New York, NY 10017

and by Routledge
2 Park Square, Milton Park, Abingdon, Oxon, OX14 4RN

Routledge is an imprint of the Taylor & Francis Group, an informa business

Library of Congress Cataloging-in-Publication Data
Names: Almarode, John, author.
Title: Inclusive teaching in the early childhood science classroom / John T. Almarode.
Description: New York, NY : Routledge, 2021. | Includes bibliographical references and index.
Identifiers: LCCN 2020044944 (print) | LCCN 2020044945 (ebook) | ISBN 9780367197896 (hardback) | ISBN 9780367197926 (paperback) | ISBN 9780429243295 (ebook)
Subjects: LCSH: Science—Study and teaching (Early childhood) | Inclusive education.
Classification: LCC LB1139.5.S35 A56 2021 (print) | LCC LB1139.5.S35 (ebook) | DDC 371.9/046—dc23
LC record available at https://lccn.loc.gov/2020044944
LC ebook record available at https://lccn.loc.gov/2020044945

ISBN: 978-0-367-19789-6 (hbk)
ISBN: 978-0-367-19792-6 (pbk)
ISBN: 978-0-429-24329-5 (ebk)

Typeset in Insterstate
by SPi Global, India

Access the Support Material: www.routledge.com/9780367197926

CONTENTS

CONTRIBUTORS

John T. Almarode has worked with schools, classrooms, and teachers all over the world. John began his teaching career in Augusta County. Since then, he has presented locally, nationally, and internationally on the application of the science of learning to schools and classrooms. He has worked with hundreds of school districts and thousands of teachers. In addition to his time in PreK-12 schools and classrooms, he is an associate professor and executive director of teaching and learning in the College of Education at James Madison University (JMU). At JMU, he works with preservice teachers and actively pursues his research interests, including the science of learning and the design and measurement of classroom environments that promote student engagement and learning. John and his colleagues have presented their work to the US Congress, the US Department of Education, as well as the Office of Science and Technology Policy at the White House. John has authored multiple articles, reports, book chapters, and more than a dozen books on effective teaching and learning in today's schools and classrooms. However, what really sustains John and is his greatest accomplishment is his family. John lives in Waynesboro, Virginia, with his wife Danielle, a fellow educator; their two children, Tessa and Jackson; and Labrador retrievers, Angel, Bella, and Dukes.

John can be reached at almarojt@jmu.edu or through Twitter: @jtalmarode.

Katy Campbell is a teacher in Hanover County Public Schools. She has taught both fifth grade and first grade over the last seven years. She is passionate about inspiring a love of learning in her students through STEM and hands-on science experiences as well as through reading and literacy. Her greatest joy and motivation to continue growing as a teacher is watching her toddler become a learner as he explores the world around him. Katy lives in Mechanicsville, Virginia with her husband and fellow educator, Russ; their son, Rowan; and their service dog, Paxton.

Cheryl Lamb Is a recently retired early childhood educator. She was the lead pre-k teacher at Orange County Public Schools Head Start Program for over thirty years. She has spent her teaching career incorporating science into all areas of childhood development and engaging students with hands-on everyday experiences relevant to their world. Her greatest passion as a teacher has been helping young learners build a strong foundation that will lead to a lifelong love of learning and contribute to future success. Cheryl lives in Orange, Virginia with her husband, Kevin; their son, William; and their dog, Alora Lou.

Introduction

This is a book about the teaching and learning of science. Not only about teaching and learning science in general but also about a group of young learners, preschool to grade 3, who arrive in our schools and classrooms across the globe with their own experiences and ideas about how the world works.

These experiences and ideas are shaped by their home environments, parents/guardians, friends, interests, and prior knowledge. Each learner enters our classroom with their own personal abilities and interests. Therefore, each young learner who passes through the frame of your door brings their own dispositions, characteristics, and perspectives to the teaching and learning in your inclusive early childhood science classroom. At the same time, each young learner represents potential - potential learning opportunities in knowing and understanding how the world works. Our role is to work alongside these young learners to activate, guide, and support the actualization of this potential.

Five Major Areas of Teaching and Learning Science

So, let's return to the opening sentence of this introduction - this book is about the teaching and learning of science. The teaching and learning of science involve a careful look at five major areas that can be represented by the familiar five question words: why, what, how, who, and when.

1. Why should we teach science, and why should students learn science in the early childhood classroom?
2. What do we teach, and what are they expected to know, understand, and be able to do?
3. How do we teach science, and how do our students learn science?
4. Who are we as teachers, and who are the learners in our classrooms?
5. When do we teach science, and when is it best to engage our students in science learning?

These five major areas are not intended to be sequential, addressing one area before moving into another. Instead, these five areas, represented by these five questions, are interwoven into the execution of effective teaching and learning in inclusive early childhood science. Let's eavesdrop on a pre-kindergarten class to see these five major areas in action.

Figure 0.1 Jackson feeding a rabbit.
Credit: Author.

Meet Jackson. Jackson is a preschooler in Ms. Roger's classroom where, today, they are engaging in *science*. Standing at his table with two of his classmates, each in their own youth-sized laboratory coats and safety goggles, they carefully count out loud 20 drops of food coloring as they drop into a plastic test tube filled with vegetable oil. One of his peers keeps count.

"1, 2, 3,...20. That's enough. We're done."

Ms. Rogers asks them, as well as the other young learners in her classroom, to make observations.

"Girls and boys, let's make some observations. What do you see happening as you drop the food coloring into the test tube?"

As they share their thinking out loud, she records their observations next to the letter *S* on poster paper placed in front of the room.

Prior to the start of the science block, Ms. Rogers prepared a larger poster paper with three letters down the left side.

The *S* stands for *see* and provides a place for her to record the observations of her young learners. What they observe or notice can be documented for everyone to see. At the same time, with each "I see" comment from her learners, Ms. Rogers can provide immediate and just-in-time feedback to her learners. We will talk more about that later. Returning to the chart, the *T* stands for *think*. As we will see in a moment, this is where Ms. Rogers will document students' ideas about the phenomenon they are investigating today. She wants to visually represent learners' ideas about this investigation as a formative assessment of the learners' background knowledge. Finally, the *W* stands for *wonder* - a place for learners to record their own questions about this specific phenomenon.

These *wonders* springboard her class into their own investigation of sinking and floating that requires them to engage in multiple science stations throughout the classroom. One station is designed for learners to experiment with a variety of objects to identify the characteristics of objects that float and objects that sink. Another station is a literacy-rich station that offers learners the opportunity to read and write about sinking and floating. Filled with a variety of picture books and print books, Ms. Rogers's young learners interact with a variety of images and words as they work on emergent literacy skills (i.e., letter recognition, phonological awareness, word recognition). There is a station that links mathematics to sinking and floating that has learners graph data related to how many pennies a container can hold before it sinks - not to mention an art station as well. The final culminating task requires that learners design and construct their own objects and test to see if they sink or float. As you might suspect, learners will get to make revisions and adjustments to their design (e.g., repeated trials). And this all started with food coloring and vegetable oil.

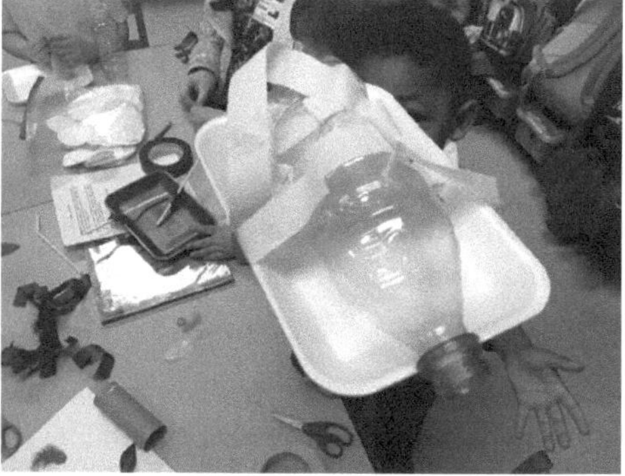

Figure 0.2 Student-designed and created object for sinking or floating test.
Credit: Author.

For Ms. Rogers, these learning experiences each have a very specific purpose that is targeted toward very specific academic, behavioral, and social-emotional learning outcomes.

Besides having a strong belief that teaching science in the early childhood classroom is important, Ms. Rogers has a clear focus on what her learners must know, understand, and be able to do as a result of this learning experience (Bell, 2005):

- For an object to float, there must be a balance between the weight of the object and the upward push of the water on the object.
- The amount of material and the type of material affect the weight of the object.
- The volume of the object can be changed by adjusting the shape of the object.
- The volume of the object affects the upward push of the water on the object.

From this vantage point, she has designed and implemented a learning experience that leverages instructional approaches that have been demonstrated through research to work best in the teaching and learning of science. Selecting instructional approaches that have the highest probability to accelerate student learning in science is important. Each of the instructional approaches is integrated across multiple content areas, sending a strong message that science is connected to other content areas and is valuable all of the time, not just during a set block of time. What Ms. Rogers also factors into the teaching and learning of science for Jackson and his classmates are the dispositions, characteristics, perspectives, and potential learning opportunities to the classroom. Ms. Rogers makes decisions about the learning experiences as a whole group, and then at each station, she pivots on who her learners are and how that drives inclusive early childhood science teaching and learning.

Our Purpose

This brief look into Ms. Rogers's classroom demonstrates the major areas of why, what, how, who, and when. This brings us to the purpose of this book. This book is designed to support your journey toward high-quality, high-impact teaching and learning in the inclusive early childhood science classroom. Whether you are currently teaching and expanding your knowledge base or making progress toward your first teaching position, the contents of these pages seek to add to your pedagogical content knowledge so that you can meet each young learner who passes through the frame of your door and leverage his or her dispositions, characteristics, and perspectives in the teaching and learning in your inclusive early childhood science classroom so that you can also see each young learner's potential and activate, guide, and support the actualization of his or her potential.

The *learning intention* for this book is to

> **understand what defines effective inclusive early childhood science teaching and learning and implement effective inclusive early childhood science instruction in the PreK-3 classroom.**

Over the next several chapters, we will unpack these five major areas with the overall goal of translating them into the implementation of high-quality, high-impact teaching and learning in the inclusive early childhood science classroom. Let's review each of those five areas and how they will be specifically addressed in the subsequent chapters – keep in mind that these are not to be treated as a sequential recipe or checklist but an interconnected way of thinking about teaching and learning in the inclusive early childhood science classroom.

1. *Why should we teach science, and why should students learn science in the early childhood classroom?* The teaching and learning of science in the early childhood classroom are important and should not be postponed to later years. Early experiences in science are correlated with later outcomes in student growth and achievement. The assumption that young learners have access and exposure to science in the early childhood classroom is not valid. Pianta et al. (2007) found that only 11% of the time in a fifth-grade classroom was allotted for science teaching and learning. Given that 17% of the time in fifth grade was set aside for instructing students on managing materials and time, 11% for science is very small. This reduced time allotted for science is likely prevalent in the early childhood classroom as well. How do science content, skills, and understandings provide a foundation for later growth and learning across academic, behavioral, and social-emotional outcomes? We will explore the *why* in Chapter 1 and then weave this purpose throughout the rest of the book.
2. *What do we teach, and what are our learners expected to know, understand, and be able to do?* To have high-quality, high-impact teaching and learning, we have to have a clear understanding of what success looks like. What exactly do we expect our students to learn? This particular area lays the foundation for all subsequent decisions about teaching and learning. High-quality, high-impact teaching requires purposeful, intentional, and deliberate decisions. These decisions must be based on where we are headed in our classrooms. Without having clarity around the academic, behavioral, and social-emotional learning outcomes, we cannot make informed decisions about how to teach or how our students will learn (see Almarode & Vandas, 2019). We cannot create inclusive access and opportunity for that learning because we will have no way to determine where our students are in their learning journey. Chapter 2 will provide a process for addressing this question so that our decisions about how, who, and when will move learning toward the targeted outcomes - what we expect them to know, understand, and be able to do.
3. *How do we teach science, and how do our students learn science?* There are several chapters for addressing the area of implementation. Knowing what to teach is very different from knowing how to teach it. Chapters 3-7 will look at different aspects of implementation, including preassessment, making learning visible to students, selecting the right level of challenge, and selecting the best approach for moving science learning forward. There is an ever-growing body of research on evidence-based practices. As teachers, how do we discern which strategy, approach, or intervention to use at what time? As we develop clarity around the academic, behavioral, and social-emotional learning outcomes, we must also deliberately implement the specific strategies, approaches, and interventions in such a way that our learners will engage in the content and skills (see Almarode et al., 2018). At the conclusion of this set of chapters, we want to know how we successfully match evidence-based practices with our targeted outcomes.
4. *Who are we as teachers, and who are the learners in our classrooms?* This area of science teaching and learning is tightly connected to our *how*. Knowing who we are as teachers, and who our students are as learners, allows us to provide an inclusive environment that offers equity of access and opportunity to learn. This requires that we assess. Assessment plays a vital role in teaching and learning when the assessments generate information about us and our learners. Specifically, when we use assessment of learning, assessment for learning,

and assessment as learning, we can better monitor the learning journey toward the targeted outcomes and make in-the-moment or just-in-time adjustments to how we are teaching and how are students are learning (Earl, 2003). Chapter 8 looks at the *who* by exploring how we must measure our effect on student learning while at the same time evaluating our students learning progress toward academic, behavioral, and social-emotional outcomes.

5. *When do we teach science, and when is it best to engage our students in science learning?* The final area seeks to broaden our view of when science teaching and learning take place. In the closing chapter of this book, we will explore the integration of science content across other disciplines within the walls of the school. Then we will take a look at how to expand this learning beyond the traditional school day and outside of the walls of the classroom. Out-of-school-time science provides opportunities for our young learners to engage in authentic science experiences that help them develop skills and understandings about how the world works by engaging with the world as it works. How do we collaborate with parents, guardians, and other valuable resources to extend the hours and the walls of our early childhood classrooms?

What This Book Is Not

We do not want to strike a negative tone this early in the book. However, we do believe it is important to ensure that expectations are clear both about our purpose together and what is beyond the scope of this book. As we stated in the opening sentence, this is a book about the teaching and learning of science in the inclusive early childhood science classroom. Although the areas of child development, play pedagogy, health and medical aspects of early childhood, delivery services, early intervention, special education, and educational philosophy are essential and non-negotiable aspects of our passion, those disciplines are beyond the scope of this book. To produce a text that comprehensively incorporates each of the aforementioned areas would result in a book that would exceed the reading capacity of any individual and certainly exceeds our expertise. Furthermore, these areas are essential and non-negotiable because of the contributions of world-renowned thinkers and practitioners who are the top scholars in those fields. Thus, we leave that to them. This book represents one small piece of the bigger picture of inclusive early childhood education. Therefore, we will stick to the science. There will be here many references and connections to those specialized areas of inclusive early childhood education and how the teaching and learning of science is a part of this highly complex and integrated environment. For example, child development matters, and we will point out where that body of work informs decisions about teaching and learning science. Special education, delivery services, and medical and health aspects of inclusive early childhood education inform our decisions as well. Again, we point that out but rely on experts in those fields to provide a focused and comprehensive treatment of those areas. Our focus is to bring those areas into the teaching and learning of science in the inclusive early childhood classroom. High-quality, high-impact teaching and learning in the inclusive early childhood science classroom require it.

Our Criteria for Success

By the end of this book, you will be one step closer to planning, designing, and implementing high-quality, high-impact teaching and learning in the inclusive early childhood science classroom. To monitor our own learning journey and model the why, what, how, who, and when in our own learning, the following success criteria lay out exactly what comes from your active engagement with each of the aforementioned five major areas. By the end of this book, you will be able to make the following statements:

I can explain the way in which children's cognitive development and the individual child's experiences and capabilities affect science teaching and learning.

I can demonstrate knowledge of the Next Generation Science Standards (NGSS) for pre-K to third grade.

I can match evidence-based practices to the teaching and learning of specific NGSS for pre-K to third grade.

I can create the essential aspects of an inclusive environment for science learning.

I can select, develop, and organize activities that foster attitude, process, and concept development in appropriate science areas.

I can demonstrate effective educational decision making regarding teaching inclusive early childhood science in pre-K to third grade.

I can integrate science content into other content areas.

I can design assessments for the monitoring of student progress.

I can identify and use available professional resources that are appropriate for teaching and learning science in pre-K to third grade.

What to Expect in This Book

Learning is an active process. As we begin to dive into each of the major areas and topics in this book, which we are almost ready to do, here are a few features that will support the journey.

- *Professional Learning Tasks:* Throughout the pages of this book, there will be opportunities to stop reading and engage in the deliberate practice of things presented in the chapter. For example, as we unpack what we want our learners to know, understand, and be able to do, you will be encouraged to stop and go through the process on your own. Look for these callout boxes throughout the book.
- *Research-to-Classroom Practice Tasks*: We will explore various strategies, approaches, and interventions for moving learning forward. Beyond the vignettes and examples in the text, you will be encouraged to take the various strategies, approaches, and interventions and adjust them for the learners in your specific context. This is to support you in translating research into practice.
- *Opportunities for Reflective Practices*: Reflectively thinking about your future classroom will help enhance your own learning. There will be times over the next several chapters where we will pause and reflect on our own views of teaching and learning and how the topics in this book align or challenge those views.

- *Moving to Implementation:* Beyond the "Professional Learning Tasks," there are several opportunities at the end of each chapter that move you closer to implementation. Whether identifying community resources, completing an assignment analysis, or taking a deeper dive into unpacking what learners need to know, understand, and be able to do, these *moving to implementation* tasks are more rigorous opportunities to practice.
- *Engaging the Family and Community:* The power of engaging families or other role models outside of the classroom cannot be overstated. With that in mind, we will close each chapter with ideas for engaging the family and the community in the teaching and learning in your inclusive early childhood science classroom.

With all that being said, let's get started!

1 The Role of the Teacher in Inclusive Early Childhood Science Teaching and Learning

As teachers of young children, we play a pivotal role in how students approach, engage, and come to understand science. This role is wrapped up in our beliefs about what science is or is not, why all young children should learn science, our beliefs or mindsets about science teaching and learning, and, lastly, what makes a "good science learner" in our schools and classrooms. In this chapter, we will unpack each of these through the lens of Ms. Campbell and her first-grade students.

> **Opportunities for Reflective Practices**
>
> Before reading on, what do you think the role of the teacher is in inclusive early childhood science teaching and learning?

On Tuesday morning, Katy Campbell's first-grade learners begin their day by joining her on the carpet to participate in a read-aloud. Today's book, *Moja Means One* by Muriel Feelings, not only allows her learners to get a glimpse of East African culture but also provides a context for the use of Kalimbas, an African thumb piano made of thin pieces of metal of different lengths attached to a wooden block.

While engaged in the read-aloud, Ms. Campbell strategically asks her learners text-dependent questions. For example, she asks them to think about the setting of the book. "Boys and girls, why is the setting important in understanding this book?" Or, "Who can tell me what a kalimba is?" She also incorporates text-independent questions, such as "How do you think a kalimba works?" As you might have guessed, her learners enthusiastically raise their hands to share their ideas about how a kalimba works. After Ms. Campbell uses their responses as a way to preassess her learners' understanding of sound, she introduces the day's driving question: How can we, as musicians, create a variety of sounds with our instruments? (Figure 1.1)

From there, learners gather in their science learning communities (see Fisher, Frey, & Almarode, 2020) to move through multiple learning centers that provide them with different opportunities to "create a variety of sounds with instruments."

Center 1: Xylophones

5 different length metal tubes on a piece of ridged foam and a small wooden mallet form the xylophone for this rotation. Students use the mallet to explore how the length of the tube relates to the pitch. A longer tube has a lower pitch compared to a shorter tube. Journal questions for this rotation are: How are the bars different? How did the bars sound different?

Center 2: Kalimbas

Kalimbas are African thumb pianos made of thin pieces of metal of different lengths held onto a wooden block. When flicked with the thumb, they vibrate producing sound. Based on the length of the metal strip, different pitches of sound are created. Journal questions for this rotation are: How are the bars different? How did the bars sound different?

Center 3: Rubber Band Guitar

3 different thicknesses of rubber bands wrapped around a plastic storage container or metal loaf pan form a makeshift guitar. When plucked, the bands vibrate and produce different pitches of sound. The thicker the band, the lower the pitch. Journal questions for this rotation are: How are the bands different? How did the bands sound different?

Center 4: Cans

Students can make sounds whatever ways they want using a popsicle stick and metal can. For example, they can bang the stick on the bottom or sides of the can, run the stick up and down the ridges of the can, or rattle it around the inside of the can. The journal page for this rotation had a space for students to draw or write how they made sounds with the can.

Center 5: What Makes the Sound?

Place objects in small containers and number the bottoms. Be sure students cannot see what is inside the containers. Students shake the containers and guess what objects are inside. The journal page for this station had a table with pictures of the 6 objects in the canisters. Students wrote the number on the canister next to their guess of what it contained.

Figure 1.1 Descriptions of the Learning Centers That Will Engage Learners in Developing Their Answers to the Day's Driving Question.

Source: Katy Campbell, first-grade teacher, Hanover County Public Schools, Virginia.

We will return to the rest of the day's learning as we move through the chapter. But for now, let's spend just a few moments on Ms. Campbell's decision to use a driving question, as this specific aspect of her teaching will provide the context of this chapter. Driving questions engage students by focusing on the *why* of the learning behind the *what* (Pijanowski, 2018). For example, the *what* in Ms. Campbell's classroom is that moving objects exhibit different kinds of motion; objects may vibrate and produce sound. Her decision to use a driving question in her science teaching is deliberate, purposeful, and intentional. Ms. Campbell could just as easily have presented a traditional objective (e.g., The student will...) on the interactive whiteboard or written the topic on poster paper. She could also have posed what is often called an essential question that asked her learners, "What is sound?" However, using a driving question as the lead-in to today's learning reflects the context of this chapter and focuses our attention on the role of the teacher in inclusive early childhood science teaching and learning. Table 1.1 contains a side-by-side comparison of objectives, essential questions, and driving questions.

Table 1.1 A Comparison of Objectives, Essential Questions, and Driving Questions in Science

Objective	*Essential Question*	*Driving Question*
The student will understand that moving objects vibrate and produce sound.	What is sound?	How can I, as a musician, create a variety of sounds with my instruments?
The student will understand the impact of humans on the environment.	How do humans impact the environment?	How can I, as a good citizen, encourage others to take care of our environment?
The student will understand how parents help their offspring survive.	How do parents interact with their environment?	How can I, as a scientist, figure out how animals communicate with their young?
The student will understand how matter changes.	How does heating and cooling change matter?	How can I, as a chef, explain the role of the heat in preparing a meal?

Source: Adapted from Pijanowski, L. (2018). *Architects of deeper learning. Intentional design for high-impact instruction.* Rexford, NY: International Center for Leadership in Education, Inc.

Research to Classroom Practice Tasks

Take some time and develop learning objectives, essential questions, and driving questions for a science topic or content.

Considering each of the previous examples, there is a clear difference between simply providing an objective and starting with an essential question. In both of those instances, teachers and learners could quickly drift into a quest for copious facts or the accumulation of content.

However, science is more than just facts, and we want our learners to be more than just walking encyclopedias of science trivia. Although there is a time and place for both an objective and essential question, Ms. Campbell's decision to use a driving question leverages her learners' interests and motivates their learning to include the content, the processes of science, and the unique ways of knowing in science (e.g., evidence).

Opportunities for Reflective Practices

What is the difference between a driving question and an essential question and objective? When is one better than the other? When might you use one over the other?

This brings us to the main focus of this chapter. What exactly is science, and what role do we as teachers play in the inclusive early childhood science teaching and learning?

Ms. Campbell's decision making around how to initially engage her learners in the concept of sound reflects her beliefs about what science is, why her learners should engage in the learning of science, and her understanding and expectations of who they are as learners. Let's look at each one of these beliefs, starting with what science is and is not.

Definition of Science

For many of our learners, and us if we are completely honest, science is viewed as a collection of facts and figures. There are nine planets. Wait, now eight planets. The parts of a plant include the roots, stem, and leaves. Living things need water, air, and nutrients. There is no such thing as centrifugal force. Returning to Ms. Campbell's classroom, these facts are easy to pull out of the day's learning, as sound, vibrations, compressions, wavelength, frequency, and amplitude are well-defined and understood terms in science. There must be more - and there is more to science than facts. Bell (2008) articulates a three-point definition of science that, when applied to our teaching and learning, moves us beyond a list of facts. He defines science as a body of knowledge, a set of processes, and a way of knowing.

The body of knowledge includes the science. For Ms. Campbell, the body of knowledge is clear. She strives for her learners to know and understand the developmentally appropriate content associated with sound, vibrations, compressions, wavelength, frequency, and amplitude. These are the laws, principles, and ideas she expects her learners to know and understand. However, she also recognizes that the body of science knowledge is built through a set of processes (see Table 1.2). In other words, doing science builds, or even refines, that body of knowledge.

For Ms. Campbell's learners, as indicated by the driving question, they will be engaged in the body of knowledge around science, as well as the processes associated with that knowledge. Her learners will observe, communicate, hypothesize, infer, experiment, analyze, evaluate, and model this body of knowledge during this learning experience.

Finally, the discipline of science is associated with a distinct way of knowing. The accumulation of knowledge through the application of a set of processes comes from the accumulation of empirical evidence. In general, scientists assume that we can better understand our world and that the current knowledge about how the world works is tentative and does not represent absolute truth. Thus science, as a way of knowing, involves the use of empirical evidence generated from experiments that can be replicated by other scientists to see if the body of knowledge withstands continued inquiry - not assumptions.

Table 1.2 Processes of Science

Observing
Classifying and Sequencing
Communicating
Measuring
Predicting
Hypothesizing
Inferring
Experimenting
Interpreting
Analyzing
Evaluating
Modeling

Source: Adapted from Virginia Department of Education (VDOE). (2012). *Practices for science investigation: Kindergarten-physics progression*. Richmond, VA: Author.

For young children, this is a different way of thinking. For example, when a five-year-old comes up with a hypothesis that "doggies are nice", he or she will naturally seek evidence to confirm his or her belief. This is evidenced by the learner's use of phrases like, "See, I told you doggies were nice." Or, "Let me show you my dog." However, only looking for confirming evidence will likely lead to the development of misconceptions, as the child is only focused on confirming his or her hypothesis. Not to mention the fact that the young child would likely only be allowed around "doggies that are nice." The way we know something in science is not from seeking evidence that confirms our hypotheses but attempting to verify them through replication. In other words, we use the processes of science to test and see if our hypothesis holds up to repeating experiments across multiple contexts and time. In our example, the child would demonstrate this way of knowing by purposefully seeking a dog that does not align with his or her hypothesis.

Opportunities for Reflective Practices

Compare and contrast this definition of science with the one you had in your own mind prior to reading this section.

In the end, the replication of scientific experiments, through the use of scientific processes, builds the current body of knowledge. Returning to Ms. Campbell's classroom and her use of a driving question, we see that her decision reflects all three aspects of science. When her first graders approach, tackle, and address the driving question, they will accomplish the following:

- Apply the processes of observing, communicating, hypothesizing, inferring, experimenting, analyzing, evaluating, and modeling
- Have multiple opportunities to verify their hypotheses through replication
- Build their body of knowledge about sound, vibrations, compressions, wavelength, frequency, and amplitude

Yes, Ms. Campbell is an exceptional teacher, and even in this brief visit to her classroom, you have likely noticed the time and attention she gives to her teaching and her students' learning. What she does each and every day is the result of her beliefs about why her learners should engage in the learning of science and her beliefs about science teaching and learning.

Why We Teach, and Why All Young Children Should Learn Science

Science learning provides many benefits to learners above and beyond developing their understanding of how the world works. For many of us, learning about cells, plants, animals, chemical reactions, forces, stars, and galaxies is benefit enough in our interconnected and ever-complex world. However, the teaching and learning of science provide benefits beyond the core content, skills, and understandings of the discipline. These are as follows:

- supporting the development of problem-solving skills, critical thinking, higher-order thinking, and reasoning in young children;
- enhancing the language development in young children; and
- increasing interest and persistence in science.

Problem-Solving, Critical Thinking, Higher-Order Thinking, and Reasoning. Much attention has been given to the development of 21st-century skills or what is more commonly called the profile of a graduate (Battelle for Kids, 2020). There are many variations of these skills based on how schools around the globe assimilate them into their own visions for their learners (see Battelle for Kids, 2020). At the root of each variation of each profile are four skills, often referred to as the 4Cs: critical thinking, communication, creativity, and collaboration. Yes, our focus is on inclusive in early childhood science, but research has strongly indicated that the foundational learning with our youngest students lays the foundation for subsequent growth and development (e.g., Samarapungavan, 1992; Schulz & Bonawitz, 2007; Sodian, Zaitchik, & Carey, 1991). In other words, it is never too early to begin working on the 4Cs, and science provides the ideal context for this start.

Science teaching and learning in the inclusive early childhood classroom contributes to the building of problem-solving skills (see Rahayu & Tytler, 1999). When learners engage in the processes of science within the context of authentic interactions with scientific phenomena, they begin to develop and apply problem-solving skills (e.g., Tytler & Peterson, 2003). In addition to critical thinking, young learners develop processes of higher-order thinking and reasoning (Gelman & Brenneman, 2004; Stein & McRobbie, 1997). For teachers like Ms. Campbell, science is a valued part of the day, as well as a vehicle for scaffolding and enhancing the level of thinking in her first graders. She recognizes that the progression of thinking in her learners requires that they not only learn about higher-order thinking skills (e.g., predicting, inferring, analyzing) but also have multiple opportunities to practice these thinking skills within the context of authentic content. For first graders, the opportunity to experiment with musical instruments is a way to scaffold and support their problem-solving skills, higher-order thinking, and reasoning. Not to mention, the intentional, purposeful, and deliberate decisions of Ms. Campbell offer learners the opportunity to be creative and collaborate with their peers. In the end, science experiences from the earliest grades are essential for developing processes of thinking.

Language Development. Communication, both as one of the 4Cs and as an essential part of student learning, requires that learners effectively exchange ideas. For young children, oral language development lies at the heart of the effective exchange of ideas. Science teaching and learning enhance the vocabulary of learners by putting words into context and creating opportunities for learners to engage in academic discourse around science phenomena. This academic discourse will use three tiers or types of academic vocabulary (Beck, McKeown, & Kucan, 2013):

Tier 1 Vocabulary – These are words or terms that are used in everyday life and are common in spoken language. In many cases, this vocabulary is built through conversation. For Ms. Campbell, examples of Tier 1 vocabulary include notebook, book, happy, walk, animal, red, teacher, door, school, and room.

Tier 2 Vocabulary – This cluster of terms are academic vocabulary that cross multiple subject areas. For example, the processes of science (e.g., predict, infer, analyze, evaluate). Students need to know and understand these terms, as they will be part of their learning experience across all content areas and outside of the classroom.

Tier 3 Vocabulary – This set of words includes terms that are domain specific. This means that these terms mean something within the context of science, for example, and are key to understanding specific concepts in science. Examples of these words in Ms. Campbell's classroom include sound, vibrations, compressions, wavelength, frequency, and amplitude.

Through the planning, designing, and implementing of high-quality, high-impact teaching and learning in the inclusive early childhood science classroom, we foster the effective exchange of ideas through academic discourse that helps learners build their Tier 1, Tier 2, and Tier 3 vocabulary. Science provides a context for oral language development that is foundational for growth in reading and writing. As our young learners develop their writing skills, the combination of academic discourse and academic writing further enhances academic vocabulary (see Graham, Kiuhara, & MacKay, 2020).

Interest and Persistence. High-quality, high-impact teaching and learning in the inclusive early childhood science classroom is correlated with the development of interest in science-related areas. A significant collection of empirical evidence suggests that by age 15, students are less engaged in science than at earlier ages (Osborne, 2008). Prior to age 15, student interest in science is quite high with little difference between boys and girls (Murphy & Beggs, 2005). Thus the research literature points to the idea that interest in science starts early. Much of the research suggests that the development of interest in science is early and that this interest has long-range educational outcomes (Tai et al., 2006). Some studies attribute early interest development in science with school-based experiences (Maltese & Tai, 2010) while others do not address the source of this interest and instead just show that the interest in science develops early (Hadden & Johnstone, 1982). Regardless of the studies' perspectives on the timing of interest, by age 14, an interest in science or lack thereof is set in a majority of students (Osborne, 2008).

Let's look at specific examples that point out why we should teach science and why students should engage in science learning. In a subsequent study, Maltese and Tai (2010) used data obtained from interviews of current graduate students in physics or chemistry, along with current physical scientists. The transcripts generated from these interviews were analyzed for the timing, source, and nature of the participants' earliest interest in science. The study found that 65% of those interviewed indicated that their initial interest in science occurred before middle school. Forty percent of the scientists and graduate students mentioned that the source of their initial interest was a school-based experience. Within these school-based experiences, 24% stated that class content was the key source, 18% stated that demonstrations, laboratories, and projects were the source of primary interest, and 22% mentioned enrichment experiences in science. Maltese and Tai (2010) also noted a gender difference in their results. Specifically, female scientists and graduate students referenced school-based experiences (52%) more frequently than males, who more frequently noted individually motivated interests (57%).

What is most interesting about these results is that the data comes from practicing scientists and graduate students, people who have persisted in science-related interests and have earned or are earning an advanced degree in a science-related field. Most notable is that a large percentage of these individuals indicated early timing and school-related experiences as their primary or initial source of interest in science. Thus the lack of exposure to school-based science experiences may actually be a missed opportunity for sparking the interest of future scientists. In particular, these results suggest that females may be most influenced by this lack of early exposure, which is not surprising given the current gender gap that exists within the physical sciences.

Opportunities for Reflective Practices

In your own words, summarize why we should teach science and why young children should learn science.

Why We Avoid Teaching Science in the Early Years

In spite of the relatively strong case for why science is an important part of the early childhood years, there is the indication that primary classroom teachers are avoiding the teaching of science (Goodrum, Hackling, & Rennie, 2001; Osborne & Simon, 1996). For example, Harlen (1997) interviewed 33 teachers by telephone about their teaching of science during a ten-week period. This study identified six strategies used by teachers to avoid teaching science:

1. Some classroom teachers exercise outright avoidance by simply not including science as part of the learning experience for their students.
2. Many classroom teachers only taught science content that they were comfortable with, and that content may or may not be part of the expectations for that particular grade level.
3. Teachers often focused on experiments and did not include any content in the instruction.
4. Some classrooms relied on prepackaged curricula, using only lecture-based instruction to avoid questions or discussion that drifts into material with which the teacher is not comfortable.
5. Teachers used the simplest of activities to avoid things going wrong.

When we avoid teaching science in the early childhood classroom, there are implications to that decision. When we avoid teaching science content outright or only teaching content with which we are most comfortable, we obviously leave parts of the curriculum untouched that are key to subsequent content, skills, and understandings. Therefore, there is the strong possibility that the learning progressions of your youngest students are disrupted or delayed, which influences future growth and achievement. Even if learners had science on a regular basis, teaching what we thought was "neat" to know may be different from what learners "need" to know. In addition, when we rely too heavily on prepackaged materials or curricula, we rely on ready-made experiences that may or may not be appropriate for all learners in your classroom. Scripted or programmed instruction leaves little room for us to differentiate our instruction based on who our learners are and how they see themselves as learners. Along those same lines, relying solely on the textbook is often associated with an emphasis on vocabulary learning and the memorization of facts (Mastropieri & Scruggs, 1994). What activities do exist within many textbook-based curricula do not truly represent authentic science (Chinn & Malhotra, 2002).

The avoidance behavior of using only lectures while avoiding questions or discussion speaks to the overall quality of early science instruction rather than just the quantity. In this case, students' exposure to early science instruction may not be beneficial, even though time has been allotted for such instruction. With regard to lecturing or expository teaching, the literature supporting or refuting the use of expository teaching when compared to other methods (e.g., laboratory methods, inquiry) is often contradictory and thus not helpful. As far back as 1971, researchers were looking at the relative effectiveness of the expository method versus the laboratory method and the discovery method (Babikian, 1971). However, literature does exist on other methods for teaching elementary school science that highlights the need for a variety of approaches, such as inquiry, conceptual change, cognitive conflict, small-group interaction, and models and analogies, as well as writing or science notebooks rather than limiting science lessons to expository teaching (Barnett & Moran, 2002; Carter, Jones, & Rua, 2003; Tomkins & Tunnicliffe, 2001).

Let's take a moment and review where we have been in our understanding of the role of the teacher in planning, designing, and implementing high-quality, high-impact teaching and learning in the inclusive early childhood science classroom. Using Ms. Campbell as our example, we acknowledge that the decisions she made about her lesson on sound were driven by her understanding of what science is and is not, as well as her strong beliefs about the value of science and why this type of learning should not be avoided. Now we want to explore what Ms. Campbell believes about her learners and what makes a good learner in science.

Our Beliefs about Science Teaching and Learning

Opportunities for Reflective Practices

What are your beliefs about science teaching and learning? What does high-quality, high-impact teaching and learning in the inclusive early childhood science classroom look like?

How we see our learners and our beliefs about their abilities, interests, and dispositions as learners informs the decisions we make on a daily basis. The National Science Teachers Association (2014), or NSTA, explicitly state these beliefs through a series of declarations about the teaching and learning of science in early childhood. These beliefs, in the form of declarations, assert that teachers of young children should (adapted from the National Science Teacher Association, 2014) accomplish the following:

1. Provide experiences in science that recognize the value and importance of nurturing learners' curiosity around science content, skills, and understandings.
2. Provide a learning environment that promotes the asking of questions, the planning of investigations, and the analyzing of findings.
3. Recognize that young children are already experiencing the world and thus have prior conceptions about how the world works. These experiences should be incorporated into their learning experiences.
4. Leverage learners' interests, abilities, and dispositions through carefully selected opportunities to engage with scientific phenomena in open-ended or driving questions.
5. Engage learners in a balanced approach to science - science as a body of knowledge, a set of processes, and a way of knowing.
6. Recognize that science provides a context for developing literacy skills, the use of math skills and concepts, and the integration of social studies content.

These beliefs, or mindsets, about learners' abilities, interests, and dispositions inform the decisions we make in our early childhood classrooms. Referring back to Ms. Campbell, you can see how each aspect of her instruction, even though we have only seen a small snippet of the overall lesson, reflects these beliefs. From recognizing their curiosity to providing a context for literacy skills, embracing why we should teach science and possessing specific beliefs about our learners is key to our role in teaching and learning in the inclusive early childhood science classroom.

In the shaded box that follows, we have provided the principles NSTA has developed based on research on how students learn to guide the teaching and learning of science in the early childhood classroom.

NSTA Position Statement on Early Childhood Science

1. Children have the capacity to engage in scientific practices and develop understanding at a conceptual level.

   Current research shows that young children have the capacity for conceptual learning and the ability to use the skills of reasoning and inquiry as they investigate how the world works (NRC, 2007, 2012). For example, their play with blocks, water, and sand shares some science-relevant characteristics. Young children also can learn to organize and communicate what they learn and know the difference between concrete and abstract ideas (Carey, 1985). Adults who engage children in science inquiry through the process of asking questions, investigating, and constructing explanations can provide developmentally appropriate environments that take advantage of what children do as part of their everyday life prior to entering formal school settings (NAEYC, 2013, p. 17; NRC, 2007). These skills and abilities can provide helpful starting points for developing scientific reasoning (NRC, 2007, p. 82).

2. Adults play a central and important role in helping young children learn science.

   Everyday life is rich with science experiences, but these experiences can best contribute to science learning when an adult prepares the environment for science exploration, focuses children's observations, and provides time to talk about what was done and seen (NAEYC, 2013, p. 18). It is important that adults support children's play and direct their attention, structure their experiences, support their learning attempts, and regulate the complexity and difficulty of levels of information (NRC, 2007, p. 3). It's equally important for adults to look for signs from children and adjust the learning experiences to support their curiosity, learning, and understanding.

3. Young children need multiple and varied opportunities to engage in science exploration and discovery (NAEYC, 2013).

   Young children develop science understanding best when given multiple opportunities to engage in science exploration and experiences through inquiry (Bosse, Jacobs, & Anderson 2009; Gelman, Brenneman, Macdonald, & Roman, 2010). The range of experiences gives them the basis for seeing patterns, forming theories, considering alternate explanations, and building their knowledge. For example, engaging with natural environments in an outdoor learning center can provide opportunities for children to examine and duplicate the habitats of animals and insects, explore how things move, investigate the flow of water, recognize different textures that exist, make predictions about things they see, and test their knowledge.

4. Young children develop science skills and knowledge in both formal and informal settings.

   Opportunities to explore, inquire, discover, and construct within the natural environment and with materials that are there need to be provided in formal education settings, such as preschool and early care and education programs through intentional lessons planned by knowledgeable adults. In addition, children need to have opportunities to engage in science learning in informal settings, such as at home with cooking activities and outdoor play or in the community exploring and observing the environment.

5. Young children develop science skills and knowledge over time.

   To effectively build science understanding, young children need opportunities for sustained engagement with materials and conversations that focus on the same set of ideas over weeks, months, and years (NRC, 2007, p. 3). For example, investigating the concept of light and shadows over several weeks indoors and out with a variety of materials and multiple activities will allow children to re-visit and re-engage over time, building on observations and predictions from day to day.

6. Young children develop science skills and learning by engaging in experiential learning.

   Young children engage in science activities when an adult intentionally prepares the environment and the experiences to allow children to fully engage with materials. The activities allow children to question, explore, investigate, make meaning, and construct explanations and organize knowledge by manipulating materials.

Reprinted with permission. *Source:* National Science Teachers Association (NSTA, 2014). *NSTA Position Statement: Early Childhood Science Education.*

All Means All – Inclusion in Early Childhood Science

What happens, in the end, is that our decisions within the role of teaching inclusive early childhood science ensure that all of our learners have equity of access and opportunity to science content, skills, and understandings. *And by all, this means all learners, regardless of their personal or social circumstances, have the access and opportunity to achieve their personal potential.* Thus we must seek to provide an inclusive environment for all learners – an environment that actively engages all learners, welcomes and embraces every learner as an important member of the community, and provides the necessary support to each learner so that they have an equal opportunity for success (see Jimenez et al., 2012; Spooner et al., 2011).

> Early childhood inclusion embodies the values, policies, and practices that support the right of every infant and young child and his or her family, regardless of ability, to participate in a broad range of activities and contexts as full members of families, communities, and society. The desired results of inclusive experiences for children with and without disabilities and their families include a sense of belonging and membership, positive social relation-ships and friendships, and development and learning to reach their full potential. The defining features of inclusion that can be used to identify high quality early childhood programs and services are access, participation, and supports. (DEC/NAEYC, 2009, p. 1)

For early childhood science teaching and learning, this means that we have to provide a wide range of experiences, tasks, and centers that are accessible to every learner regardless of his or her unique identity profile. The experiences, tasks, and centers engage learners beyond compliance but with a strong sense of belonging and efficacy. And, finally, there are strategic supports in place to ensure access and participation (DEC/NAEYC, 2009).

Opportunities for Reflective Practices

What is inclusion? Describe inclusion in your own words. Compare and contrast this with what you witnessed or with your experiences in your own school.

This moves beyond rattling off facts about the nine planets, now eight planets; the parts of a plant; the needs of living things; or centripetal force. The NSTA, along with the National Association for the Education of Young Children (NAEYC) both emphasize the continuity of growth in learning for each and every student in our classrooms (NSTA, 2014, DEC/NAEYC, 2009). Put differently, every parent, guardian, administrator, teacher leader, and teacher must strive to build lifelong learners by ensuring that the content, skills, and knowledge acquired during a single school year continues on beyond the walls of the school or classroom and beyond the academic calendar. This idea of lifelong learning is a long-sought-after goal in education (NSTA, 2014). So what does this look like? What is the outcome we are striving for in our young learners? The answer: assessment-capable visible science learners.

Assessment-Capable Visible Science Learners

The characteristics of an assessment-capable visible science learner draw from the key findings from John Hattie's Visible Learning database (Visible Learning Meta X, 2020). The Visible Learning research allows us to gain a perspective on what works best in teaching and learning science in the early childhood classroom. The Visible Learning database is composed of more than 1,800 meta-analyses of studies that include more than 80,000 studies and 300 million students. With that many studies and so many influences on student learning in our schools and classrooms, this database focuses on meta-analyses – the combination of results from a collection of studies. In other words, a meta-analysis is a study of studies. From these studies of studies, we can calculate an effect size that represents the magnitude or relative size of the particular influence. We will come back to this database and the list of effect sizes when we look at strategies for teaching and learning. For now, it is important to understand that an effect size not only helps us to discern whether something does or does not have an influence on learning but also we can look at a particular influence and see its relative impact compared to other influences (e.g., phonics versus whole-language instruction). For the purposes of our current discussion, planning, designing, and implementing high-quality, high-impact teaching and learning in the inclusive early childhood science classroom should build and support assessment-capable visible learners (Frey, Hattie, & Fisher, 2018). As we return to Ms. Campbell's classroom one more time, we will look at an example of an assessment-capable visible learner.

Mirya is one of Ms. Campbell's learners and is quite enthusiastic about getting right to work on answering the driving question for the day: How can I, as a musician, create a variety of sounds with my instruments? Mirya has been diagnosed with a learning disability and has no intention of letting that slow down her passion for learning. She is an energetic first grader who enjoys science, math, or any subject she encounters. During her most recent one-on-one conference with Ms. Campbell, Mirya demonstrated a strong conceptual understanding of sound but is not quite sure about hypothesizing and inferring. This does not completely surprise Ms. Campbell, because she also needs additional support in making inferences during the literacy block. During a discussion with Ms. Campbell, Mirya is able to articulate where she is in her learning and where she is going next in her learning journey. She tells Ms. Campbell, "I read a book about sound, but I don't really know what you mean by infer. So, I need to make sure I ask for help and make sure you check my work until I get it." Mirya demonstrates two characteristics of an assessment-capable learner in science:

1. Assessment-capable visible science learners know their current level of understanding in science content, skills, and understandings.
2. Assessment-capable visible science learners know where they are going next in their science learning and are confident to take on the challenge.

As Mirya engages in her first center, she struggles a bit with the task at the kalimba center. She is not clear on how to communicate her learning in her science notebook or record her thinking into the graphic organizer provided by Ms. Campbell. Her group discusses how to get around this challenge so that they can move forward in the tasks. They quickly discuss their options. Mirya speaks up and says, "Before we ask Ms. Campbell, why don't we look at the examples on Google classroom." One of her peers speaks up and says, "I will go get the book from the story and find it in there. He uses a kalimba in the book, remember?"

- Assessment-capable visible science learners have the tools to move learning forward and know when and how to use them.

Mirya and her science learning community stop their work at one of the centers. A member of the group has pointed out that "something does not look right here. I am not sure we did this the way Ms. Campbell wants us to. We have not used any of the science terms we talked about on the carpet. Let's go back and put those in." After they made edits and revisions to their science notebooks and graphic organizers, they compared their responses among themselves and made a few additional edits before moving forward to the next center.

- Assessment-capable visible science learners recognize that errors are learning opportunities and seek feedback.
- Assessment-capable visible science learners monitor their learning and make adjustments when necessary.

Finally, the most endearing aspect of this lesson comes when Mirya recognizes that another group is struggling with the kalimba center. She moves to provide them with help and begins to teach them about inferring.

- Assessment-capable visible science learners recognize when they have learned something and act as teachers to others.

Research to Classroom Practice Tasks

Brainstorm: What specific decisions build and support assessment-capable visible science learners?

Table 1.3 Characteristics of Assessment-Capable Visible Science Learners

- Assessment-capable visible science learners know their current level of understanding in science content, skills, and understandings.
- Assessment-capable visible science learners know where they are going next in their science learning and are confident to take on the challenge.
- Assessment-capable visible science learners have the tools to move learning forward and know when and how to use them.
- Assessment-capable visible science learners recognize that errors are learning opportunities and seek feedback.
- Assessment-capable visible science learners monitor their learning and make adjustments when necessary.
- Assessment-capable visible science learners recognize when they have learned something and act as teachers to others.

Source: Adapted from Frey, N., Hattie, J., & Fisher, D. (2018). *Developing assessment-capable visible learners.* Thousand Oaks, CA: Corwin.

These six characteristics did not come to fruition on their own (Table 1.3).
The actions of Mirya bring us to the end of this chapter and offer us an opportunity to tie everything together. Mirya is an assessment-capable visible learner because of the intentional, purposeful, and deliberate decisions of Ms. Campbell. Those decisions reflect her beliefs about what science is or is not, why all young children should learn science, and what her beliefs or mindset about science teaching and learning are. And this brings to light the role of the teacher in inclusive early childhood science teaching and learning. Where we go next addresses how Ms. Campbell decided on the body of knowledge (moving objects exhibit different kinds of motion; objects may vibrate and produce sound), the set of processes (observing, communicating, hypothesizing, inferring, experimenting, analyzing, evaluating, and modeling), and a specific aspect of a way of knowing (verify their hypotheses through replication).

Professional Learning Tasks

1. Return to the discussion of tiered vocabulary. Develop a list of Tier 1, 2, and 3 vocabulary terms for a science topic. Using resources available to you, explore and record strategies that support the acquisition and application of Tier 3 vocabulary.
2. What does the research say about the effect of the teacher on student learning? Using resources available to you, complete a miniature literature review of empirical research that explores the influence of a teacher on a student learning in science.
3. Inclusion, culturally responsive teaching, and differentiation are common terms in education. Develop your own definitions for each of these terms. Then compare and contrast these terms.

Engaging the Family and Community

1. **Focus on the Positive:** Everyone likes to hear something positive about their children, grandchildren, or any family member for that matter. Just as we begin our journey into inclusive early childhood science teaching and learning, this is our first discussion concerning engaging the family and community. As we devote time in each chapter to ideas, approaches, and strategies for extending teaching and learning beyond the walls of your classroom, one principle should be at the forefront of each of these efforts: focus on the positive. Successful family and community engagement are built on strong family-teacher relationships. These are initiated by engaging with them for positive reasons and not just when there is a problem. For example, make contact before the year begins and within the first two weeks of school. Whether by phone or by email, have the parent/guardian share something positive about their child before the year begins. Then, during the first two weeks of school, share something positive with them.

   The extra touch point or connection takes only a few moments but sets the tone for the rest of the year. This extra touch point connection increases the likelihood that our students will share future experiences from our classrooms with their parents or guardians. Plus, the parents or guardians are more likely to engage in constructive conversations if a tough conversation is necessary in the near or distant future.
2. **Share School Experiences:** Although we will continue to come back to the sharing of school experiences, we want to set the stage here and then go into specifics later on in the book. Before embarking on the mission of teaching and learning in the inclusive early childhood science classroom, set up a process and procedure for sharing the school experience beyond the walls of the classroom. Set aside some time for mapping out ways to encourage students to share their experiences and for parents, guardians, and other community members to share their experiences with our learners. Locate examples of newsletters and plan how you will use newsletters to share school experiences. How will you integrate student voice and parent/guardian voice into the newsletters?

   Then, locate technology that will support the sharing of experiences. Do not try to use all of the available options (e.g., Animoto, Storybird, TikTok, Remind, WeVideo, YouTube, Flipgrid, Facebook, Twitter, or Instagram). You do not need them all. Too much or too many can be overwhelming for you, your students, and their parents or guardians. Pick one piece of technology and stick with that for the quarter, semester, or even the year. Then plan how you will use that technology to share school experiences. Again, how will you integrate student voice and parent/guardian voice?
3. **Find Common Ground:** Engaging the family and community comes down to finding common ground. As you know, engaging with anyone is easier if we have something in common (e.g., current events, travel, food). When it comes to the families of our learners, the same rule applies. However, we already have common ground in that we will be sharing their child's time this school year. Take time to get to know the

families of your children. For example, set up regular opportunities for families to visit your classroom, face-to-face or remotely using Zoom, WebEx, Google Hangout, etc. This provides a forum for them to see the learning environment and hear about what their child is doing at school. What is even more powerful is when our learners lead the visits, sharing what they think is important about the classroom. Families should be visitors in our rooms, face-to-face or remotely, beyond back-to-school night. The more we interact with families, the better the chances that we will find the common ground that helps us see each other as individuals with the same end goal in mind: what's best for their child and our student.

Sometimes the best approach is to offer families the option of meeting with you in their homes – their turf so to speak. This is an excellent way to learn about the lives of students and their families.

In any of these ideas, approaches, or strategies for engaging families and community, always consider how you would respond if you were in their shoes. Understanding is one of the keys to unlocking a successful relationship with families and communities. What if this were your child? We should approach teaching and learning in the inclusive early childhood science classroom as if our own children were in the class.

Look for the other "Engaging the Family and Community" sections in subsequent chapters. Each of these special, highlighted sections will provide practical ways to move teaching and learning beyond the walls of your classroom. Sometimes we will focus on families, sometimes the community. In some sections, we will weave the two together. Each of these sections delivers a consistent message: We are partners in teaching and learning in the inclusive early childhood science classroom.

2 Analyzing What to Teach in Inclusive Early Childhood Science

As teachers of young children, we play a pivotal role in how students approach, engage, and come to understand the world around them. But there is a distinct difference between what we teach and how we teach. Placed in the context of the two exemplary teachers we have met thus far, how did Mrs. Rogers and Mrs. Campbell know what they needed to teach and what their students needed to learn? How did Ms. Rogers decide on sinking versus floating, the centers in her classroom, and the opening activity using the S-T-W strategy? Likewise, how did Ms. Campbell decide on her learning stations and read aloud? Diving deeper into this line of questioning, how did Mrs. Campbell develop her driving question and learning intention? These two vignettes in the previous chapters are the results of intentional, deliberate, and purposeful planning. In this chapter, we look at the first part of this planning - analyzing what we expect our students to know, understand, and be able to do. These expectations should encompass cognitive, social-emotional, psychomotor, and behavioral outcomes, as these interconnected domains contribute to the development of assessment-capable visible science learners.

Opportunities for Reflective Practices

Take a moment and revisit the six characteristics of an assessment-capable visible science learner.

Although we are teaching science, as teachers of young children, we are teaching the whole child. For example, Ms. Rogers not only wants learners to develop conceptual understanding about sinking and floating, she also wants learners to enhance their reasoning skills and use academic language within the context of sinking and floating. These are expectations within the cognitive domain. We also want learners to engage in collaborative learning where each student interacts with his or her peers in a prosocial manner. In other words, Ms. Campbell has social-emotional expectations for her learners as they work within each of the learning centers. Each of us must take into consideration the gross and fine motor skills in our teaching and learning. Whether writing, constructing models, or executing a scientific experiment, we must include psychomotor outcomes with young children. Finally, classroom management involves the establishment of norms and processes that ensure a learning-focused environment. These expectations are also a part of what we want our young learners to know, understand, and be able to do in science.

To establish expectations of student learning in science, we have to analyze the standards of learning associated with our particular grade level and topic of focus. Teaching and learning in the inclusive early childhood science classroom begin with the process of analyzing the standards of learning at the national, state, or local level. This process leads us to learning outcomes across each domain of student growth and learning.

Standards Tell Us What to Teach, Not How

Before we move through the process of analyzing the standards, we want to tackle an area of concern regarding the standards-based movement. Whether we are talking about national standards or state and local standards, there has been considerable criticism about the development and implementation of standards, specifically the quantity, lack of depth, and developmental appropriateness of standards (see Hamilton, Stecher, & Yuan, 2008). The perspective we are taking here and throughout this book is that standards tell us what to teach but not how to teach. In other words, standards clearly articulate what learners are expected to know, understand, and be able to do at each point of their learning progression. However, the standards do not tell us how to implement what needs to be taught in our classrooms. For example, in the Next Generation Science Standards (NGSS), kindergartners are expected to identify and describe the given evidence to support a claim about plants and animals (NGSS Lead States, 2013). However, this statement says nothing about the instructional approach and strategies used by kindergarten teachers to move learners toward proficiency in this area. It does not insist on us asking learners to construct descriptive sentences with complex scientific vocabulary or engage in other exercises or tasks that might not yet be developmentally appropriate. The instructional approach and strategies are left to our professional judgment and decisions about how to teach. Again, the approaches, strategies, and decisions should reflect who are learners are, where they are in their own learning progression, and how to move their learning forward.

Much effort has been devoted to the new generation of standards to ensure that they are developmentally appropriate; reflect a progression toward deeper learning of content, skills, and understanding; and focus on the essential knowledge, skills, and understandings and not a "laundry list" of topics (NGSS Lead States, 2013).

There are several benefits to the standards-based approach to teaching and learning science, but before we look at those benefits, consider the following "Opportunity for Reflective Practices."

Opportunities for Reflective Practices

If you were preparing to design and implement a lesson on the parts of a plant, what parts would you include? Make a mental list or a list in the margin. Hang on to that list. We will come back to your list soon.

One of the primary benefits to a standards-based approach is the establishment of a shared language of learning. When teachers and learners can identify a shared language of learning, we can focus on the academic vocabulary necessary for academic discourse. Furthermore, learners will have consistent expectations about what they are learning, why they are learning it, and what success looks like regardless of who they have as a teacher. This, then, leads to a greater likelihood of providing a truly inclusive learning environment - one where a shared language of learning and consistent expectations lead to high expectations for all learners. This is exemplified by the previous "Opportunity for Reflective Practices." When this question is posed to a room or auditorium full of teachers, there are as many differences in the lists as there are teachers in the room. Some lists include roots, stems, and leaves, while others include flowers, fruits, pollen, and seeds. Other lists include the parts of a flower, while others do not. If these learners were to demonstrate their knowledge, skills, and understandings, we would have a hard time assessing where learners are in their learning. This includes identifying the prior knowledge and experiences of the learners, as well as their growth in learning about the parts of a plant and how those parts work together to help the plant survive. Furthermore, how would we ensure that learners are developing the academic language and literacy skills necessary for academic discourse without agreeing on that language?

Finally, standards ensure that we focus on what learners need to know and not get distracted by what is neat to know. In other words, standards provide the guardrails around topics in science. Given the engaging nature of science as a discipline, we can easily find ourselves focusing on content, skills, and understandings that are neat to know but are not needed for learners to progress toward the learning.

Without standards, there is a greater likelihood that we could unintentionally lower expectations because of our misconceptions or beliefs about what learners cannot do rather than focus on the standards or expectations and then scaffolding learning experiences to support them in meeting those standards or expectations. A standards-based approach ensures that all of our learners have equity of access and opportunity to science content, skills, and understandings. *And by all, this means all learners, regardless of their personal or social circumstances, have the access and opportunity to achieve their personal potential.*

Now, let's work through the process of analyzing the standards of learning to establish a shared language of learning in science and establish expectations for all learners across all domains (Figure 2.1).

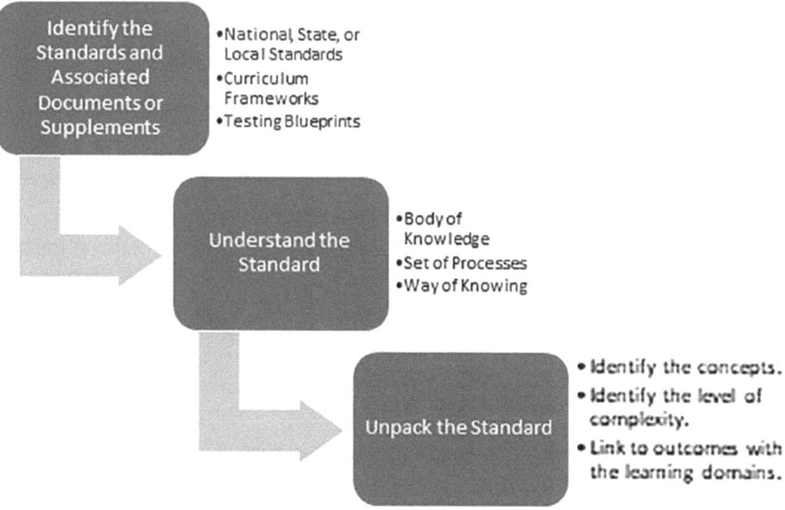

Figure 2.1 The Process for Analyzing the Science Standards of Learning.

Identifying the Science Standards of Learning

Standards of learning in early childhood science come from three possible sources:

1. National standards
2. State standards
3. Local standards

In the United States, some state departments of education use the national science standards, the NGSS (NGSS Lead States, 2013). States like California, Kentucky, and Maryland adopted these standards and thus are the sources for establishing expectations in science for grades K–12. Other states adopted their own state-level standards, but they were likely informed by the NGSS and contain very similar expectations of knowledge, skills, and contents. Again, this is for grades K–12. At this time, there is not a national set of standards for prekindergarten teaching and learning above and beyond position statements and accreditation standards provided by organizations that support inclusive early childhood education or science education (e.g., NAEYC and NSTA). However, many of the states have worked to establish early learning standards and guidelines that integrate developmental milestones with the knowledge, skills, and understandings that support learners' transition into kindergarten. Thus when we set to analyze the standards for our youngest learners, we may find that we have to look to state standards and, in some cases, local standards.

Local standards, in this case, are a more detailed set of expectations above and beyond state-level early learning standards or guidelines around early childhood learning. For example, they may take the standards and guidelines presented by the Department of Health and Human Services and provide more specific insight into what learners in, say, Virginia, should know, understand, and be able to do prior to kindergarten. Digging even deeper into the standards of learning, we may find that specific school districts or divisions have adopted a specific early childhood curriculum and thus the specific content, skills, and understandings are unique to that locality.

Outside of the United States, many countries have national standards. For example, in the United Kingdom, they have a national curriculum (https://www.gov.uk/national-curriculum) that provides clear standards at different stages in compulsory schooling. Australia (https://www.australiancurriculum.edu.au/) and New Zealand (http://nzcurriculum.tki.org.nz/The-New-Zealand-Curriculum) are similar to the United Kingdom. In Canada, the standards vary by province. For example, the specific content, skills, and understandings differ between Ontario (http://www.edu.gov.on.ca/eng/teachers/curriculum.html) and, for example, Alberta (https://www.alberta.ca/k-12-education.aspx). Although there are commonalities, knowing which standards apply to your classroom is essential for establishing expectations of student learning in science.

Regardless of which standards of learning are used by the state or district, locating them is the first step in analyzing the standards of learning to establish a shared language of learning in science and establish expectations for all learners across all domains.

Opportunities for Reflective Practices

Locate the standards of learning for science in your current school district/division or state. Spend some time looking through the standards for your grade level. Then take a look at the previous grade-level science standards and the one grade level above yours. Make a note of your observations, thoughts, and/or questions.

In our analysis of the standards, we will use an example from the NGSS and a state-level standard. The process for analyzing the standards of learning works regardless of whether your state, district, or school uses national, state, or local standards.

Curriculum Frameworks and Test Blueprints. As we located the standards of learning for science for your specific classroom, we likely found other documents that support each specific standard and then the standards in their entirety. For example, we likely located what is often called a curriculum framework. A curriculum framework is a document that accompanies the standards of learning and articulates the measurable outcomes that learners must demonstrate to, at a minimum, meet the standard. For example, consider the following second-grade NGSS (Figure 2.2).

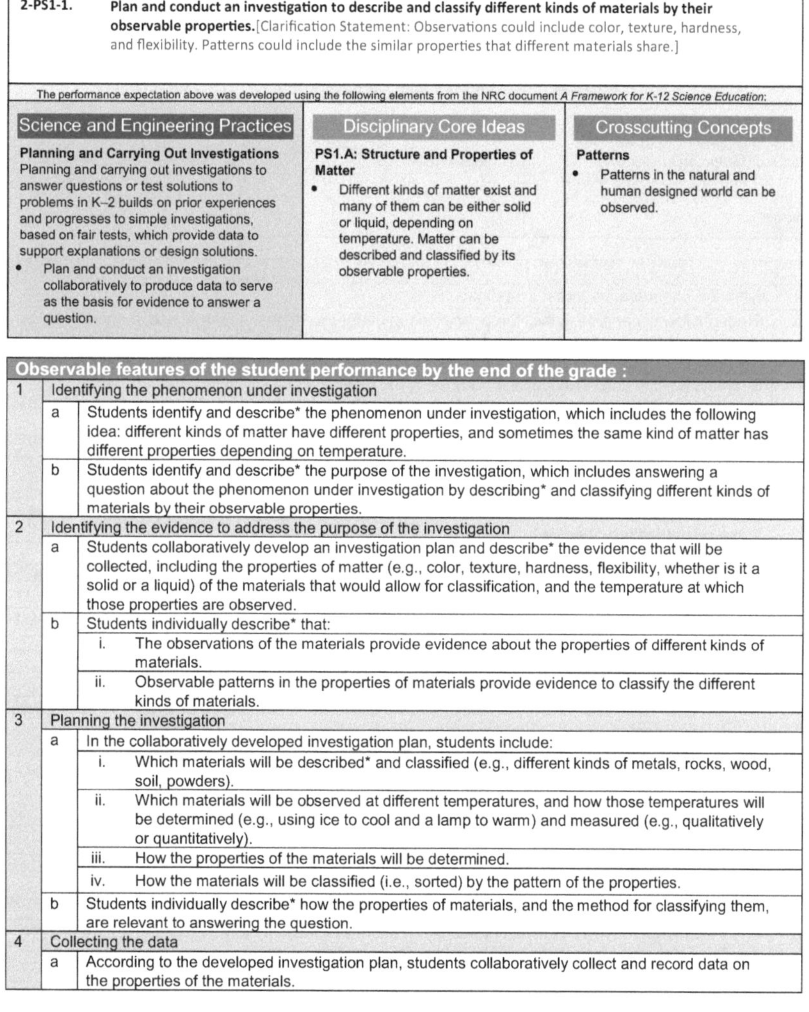

Students who demonstrate understanding can:

2-PS1-1. Plan and conduct an investigation to describe and classify different kinds of materials by their observable properties. [Clarification Statement: Observations could include color, texture, hardness, and flexibility. Patterns could include the similar properties that different materials share.]

The performance expectation above was developed using the following elements from the NRC document *A Framework for K-12 Science Education:*

Science and Engineering Practices	Disciplinary Core Ideas	Crosscutting Concepts
Planning and Carrying Out Investigations Planning and carrying out investigations to answer questions or test solutions to problems in K–2 builds on prior experiences and progresses to simple investigations, based on fair tests, which provide data to support explanations or design solutions. • Plan and conduct an investigation collaboratively to produce data to serve as the basis for evidence to answer a question.	**PS1.A: Structure and Properties of Matter** • Different kinds of matter exist and many of them can be either solid or liquid, depending on temperature. Matter can be described and classified by its observable properties.	**Patterns** • Patterns in the natural and human designed world can be observed.

Observable features of the student performance by the end of the grade :			
1	Identifying the phenomenon under investigation		
	a	Students identify and describe* the phenomenon under investigation, which includes the following idea: different kinds of matter have different properties, and sometimes the same kind of matter has different properties depending on temperature.	
	b	Students identify and describe* the purpose of the investigation, which includes answering a question about the phenomenon under investigation by describing* and classifying different kinds of materials by their observable properties.	
2	Identifying the evidence to address the purpose of the investigation		
	a	Students collaboratively develop an investigation plan and describe* the evidence that will be collected, including the properties of matter (e.g., color, texture, hardness, flexibility, whether is it a solid or a liquid) of the materials that would allow for classification, and the temperature at which those properties are observed.	
	b	Students individually describe* that:	
		i.	The observations of the materials provide evidence about the properties of different kinds of materials.
		ii.	Observable patterns in the properties of materials provide evidence to classify the different kinds of materials.
3	Planning the investigation		
	a	In the collaboratively developed investigation plan, students include:	
		i.	Which materials will be described* and classified (e.g., different kinds of metals, rocks, wood, soil, powders).
		ii.	Which materials will be observed at different temperatures, and how those temperatures will be determined (e.g., using ice to cool and a lamp to warm) and measured (e.g., qualitatively or quantitatively).
		iii.	How the properties of the materials will be determined.
		iv.	How the materials will be classified (i.e., sorted) by the pattern of the properties.
	b	Students individually describe* how the properties of materials, and the method for classifying them, are relevant to answering the question.	
4	Collecting the data		
	a	According to the developed investigation plan, students collaboratively collect and record data on the properties of the materials.	

Figure 2.2 Second-Grade Physical Science Standard.
Source: NGSS Lead States. (2013). Next generation science standards: For states, by states. Washington, DC: The National Academies Press.

This standard, alone, without any clarification, leaves us in a situation similar to the earlier "Opportunity for Reflective Practices" section on teaching about the parts of the plant. The ambiguity in this standard will likely hinder our ability to arrive at a shared language of learning and thus clear expectations across cognitive, social-emotional, psychomotor, and behavioral outcomes. However, a curriculum framework (Figure 2.3) accompanies the NGSS

2-PS1-1 Matter and Its Interactions

Students who demonstrate understanding can:

2-PS1-1. **Plan and conduct an investigation to describe and classify different kinds of materials by their observable properties.** [Clarification Statement: Observations could include color, texture, hardness, and flexibility. Patterns could include the similar properties that different materials share.]

The performance expectation above was developed using the following elements from the NRC document *A Framework for K-12 Science Education*:

Science and Engineering Practices	Disciplinary Core Ideas	Crosscutting Concepts
Planning and Carrying Out Investigations Planning and carrying out investigations to answer questions or test solutions to problems in K–2 builds on prior experiences and progresses to simple investigations, based on fair tests, which provide data to support explanations or design solutions. • Plan and conduct an investigation collaboratively to produce data to serve as the basis for evidence to answer a question.	**PS1.A: Structure and Properties of Matter** • Different kinds of matter exist and many of them can be either solid or liquid, depending on temperature. Matter can be described and classified by its observable properties.	**Patterns** • Patterns in the natural and human designed world can be observed.

Observable features of the student performance by the end of the grade :

1	Identifying the phenomenon under investigation		
	a	Students identify and describe* the phenomenon under investigation, which includes the following idea: different kinds of matter have different properties, and sometimes the same kind of matter has different properties depending on temperature.	
	b	Students identify and describe* the purpose of the investigation, which includes answering a question about the phenomenon under investigation by describing* and classifying different kinds of materials by their observable properties.	
2	Identifying the evidence to address the purpose of the investigation		
	a	Students collaboratively develop an investigation plan and describe* the evidence that will be collected, including the properties of matter (e.g., color, texture, hardness, flexibility, whether is it a solid or a liquid) of the materials that would allow for classification, and the temperature at which those properties are observed.	
	b	Students individually describe* that:	
		i.	The observations of the materials provide evidence about the properties of different kinds of materials.
		ii.	Observable patterns in the properties of materials provide evidence to classify the different kinds of materials.
3	Planning the investigation		
	a	In the collaboratively developed investigation plan, students include:	
		i.	Which materials will be described* and classified (e.g., different kinds of metals, rocks, wood, soil, powders).
		ii.	Which materials will be observed at different temperatures, and how those temperatures will be determined (e.g., using ice to cool and a lamp to warm) and measured (e.g., qualitatively or quantitatively).
		iii.	How the properties of the materials will be determined.
		iv.	How the materials will be classified (i.e., sorted) by the pattern of the properties.
	b	Students individually describe* how the properties of materials, and the method for classifying them, are relevant to answering the question.	
4	Collecting the data		
	a	According to the developed investigation plan, students collaboratively collect and record data on the properties of the materials.	

Figure 2.3 Second-Grade Physical Science Standard with Curriculum Framework.
Source: NGSS Lead States. (2013). Next generation science standards: For states, by states. Washington, DC: The National Academies Press.

and provides measurable outcomes that define what learners are expected to know, understand, and be able to do.

In addition to a curriculum framework, we might also find a test blueprint or released test items. Much like a blueprint informs a builder about specific characteristics (e.g., dimensions and location) of a building that guide the construction of that building, a test blueprint informs the teacher about the characteristics and dimensions of the assessment that will be used to evaluate student learning. For example, if a particular room in a building has specific dimensions, the builder can see both the size and location of the room relative to the other rooms in the building. If a test blueprint indicates that 25% of the assessment questions will focus on matter and its interactions, then a teacher can see the size and importance of that particular content and understanding relative to the other content, skills, and understandings in that grade level. The test blueprint or released test items provide additional clarity about which standards need the highest level of priority or focus during that particular school year.

Simply because a standard in second grade accounts for only 5% of the assessment does not mean that the learning within that standard is not important. What it does mean is that in the second grade, the emphasis is on other areas of science. When learners move into the third grade and beyond, there is a high likelihood that the standard accounting for 5% of the assessment in second grade will take center stage in subsequent years. What they know, understand, and are able to do in second grade serves as the foundation for those subsequent years and thus requires that we plan, design, and implement high-quality, high-impact teaching and learning experiences around each standard. What changes is the time devoted to that standard.

Opportunities for Reflective Practices

Locate the supplemental documents associated with your science standards of learning. What do they tell you about the priority of certain standards for your grade level? How will this influence the amount of time you devote to each standard? Do you see any commonalities between those that are a greater priority? Less of a priority?

The time devoted to that standard is strongly influenced by what we find when we unpack the standard. This is the second part of the process for analyzing the science standards of learning.

Understanding the Science Standards of Learning

To unpack the NGSS, we have to first look at how these standards, along with the framework, are organized. Consider the following NGSS.

In addition to the actual statement of the standard, in Figure 2.4, Kindergarten Earth's Systems Second-Grade Standard, Number Two (K-ESS2-2), we are provided essential information that clarifies the expectations for this standard. This information includes a clarifying statement and observable outcomes. However, we want to look closer at the science and engineering practices, disciplinary core ideas, and crosscutting concepts. These are the three dimensions of science learning (Figure 2.5).

These three dimensions are highly correlated with the definition of science we explored in Chapter 1 of this book. Recall that science is a body of knowledge, a set of processes, and a way of knowing

K-ESS2-2 Earth's Systems		
Students who demonstrate understanding can: **K-ESS2-2. Construct an argument supported by evidence for how plants and animals (including humans) can change the environment to meet their needs.** [Clarification Statement: Examples of plants and animals changing their environment could include a squirrel digs in the ground to hide its food and tree roots can break concrete.]		
The performance expectation above was developed using the following elements from the NRC document *A Framework for K-12 Science Education*:		
Science and Engineering Practices	**Disciplinary Core Ideas**	**Crosscutting Concepts**
Engaging in Argument from Evidence Engaging in argument from evidence in K – 2 builds on prior experiences and progresses to comparing ideas and representations about the natural and designed world(s). • Construct an argument with evidence to support a claim.	**ESS2.E: Biogeology** • Plants and animals can change their environment. **ESS3.C: Human Impacts on Earth Systems** • Things that people do to live comfortably can affect the world around them. But they can make choices that reduce their impacts on the land, water, air, and other living things. *(secondary)*	**Systems and System Models** • Systems in the natural and designed world have parts that work together.

Observable features of the student performance by the end of the grade:			
1	Supported claims		
	a	Students make a claim to be supported about a phenomenon. In their claim, students include the idea that plants and animals (including humans) can change the environment to meet their needs.	
2	Identifying scientific evidence		
	a	Students identify and describe * the given evidence to support the claim, including:	
		i.	Examples of plants changing their environments (e.g., plant roots lifting sidewalks).
		ii.	Examples of animals (including humans) changing their environments (e.g., ants building an ant hill, humans clearing land to build houses, birds building a nest, squirrels digging holes to hide food).
		iii.	Examples of plant and animal needs (e.g., shelter, food, room to grow).
3	Evaluating and critiquing evidence		
	a	Students describe * how the examples do or do not support the claim.	
4	Reasoning and synthesis		
	a	Students support the claim and present an argument by logically connecting various needs of plants and animals to evidence about how plants/animals change the irenvironments to meet their needs. Students include:	
		i.	Examples of how plants affect other parts of their systems by changing their environments to meet their needs (e.g. , roots push soil aside as they grow to better absorb water).
		ii.	Examples of how animals affect other parts of their systems by changing their environments to meet their needs (e.g. , ants, birds, rabbits, and humans use natural materials to build shelter; some animals store food for winter).

Figure 2.4 Kindergarten Earth's Systems Standard with Curriculum Framework.
Source: NGSS Lead States. (2013). Next generation science standards: For states, by states. Washington, DC: The National Academies Press.

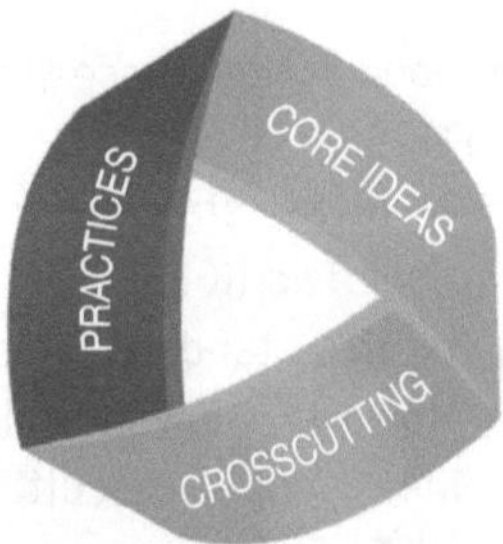

Figure 2.5 The Three Dimensions of Science Learning.
Source: NGSS Lead States. (2013). *Next generation science standards: For states, by states.* Washington, DC: The National Academies Press.

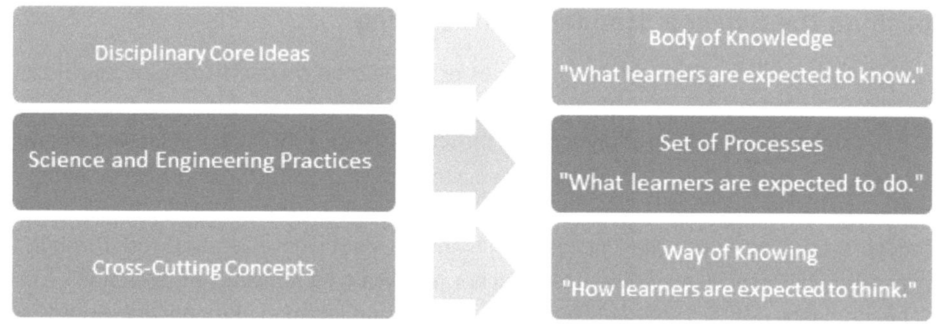

Figure 2.6 Connecting the three dimensions of the Next Generation Science Standards and the definition of science.
Source: Author created.

(Bell, 2008). From this perspective, the three dimensions of learning provide guidance on what learners are expected to know, understand, and be able to do across each aspect of science (Figure 2.6).

Disciplinary core ideas reflect the specific content within the standards. This includes the laws, principles, theories, and ideas within the particular topic of the standard (e.g., Earth's systems). These provide us with the information we need to identify and establish cognitive learning outcomes for learners, including the specific language or academic vocabulary (social-emotional outcomes) necessary to engage in academic discourse while engaging in science and engineering practices. The science and engineering practices identify the specific process skills that are best aligned with the disciplinary core ideas. These processes, or science and engineering practices, are embedded into the content and not treated as separate discrete learning experiences. For example, learners are not taught or expected to construct an argument with evidence to support a claim in isolation but within the learning experience concerning how plants and animals can change their environment (i.e., disciplinary core ideas). The science and engineering practices provide us with the information we need to identify and establish psychomotor, behavioral, and social-emotional outcomes for learners. Again, this is the expectation that learners will "do" science.

Together, the disciplinary core ideas and the science and engineering practices should leverage a way of thinking, capitalizing on specific crosscutting concepts. When we look specifically at the standard in Figure 2.4, we see that systems and system models are the crosscutting concepts. This aims to get learners to think about science from a systems perspective. The way of knowing in science requires that we see the world as systems that are composed of parts that work together. Other crosscutting concepts include patterns, cause and effect, scale, proportion, quantity, energy/matter, structure/function, and stability/change. Incorporating these concepts into our science teaching and our students' learning helps us to identify and establish cognitive and social-emotional learning outcomes.

Opportunities for Reflective Practices

Locate your standards and the supplemental documents associated with your science standards of learning. Where are the three parts of the definition for science in the standards and supplemental documents?

Now, let's get to the analysis of the standards and identifying and establishing what to teach.

Unpacking the Science Standards of Learning

The process for analyzing the standards involves extracting the concepts from the specific standard and aligning those concepts with the complexity of thinking associated with each concept. This is often referred to as unpacking or unwrapping the standard. The process for unpacking or unwrapping standards is derived from the work of Ainsworth and Donovan (2019) and is an essential part of clarifying what we want our students to learn (see Almarode & Vandas, 2019; Fisher et al., 2019).

Concepts. Let's work with the kindergarten standard from Figure 2.4 and work through this analysis with Ms. Cornish, a kindergarten teacher at William McKinley Primary School. To analyze this standard, Ms. Cornish and her team start by underlining the concepts in K-ESS2-2 (Figure 2.7). As a general rule, the concepts are the nouns found in each part of the standard.

K-ESS2-2 Earth's Systems

Students who demonstrate understanding can:

K-ESS2-2. Construct an argument supported by evidence for how plants and animals (including humans) can change the environment to meet their needs. [Clarification Statement: Examples of plants and animals changing their environment could include a squirrel digs in the ground to hide its food and tree roots can break concrete.]

The performance expectation above was developed using the following elements from the NRC document *A Framework for K-12 Science Education*:

Science and Engineering Practices	Disciplinary Core Ideas	Crosscutting Concepts
Engaging in Argument from Evidence Engaging in argument from evidence in K–2 builds on prior experiences and progresses to comparing ideas and representations about the natural and designed world(s). • Construct an argument with evidence to support a claim.	**ESS2.E: Biogeology** • Plants and animals can change their environment. **ESS3.C: Human Impacts on Earth Systems** • Things that people do to live comfortably can affect the world around them. But they can make choices that reduce their impacts on the land, water, air, and other living things. *(secondary)*	**Systems and System Models** • Systems in the natural and designed world have parts that work together.

Observable features of the student performance by the end of the grade:

1	Supported claims		
	a	Students make a claim to be supported about a phenomenon. In their claim, students include the idea that plants and animals (including humans) can change the environment to meet their needs.	
2	Identifying scientific evidence		
	a	Students identify and describe* the given evidence to support the claim, including:	
		i.	Examples of plants changing their environments (e.g., plant roots lifting sidewalks).
		ii.	Examples of animals (including humans) changing their environments (e.g., ants building an ant hill, humans clearing land to build houses, birds building a nest, squirrels digging holes to hide food).
		iii.	Examples of plant and animal needs (e.g., shelter, food, room to grow).
3	Evaluating and critiquing evidence		
	a	Students describe* how the examples do or do not support the claim.	
4	Reasoning and synthesis		
	a	Students support the claim and present an argument by logically connecting various needs of plants and animals to evidence about how plants/animals change their environments to meet their needs. Students include:	
		i.	Examples of how plants affect other parts of their systems by changing their environments to meet their needs (e.g., roots push soil aside as they grow to better absorb water).
		ii.	Examples of how animals affect other parts of their systems by changing their environments to meet their needs (e.g., ants, birds, rabbits, and humans use natural materials to build shelter; some animals store food for winter).

Figure 2.7 K-ESS2-2 with the Nouns Underlined.
Source: NGSS Lead States. (2013). Next generation science standards: For states, by states. Washington, DC: The National Academies Press.

CONCEPTS: (nouns)	COMPLEXITY: (verbs)
Change Argument Evidence Plants Animals Humans Environment Needs Ideas Representations Natural Designed Claim Phenomenon Impact Land Water Air Other Living Things Parts that work together	

Figure 2.8 Unpacking Concepts.

Once Ms. Cornish and her team have agreed on the concepts within this standard, they list them in the unpacking template (see Appendix A; Figure 2.8).

These concepts provide the ideas learners must know and understand as a result of this standard. In addition, Ms. Cornish and her team now have a shared language for this standard that represents that academic vocabulary learners must become fluent as they engage in academic discourse concerning Earth's systems. In some cases, these concepts represent Tier 1 vocabulary, while other concepts would be classified as Tier 2 and 3 vocabulary. In each case, the kindergartners in these classrooms must integrate these concepts into their daily learning experiences.

One important point to highlight in the extraction of concepts is the redundancy of some concepts. For example, the terms "argument," "evidence," "plants," "animals," "environment," and "needs" are mentioned multiple times in K-ESS2-2. In many cases, this can provide insight into the importance of a certain concept. The more frequently the concept appears in the standard, the greater the need to ensure that learners progress toward mastery in their knowledge and understanding of that concept. Another important point to make is the possible discrepancy in underlined concepts. As Ms. Cornish points out, "There are times when we do not always identify the same concepts when unpacking the standard. However, this requires us to discuss the standard and dive deeper into what the expectations truly are for this topic. In the end, we have greater clarity about what our learners are expected to know and understand."

Level of Complexity. The second part of unpacking the standard is the complexity of thinking associated with each concept. To ensure the right level of complexity, we first look to the verbs in the standard and then use those verbs alongside taxonomies of thinking. But first, let's circle the verbs in the standard. Ms. Cornish and her team circle the verbs in the standard, verbs that are linked to the specific underlined concepts (Figure 2.9).

The verbs provide the first step in understanding the level of complexity that is aligned with the concepts. Consider the concepts of "claim" and "phenomenon." What level of complexity is expected

K-ESS2-2 Earth's Systems

Students who demonstrate understanding can:

K-ESS2-2. Construct an argument supported by evidence for how plants and animals (including humans) can change the environment to meet their needs. [Clarification Statement: Examples of plants and animals changing their environment could include a squirrel digs in the ground to hide its food and tree roots can break concrete.]

The performance expectation above was developed using the following elements from the NRC document *A Framework for K-12 Science Education*:

Science and Engineering Practices	Disciplinary Core Ideas	Crosscutting Concepts
Engaging in Argument from Evidence Engaging in argument from evidence in K–2 builds on prior experiences and progresses to comparing ideas and representations about the natural and designed world(s). • Construct an argument with evidence to support a claim.	**ESS2.E: Biogeology** • Plants and animals can change their environment. **ESS3.C: Human Impacts on Earth Systems** • Things that people do to live comfortably can affect the world around them. But they can make choices that reduce their impacts on the land, water, air, and other living things. *(secondary)*	**Systems and System Models** • Systems in the natural and designed world have parts that work together.

Observable features of the student performance by the end of the grade:			
1	Supported claims		
	a	Students make a claim to be supported about a phenomenon. In their claim, students include the idea that plants and animals (including humans) can change the environment to meet their needs.	
2	Identifying scientific evidence		
	a	Students identify and describe the given evidence to support the claim, including:	
		i.	Examples of plants changing their environments (e.g., plant roots lifting sidewalks).
		ii.	Examples of animals (including humans) changing their environments (e.g., ants building an ant hill, humans clearing land to build houses, birds building a nest, squirrels digging holes to hide food).
		iii.	Examples of plant and animal needs (e.g., shelter, food, room to grow).
3	Evaluating and critiquing evidence		
	a	Students describe how the examples do or do not support the claim.	
4	Reasoning and synthesis		
	a	Students support the claim and present an argument by logically connecting various needs of plants and animals to evidence about how plants/animals change their environments to meet their needs. Students include:	
		i.	Examples of how plants affect other parts of their systems by changing their environments to meet their needs (e.g., roots push soil aside as they grow to better absorb water).
		ii.	Examples of how animals affect other parts of their systems by changing their environments to meet their needs (e.g., ants, birds, rabbits, and humans use natural materials to build shelter; some animals store food for winter).

Figure 2.9 K-ESS2-2 with the Nouns Underlined and Verbs Circled.
Source: NGSS Lead States. (2013). Next generation science standards: For states, by states. Washington, DC: The National Academies Press.

for these learners? Will are the kindergarteners in Ms. Cornish's classroom expected to do with regard to claims and phenomena. When we look specifically at the verbs associated with these concepts, we see that learners will be expected to make a claim. This is a high level of complexity, as learners must observe a phenomenon and then draw from their prior experiences, apply that prior learning, and then make a claim that can be supported by evidence. This complexity moves above and beyond simply recognizing or identifying toward the application of learners' thinking. Ms. Cornish describes this part of the process as "our way of figuring out how deep we have to go into these concepts. Simply identifying or naming is very different than learners having to construct an argument. This helps us grasp the depth we will be aiming for in our teaching and learning."

CONCEPTS: (nouns)	COMPLEXITY: (verbs)
Change	Claim
Argument	Present
Evidence	Support with
Plants	Identify and Describe
Animals	Identify and Describe
Humans	Identify and Describe
Environment	Identify and Describe
Needs	Identify and Describe
Ideas	Comparing
Representations	Comparing
Natural	Comparing
Designed	Comparing
Claim	Support
Phenomenon	Support
Impact	Know
Land	Know
Water	Know
Air	Know
Other Living Things	Know
Parts that work together	Know

Figure 2.10 Unpacking Concepts and Verbs.

Just as they did with the concepts or nouns, once Ms. Cornish and her team agreed on the verbs within this standard, they list these verbs in the unpacking template (see Appendix A; Figure 2.10). Specifically, Ms. Cornish and her team align the verbs with the specific concepts.

Notice that the last several concepts have the verb "know" linked to them. For these concepts, found primarily in the disciplinary core ideas, are parts of the body of knowledge that learners are expected to know and understand. This is the knowledge and understanding that will allow learners to construct arguments and support those arguments with evidence. This will, in the end, require learners to identify and describe examples related to plants, animals, humans, their environments, and needs.

Research to Classroom Practice Tasks

Take some time and unpack a standard that you will be teaching in the future. Follow the process of underlining the nouns, circling the verbs, and adding this information to the template in Appendix A.

Taxonomies of Thinking. There are multiple ways to make meaning of the complexity in thinking expected within the standard: Bloom's Taxonomy, Webb's Depth of Knowledge, and the structure of observed learning outcomes (SOLO) Taxonomy. These frameworks help us ensure that we are consistent in the level of complexity when engaging young students in science learning. Consider the verbs "identify" and "describe." What is the nature of learners identifying and describing within this standard?

Bloom's Taxonomy and Webb's Depth of Knowledge are common ways of looking at the level of complexity, but they both do so through the lens of assessment. In other words, the six levels of Bloom's Taxonomy and the four levels of Webb's Depth of Knowledge provide insight into the questions we ask, the formative assessments we design, and the summative assessments we administer.

Research to Classroom Practice Tasks

Spend some time finding information about Bloom's Taxonomy and Webb's Depth of Knowledge. What did each thought leader aim to do with his framework? What are the limitations of each framework?

Let's be clear - both Bloom's and Webb's taxonomies were created to provide alignment between the level of complexity in what students must know, understand, and be able to do and our assessment of that learning. These taxonomies were not created to provide a framework for student thinking. To truly understand the level of complexity, Ms. Cornish and her team must look at the type of thinking around each verb. Only when we grasp the type of thinking expected in the standard can we plan, design, and implement high-quality, high-impact teaching and learning experiences that build that level of complexity in our young learners. For that, we must look to the SOLO Taxonomy.

In the late 1970s and early 1980s, researchers looked at many more work samples and across several disciplines, such as mathematics, English, and geography (Biggs & Collis, 1982; Kirby & Biggs, 1981). Focusing primarily on student work, researchers noted five distinct patterns in the variation of student thinking. For example, some of the learners' responses were incoherent or missed the point of the assignment. In their responses, these learners focused on irrelevant facts, concepts, or ideas. Biggs and Collis (1982) also found that other students focused on a single idea or one relevant aspect of the content, omitting other details in their responses. A third group of learners included several relevant but independent aspects of the content. That is, these learners provided lists or serial lists of information without linking the concepts, whereas some of the students were able to identify relationships between the facts, concepts, or ideas, moving beyond simply listing discrete pieces of information. The final group of students produced responses that generalized the content to a new domain, extending their learning to abstract principles or generalizable ideas.

From these five distinct patterns in the structure of learners' thinking, Biggs and Collis (1982) developed a model known as the SOLO Taxonomy (Figure 2.11). This model is based on levels of thinking that can be observed and become increasingly more complex and difficult.

The SOLO Taxonomy represents a progression of thinking that moves from single ideas, to multiple ideas, and then to relationships and transfers. In our classrooms, learners may have no prior knowledge or experience with the information and thus have no relevant structure to their

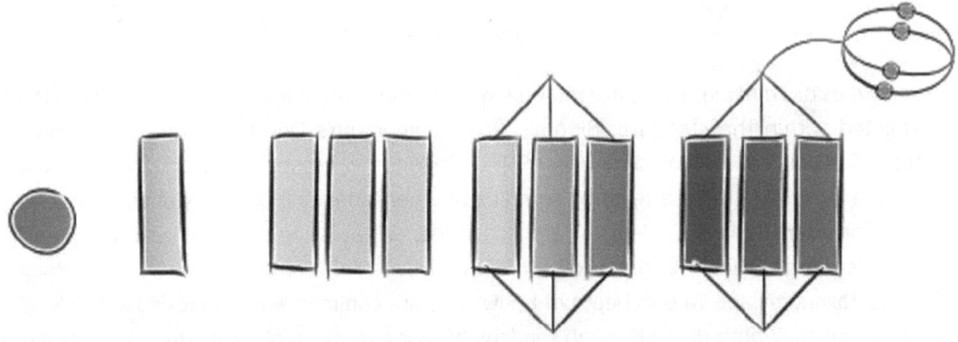

Figure 2.11 The Structure of Observed Learning Outcomes.
Source: https://pamhook.com/2012/01/20/creating-solo-taxonomy-symbols-in-many-colours/

thinking (the dot). This is referred to as the prestructural level or prestructural thinking. Learners may focus on irrelevant ideas or avoid engaging in the content, requiring the teacher to support the learner in acquiring and building background knowledge. For example, if Ms. Cornish were to show an image of a plant pushing through the sidewalk, a specific example mentioned in K-ESS2-2, a learner engaged in prestructural thinking might respond with a story that is only tangentially related to the question. Although important to the learner, the information revealed by this student, making his thinking visible, is more important to the teacher. He or she now has information that informs his or her next steps in instruction: scaffolding the learner to identify the relevant details of the photograph. A second response might be silence or disengagement. However, with the SOLO Taxonomy in mind, the interpretation of the students' responses by the teacher is not limited to "the students just don't or won't behave or participate." Instead, the learners are likely at the prestructural level, not sure what Ms. Cornish means when she says to make a claim about this picture and support your claim with evidence.

As the learners progress in their thinking, they may have a single idea or component related to the concept, represented by the single rectangle. This is referred to as the unistructural level of thinking. Learners at this level identify, name, and follow simple procedures (Hook & Mills, 2011). Referring back to the photograph of a plant pushing through the sidewalk, a student may identify "a plant," "it is green," or "that is a road or sidewalk." In multistructural thinking, learners then begin to acquire multiple ideas (three rectangles) that are combined into a coherent description. For example, "That is a plant pushing through the sidewalk on our playground." However, the learners do not see the relationship between this picture and the concepts in this standard (i.e., the needs of plants and how this plant changed the environment to meet those needs).

When learners are identifying relationships between concepts or ideas (three connected rectangles), they are said to be at the relational level or engaged in relational thinking. In Ms. Cornish's classroom, this learner might state "the plant, as it began to grow, broke through the pavement." In this case, the learner has related the growth or change in the plant to the break or change in the sidewalk. The next step in the SOLO progression is for the learner to transfer learning to different contexts (three connected rectangles with the extension). At the extended abstract level of thinking, learners formulate big ideas and generalize their learning to a new domain (Hook & Mills, 2011, 2012; Martin, 2012). For example, an extended abstract thinker in Ms. Cornish's classroom might ask about the consequences of roads and sidewalks being built near forests. Learners at this level may begin to generalize this to a human having to wear larger clothing sizes as he or she grows from a baby to a kindergartner or storing food in a refrigerator. The big idea, of course, is animals and plants change the environment to meet their needs (NGSS Lead States, 2013).

We will revisit the SOLO Taxonomy throughout the next several chapters, as this way of looking at levels of complexity will inform not only what we teach but also how we teach, why we teach certain content and skills, and when we teach certain concepts, skills, and understandings. However, at this point in analyzing what to teach, the SOLO Taxonomy supports our alignment of the levels of complexity with the concepts in the standard. In other words, don't focus solely on the verb "identify" or "describe." Instead, focus on what the standard is asking learners to identify and describe. Does this standard ask learners to identify discrete characteristics of an environment or to identify relationships between those characteristics and how plants and animals change their environment? Does the standard ask learners to describe the needs of plants and animals or to describe how they change the environment to meet their needs? Notice that there is a significant difference in the level of complexities just in what learners are asked to identify and describe.

CONCEPTS: (nouns)	COMPLEXITY: (verbs)
Change	Claim – Relational Thinking
Argument	Present – Relational Thinking
Evidence	Support with – Relational Thinking
Plants	Identify and Describe – Multitructurals Thinking
Animals	Identify and Describe – Multistructural Thinking
Humans	Identify and Describe – Multistructural Thinking
Environment	Identify and Describe – Multistructural Thinking
Needs	Identify and Describe – Multistructural Thinking
Ideas	Comparing – Relational Thinking
Representations	Comparing – Relational Thinking
Natural	Comparing – Relational Thinking
Designed	Comparing – Relational Thinking
Claim	Support – Relational Thinking
Phenomenon	Support – Relational Thinking
Impact	Know – Multistructural Thinking
Land	Know – Multistructural Thinking
Air	Know – Multistructural Thinking
Water	Know – Multistructural Thinking
Other Living Things	Know – Multistructural Thinking
Parts that work together	Know – Multistructural Thinking

Figure 2.12 Unpacking Concepts, Verbs, and Level of Complexity with SOLO.

Therefore, the final part in unpacking the standard is for Ms. Cornish and her team to understand the type of thinking called for in K-ESS2-2. "We go through each verb and discuss what level of thinking is involved. Are learners supposed to think about single ideas, multiple ideas, relationships, or applications? This informs our teaching in such a big way. We have to have this discussion instead of just looking at what the verb is in the standard." Again, this is vital if we are to plan, design, and implement high-quality, high-impact teaching and learning experiences that move student thinking forward to higher levels of complexity (Figure 2.12).

As we look at the levels of complexity, we see that this standard raises the bar by asking kindergarteners to move beyond unistructural thinking and begin to engage with multiple ideas and the relationships between those ideas.

Research to Classroom Practice Tasks

What are the levels of complexity in the standard you have unpacked? What are your observations about the type of thinking involved in the standard? How does this make you think about the how, why, when, where, and who in your classroom?

The analysis of what to teach in inclusive early childhood science leads us through an in-depth analysis of the science standards of learning. Whether we are using the NGSS, a national curriculum, or standards unique to our own province, state, or locality, before we can make high-quality decisions about how we teach, why we teach certain content and skills, where learners are in their learning, and when we teach certain concepts, skills, and understandings, we must analyze the science standards of learning. From identifying to understanding and unpacking the standard, Ms. Cornish and her team have a clear view of the cognitive, social-emotional, psychomotor, and behavioral outcomes linked to learning. For example, her team will begin planning learning experiences that build learners' cognitive capacity in understanding how plants and animals interact with their environment to meet their needs. Social-emotional outcomes will be focused on collaborative learning in relation to constructing arguments with peers and supporting those arguments in academic discourse between peers. Behaviorally, Ms. Cornish and her team will focus on creating norms and processes for engaging in collaborative learning and what prosocial behaviors will allow for equity in the access and opportunity for all learners to be successful. Finally, Ms. Cornish and her team will seek to find deliberate, intentional, and purposeful ways to integrate writing and manipulatives into their teaching and learning to work on gross and fine motor skills. As we can see, knowing what to teach springboards us into the how, why, when, where, and who in inclusive early childhood science.

There are additional examples at the end of this chapter on page 43, as well as Chapters 3 and 4. These examples are available for you and your colleagues to critically examine the analysis of a vertical progression of an NGSS standard from kindergarten to third grade. These are merely examples and are not the only way to approach each of the NGSS standards. The teachers also provided commentary and reflections about their process. They unpacked the entire standard and then, in subsequent chapters, focused on one particular strand of the standard. As you critically examine each vertical progression, consider the following reflective questions:

1. Do we see how this standard was unpacked?
2. Is this how my colleagues and I would unpack this standard?
3. What about the levels of complexity within the standard? Do you agree or disagree? How would we have approached this differently in our own analysis?
4. Did the unpacking include all three aspects of the standard (i.e., disciplinary core ideas, crosscutting concepts, and science and engineering practices)?
5. How does this example support your learning and understanding of analyzing what to teach in inclusive early childhood science?

Professional Learning Tasks

1. Identify the science standard of learning for an upcoming unit you will be teaching. Unpack the standard up to the extraction of concepts and align those concepts with the complexity of thinking associated with each concept. Complete the template in Appendix A.
2. Return once again to the discussion of tiered vocabulary. Identify whether each concept in your unpacking is Tier 1, Tier 2, or Tier 3 vocabulary. Based on the distribution of vocabulary across those tiers, what role will vocabulary play in this unit?
3. Using the SOLO Taxonomy, what observations do you have about the level of complexity expected by the standard you unpacked item #1 of this chapter's "Professional Learning Tasks."
4. Based on your unpacking, what cognitive, social-emotional, psychomotor, and behavioral outcomes are expected in this standard?

Family and Community Engagement

1. **Using social media tools to communicate beyond the walls of the classroom:** Through the power of social media, we can capitalize on Facebook, Twitter, and Instagram to communicate what students will be learning in our inclusive early childhood science classrooms. We are able to share this information quickly and in a way that engages parents, guardians, and other community members in the "what" we are teaching. Furthermore, we can use these tools to create an online community of learners that will support the disciplinary core ideas, crosscutting concepts, and science and

engineering practices. For example, we can "friend" or "follow" organizations (e.g., museums, aquariums, research centers) and individuals (e.g., scientists, mathematicians, engineers, computer scientists, authors) who will help provide authentic learning experiences and examples related to what we are teaching in our classrooms. By using these social media tools, teachers, parents, guardians, and community members can communicate instantly, privately, and as often as needed throughout the learning unit.

2. **Video tools:** Sharing information about upcoming learning can be done with tools such as Educreations (https://www.educreations.com/), Flipgrid (https://info.flipgrid.com/), or Screencastify (https://www.screencastify.com/). We can record videos of ourselves and our students sharing or announcing what we will be doing next in science. This can be done as a "preview of coming attractions" or as a big reveal. Setting up a big reveal, where learners create a mystery around the next weekly announcements or special events and then share the links with parents, creates a more supportive connection between home and school. This connection will promote dialogue at home about our students' learning. Videos can also be a great way to have students, parents, guardians, and community members to share their thinking about the topic.
3. **Blogging/class web page:** Maintaining a classroom space in the form of a blog or a class website can be done easily using tools like Kidblog (https://kidblog.org/home/), Padlet (https://padlet.com/), Edmodo (https://new.edmodo.com/), or other web-based learning platforms. As our learners engage in talking about learning and what is happening in our classrooms on a daily basis, providing a platform for students, parents, guardians, and community members a location to go and find information and resources is a great way to engage those outside of our classrooms. For example, we can provide online videos or other websites that can support learners when they are away from the classroom. This is particularly powerful if we provide resources in languages other than English or in different forms (e.g., written information, audio recordings, and visual representations). Blogging and class web pages can provide students, parents, guardians, and community members with resources that support the disciplinary core ideas, crosscutting concepts, and science and engineering practices for those who may not have a background or prior experience in science.
4. **Student as teacher**: Empowering learners to not only explain what they are learning in the science classroom but also to teach science concepts to parents, guardians, and community members further builds assessment-capable visible science learners. For example, we can partner with our students to develop a list of topics to teach at home. This list offers learners a menu of topics that allows them to fill the role of "teacher" - students share their knowledge with the parents, guardians, and community members, who then provide feedback to the classroom teacher as to how the student conveyed the information and his or her confidence in doing so. When possible, this is a great way to involve others in science teaching and learning, leading to a greater understanding of those outside of the classroom about the type of learning occurring in school. Furthermore, we get a good sense of how well our learners understand the concepts, practices, and understandings of science. Plus, this exchange can be documented using social media tools, video tools, or through a web page/class blog.

Additional Examples of the Process for Analyzing the Science Standards of Learning

Kindergarten

K-PS2-1 Motion and Stability: Forces and Interactions

Students who demonstrate understanding can:

K-PS2-1. **Plan and conduct an investigation to compare the effects of different strengths or different directions of pushes and pulls on the motion of an object.** [Clarification Statement: Examples of pushes or pulls could include a string attached to an object being pulled, a person pushing an object, a person stopping a rolling ball, and two objects colliding and pushing on each other.] [*Assessment Boundary: Assessment is limited to different relative strengths or different directions, but not both at the same time. Assessment does not include non-contact pushes or pulls such as those produced by magnets.*]

The performance expectation above was developed using the following elements from the NRC document *A Framework for K-12 Science Education*:

Science and Engineering Practices

Planning and Carrying Out Investigations

Planning and carrying out investigations to answer questions or test solutions to problems in K–2 builds on prior experiences and progresses to simple investigations, based on fair tests, which provide data to support explanations or design solutions.

- With guidance, plan and conduct an investigation in collaboration with peers.

Connections to the Nature of Science

Scientific Investigations Use a Variety of Methods

- Scientists use different ways to study the world.

Disciplinary Core Ideas

PS2.A: Forces and Motion

- Pushes and pulls can have different strengths and directions.
- Pushing or pulling on an object can change the speed or direction of its motion and can start or stop it.

PS2.B: Types of Interactions

- When objects touch or collide, they push on one another and can change motion.

PS3.C: Relationship Between Energy and Forces

- A bigger push or pull makes things speed up or slow down more quickly. *(secondary)*

Crosscutting Concepts

Cause and Effect

- Simple tests can be designed to gather evidence to support or refute student ideas about causes.

PS2.B and PS3.C are conclusions students will draw as part of the investigations they conduct (inquiry)

Observable features of the student performance by the end of the grade:			
1	Identifying the phenomenon to be investigated		
	a	With guidance, students collaboratively identify the phenomenon under investigation, which includes the following idea: the effect caused by different strengths and directions of pushes and pulls on the motion of an object.	
	b	With guidance, students collaboratively identify the purpose of the investigation, which includes gathering evidence to support or refute student ideas about causes of the phenomenon by comparing the effects of different strengths of pushes and pulls on the motion of an object.	
2	Identifying the evidence to address this purpose of the investigation		
	a	With guidance, students collaboratively develop an investigation plan to investigate the relationship between the strength and direction of pushes and pulls and the motion of an object (i.e., qualitative measures or expressions of strength and direction; e.g., harder, softer, descriptions* of "which way").	
	b	Students describe* how the observations they make connect to the purpose of the investigation, including how the observations of the effects on object motion allow causal relationships between pushes and pulls and object motion to be determined	
	c	Students predict the effect of the push of pull on the motion of the object, based on prior experiences.	
3	Planning the investigation		
	a	In the collaboratively developed investigation plan, students describe*:	
		i.	The object whose motion will be investigated.
		ii.	What will be in contact with the object to cause the push or pull.
		iii.	The relative strengths of the push or pull that will be applied to the object to start or stop its motion or change its speed.
		iv.	The relative directions of the push or pull that will be applied to the object.
		v.	How the motion of the object will be observed and recorded.
		vi.	How the push or pull will be applied to vary strength or direction.
4	Collecting the data		
	a	According to the investigation plan they developed, and with guidance, students collaboratively make observations that would allow them to compare the effect on the motion of the object caused by changes in the strength or direction of the pushes and pulls and record their data.	

(a)

K-PS2-2 Motion and Stability: Forces and Interactions

Students who demonstrate understanding can:

K-PS2-2. **Analyze data to determine if a design solution works as intended to changethe speed or direction of an object with a push or a pull.*** [Clarification Statement: Examples of problems requiring a solution could include having a marble or other object move a certain distance, follow a particular path, and knock down other objects. Examples of solutions could include tools such as a ramp to increase the speed of the object and a structure that would cause an object such as a marble or ball to turn.] [*Assessment Boundary: Assessment does not include friction as a mechanism for change in speed.*]

The performance expectation above was developed using the following elements from the NRC document *A Framework for K-12 Science Education*:

Science and Engineering Practices	Disciplinary Core Ideas	Crosscutting Concepts
Analyzing and Interpreting Data Analyzing data in K–2 builds on prior experiences and progresses to collecting, recording, and sharing observations. • Analyze data from tests of an object or tool to determine if it works as intended.	**PS2.A: Forces and Motion** • Pushes and pulls can have different strengths and directions. • Pushing or pulling on an object can change the speed or direction of its motion and can start or stop it. **ETS1.A: Defining Engineering Problems** • A situation that people want to change or create can be approached as a problem to be solved through engineering. Such problems may have many acceptable solutions. *(secondary)*	**Cause and Effect** • Simple tests can be designed to gather evidence to support or refute student ideas about causes.

Observable features of the student performance by the end of the grade:			
1	Organizing data		
	a	With guidance, students organize given information using graphical or visual displays (e.g., pictures, pictographs, drawings, written observations, tables, charts). The given information students organize includes:	
		i.	The relative speed or direction of the object before a push or pull is applied (i.e., qualitative measures and expressions of speed and direction; e.g., faster, slower, descriptions* of "which way").
		ii.	The relative speed or direction of the object after a push or pull is applied.
		iii.	How the relative strength of a push or pull affects the speed or direction of an object (i.e., qualitative measures or expressions of strength; e.g., harder, softer).
2	Identifying relationships		
	a	Using their organization of the given information, students describe* relative changes in the speed or direction of the object caused by pushes or pulls from the design solution.	
3	Interpreting data		
	a	Students describe* the goal of the design solution.	
	b	Students describe* their ideas about how the push or pull from the design solution causes the change in the object's motion.	
	c	Based on the relationships they observed in the data, students describe* whether the push or pull from the design solution causes the intended change in speed or direction of motion of the object.	

(b)

CONCEPTS: (nouns)	COMPLEXITY: (verbs)
Investigation	Plan and conduct – relational thinking
Investigation plan	Develop – relational thinking
Strength (relative strength)	Describe and compare – relational thinking
Direction (relative direction)	Describe and compare – relational thinking
Speed (relative speed)	Describe and compare – relational thinking
Motion (include start and stop)	Describe and observe – multistructural thinking
Object	Describe – multistructural thinking
Changes (in speed, direction, motion)	Describe – relational thinking
Push	Describe – multistructural thinking
Pull	Describe – multistructural thinking
Question	Answer – relational thinking
Goal	Describe – multistructural thinking
Explanation	Support – relational thinking
Tests	Design – relational thinking
Evidence	Gather – relational thinking
Ideas	Describe, support or refute – relational thinking
Causes	Support or refute – relational thinking
Phenomenon	Identify – multistructural thinking
Purpose of the investigation	Identify – multistructural thinking
Effects (on object motion)	Identify, describe, predict, and compare – relational thinking
Causal relationships	Investigate and connect – relational thinking
Observations	Describe and connect – relational thinking
Data	Recordandanalyze – relational thinking
Information	Organize – relational thinking
Design solution	Describe, determine, test – relational thinking
Graphic and visual displays	Create – relational thinking

There are a couple of spots in which "describe" has a different level of complexity based on the concept it is aligned with, hence it sometimes being listed as multistructural thinking and others as relational thinking.

Also, it is important to note that on the NGSS there is a qualification statement that reads "unless otherwise specified, "descriptions" referenced in the evidence statements could include but are not limited to written, oral, pictorial, and kinesthetic descriptions."

First Grade

1-PS4-1 Waves and Their Applications in Technologies for Information Transfer

Students who demonstrate understanding can:

1-PS4-1. **Plan and conduct investigations to provide evidence that vibrating materials can make sound and that sound can make materials vibrate.** [Clarification Statement: Examples of vibrating materials that make sound could include tuning forks and plucking a stretched string. Examples of how sound can make matter vibrate could include holding a piece of paper near a speaker making sound and holding an object near a vibrating tuning fork.]

The performance expectation above was developed using the following elements from the NRC document *A Framework for K-12 Science Education*:

Science and Engineering Practices

Planning and Carrying Out Investigations
Planning and carrying out investigations to answer questions or test solutions to problems in K–2 builds on prior experiences and progresses to simple investigations, based on fair tests, which provide data to support explanations or design solutions.

- Plan and conduct investigations collaboratively to produce evidence to answer a question.

Connections to Nature of Science

Scientific Investigations Use a Variety of Methods

- Science investigations begin with a question.
- Scientists use different ways to study the world.

Disciplinary Core Ideas

PS4.A: Wave Properties

- Sound can make matter vibrate, and vibrating matter can make sound.

Crosscutting Concepts

Cause and Effect

- Simple tests can be designed to gather evidence to support or refute student ideas about causes.

Observable features of the student performance by the end of the grade:			
1	Identifying the phenomenon under investigation		
	a	Students identify and describe* the phenomenon and purpose of the investigation, which include providing evidence to answer questions about the relationship between vibrating materials and sound.	
2	Identifying the evidence to address the purpose of the investigation		
	a	Students collaboratively develop an investigation plan and describe* the evidence that will result from the investigation, including:	
		i.	Observations that sounds can cause materials to vibrate.
		ii.	Observations that vibrating materials can cause sounds.
		iii.	How the data will provide evidence to support or refute ideas about the relationship between vibrating materials and sound.
	b	Students individually describe* (with support) how the evidence will address the purpose of the investigation.	
3	Planning the investigation		
	a	In the collaboratively developed investigation plan, students individually identify and describe*:	
		i.	The materials to be used.
		ii.	How the materials will be made to vibrate to make sound.
		iii.	How resulting sounds will be observed and described*.
		iv.	What sounds will be used to make materials vibrate.
		v.	How it will be determined that a material is vibrating.
4	Collecting the data		
	a	According to the investigation plan they develop, students collaboratively collect and record observations about:	
		i.	Sounds causing materials to vibrate.
		ii.	Vibrating materials causing sounds.

(a)

1-PS4-2 Waves and Their Applications in Technologies for Information Transfer
Students who demonstrate understanding can: **1-PS4-2.** **Make observations to construct an evidence-based account that objects in darkness can be seen only when illuminated.** [Clarification Statement: Examples of observations could include those made in a completely dark room, a pinhole box, and a video of a cave explorer with a flashlight. Illumination could be from an external light source or by an object giving off its own light.]

The performance expectation above was developed using the following elements from the NRC document *A Framework for K-12 Science Education*:

Science and Engineering Practices	Disciplinary Core Ideas	Crosscutting Concepts
Constructing Explanations and Designing Solutions Constructing explanations and designing solutions in K–2 builds on prior experiences and progresses to the use of evidence and ideas in constructing evidence-based accounts of natural phenomena and designing solutions. • Make observations (firsthand or from media) to construct an evidence-based account for natural phenomena.	**PS4.B: Electromagnetic Radiation** • Objects can be seen if light is available to illuminate them or if they give off their own light.	**Cause and Effect** • Simple tests can be designed to gather evidence to support or refute student ideas about causes.

Observable features of the student performance by the end of the grade:			
1	Articulating the explanation of phenomena		
	a	Students articulate a statement that relates the given phenomenon to a scientific idea, including that when an object in the dark is lit (e.g., turning on a light in the dark space or from light the object itself gives off), it can be seen.	
	b	Students use evidence and reasoning to construct an evidence-based account of the phenomenon.	
2	Evidence		
	a	Students make observations (firsthand or from media) to serve as the basis for evidence, including:	
		i.	The appearance (e.g., visible, not visible, somewhat visible but difficult to see) of objects in a space with no light.
		ii.	The appearance (e.g., visible, not visible, somewhat visible but difficult to see) of objects in a space with light.
		iii.	The appearance (e.g., visible, not visible, somewhat visible but difficult to see) of objects (e.g., light bulbs, glow sticks) that give off light in a space with no other light.
	b	Students describe how their observations provide evidence to support their explanation.	
3	Reasoning		
	a	Students logically connect the evidence to support the evidence-based account of the phenomenon. Students describe lines of reasoning that include:	
		i.	The presence of light in a space causes objects to be able to be seen in that space.
		ii.	Objects cannot be seen if there is no light to illuminate them, but the same object in the same space can be seen if a light source is introduced.
		iii.	The ability of an object to give off its own light causes the object to be seen in a space where there is no other light.

(b)

1-PS4-3 Waves and Their Applications in Technologies for Information Transfer

Students who demonstrate understanding can:

1-PS4-3. **Plan and conduct investigations to determine the effect of placing objects made with different materials in the path of a beam of light.** [Clarification Statement: Examples of materials could include those that are transparent (such as clear plastic), translucent (such as wax paper), opaque (such as cardboard), and reflective (such as a mirror).] [*Assessment Boundary: Assessment does not include the speed of light.*]

The performance expectation above was developed using the following elements from the NRC document *A Framework for K-12 Science Education*:

Science and Engineering Practices	Disciplinary Core Ideas	Crosscutting Concepts
Planning and Carrying Out Investigations Planning and carrying out investigations to answer questions or test solutions to problems in K–2 builds on prior experiences and progresses to simple investigations, based on fair tests, which provide data to support explanations or design solutions. • Plan and conduct investigations collaboratively to produce evidence to answer a question.	**PS4.B: Electromagnetic Radiation** • Some materials allow light to pass through them, others allow only some light through and others block all the light and create a dark shadow on any surface beyond them, where the light cannot reach. Mirrors can be used to redirect a light beam. (Boundary: The idea that light travels from place to place is developed through experiences with light sources, mirrors, and shadows, but no attempt is made to discuss the speed of light.)	**Cause and Effect** • Simple tests can be designed to gather evidence to support or refute student ideas about causes.

Observable features of the student performance by the end of the grade:			
1	Identifying the phenomenon under investigation		
	a	Students identify and describe* the phenomenon and purpose of the investigation, which include:	
		i.	Answering a question about what happens when objects made of different materials (that allow light to pass through them in different ways) are placed in the path of a beam of light.
		ii.	Designing and conducting an investigation to gather evidence to support or refute student ideas about putting objects made of different materials in the path of a beam of light.
2	Identifying evidence to address the purpose of the investigation		
	a	Students collaboratively develop an investigation plan and describe* the data that will result from the investigation, including:	
		i.	Observations of the effect of placing objects made of different materials in a beam of light, including:
			1. A material that allows all light through results in the background lighting up.
			2. A material that allows only some light through results in the background lighting up, but looking darker than when the material allows all light in.
			3. A material that blocks all of the light will create a shadow.
			4. A material that changes the direction of the light will light up the surrounding space in a different direction.
	b	Students individually describe* how these observations provide evidence to answer the question under investigation.	
3	Planning the investigation		
	a	In the collaboratively developed investigation plan, students individually describe* (with support):	
		i.	The materials to be placed in the beam of light, including:
			1. A material that allows all light through (e.g., clear plastic, clear glass).
			2. A material that allows only some light through (e.g., clouded plastic, wax paper).
			3. A material that blocks all of the light (e.g., cardboard, wood).
			4. A material that changes the direction of the light (e.g., mirror, aluminum foil).
		ii.	How the effect of placing different materials in the beam of light will be observed and recorded.
		iii.	The light source used to produce the beam of light.
4	Collecting the data		
	a	Students collaboratively collect and record observations about what happens when objects made of materials that allow light to pass through them in different ways are placed in the path of a beam of light, according to the developed investigation plan.	

(c)

1-PS4-4 Waves and Their Applications in Technologies for Information Transfer

Students who demonstrate understanding can:

1-PS4-4. **Use tools and materials to design and build a device that uses light or sound to solve the problem of communicating over a distance.*** [Clarification Statement: Examples of devices could include a light source to send signals, paper cup and string "telephones," and a pattern of drum beats.] [*Assessment Boundary: Assessment does not include technological details for how communication devices work.*]

The performance expectation above was developed using the following elements from the NRC document *A Framework for K-12 Science Education*:

Science and Engineering Practices	Disciplinary Core Ideas	Crosscutting Concepts
Constructing Explanations and Designing Solutions Constructing explanations and designing solutions in K–2 builds on prior experiences and progresses to the use of evidence and ideas in constructing evidence-based accounts of natural phenomena and designing solutions. • Use tools and materials provided to design a device that solves a specific problem.	**PS4.C: Information Technologies and Instrumentation** • People also use a variety of devices to communicate (send and receive information) over long distances.	- ***Connections to Engineering, Technology, and Applications of Science*** **Influence of Engineering, Technology, and Science, on Society and the Natural World** • People depend on various technologies in their lives; human life would be very different without technology.

Observable features of the student performance by the end of the grade:			
1	Using scientific knowledge to generate design solutions		
	a	Students describe* a given problem involving people communicating over long distances.	
	b	With guidance, students design and build a device that uses light or sound to solve the given problem.	
	c	With guidance, students describe* the scientific information they use to design the solution.	
2	Describing* specific features of the design solution, including quantification when appropriate		
	a	Students describe* that specific expected or required features of the design solution should include:	
		i.	The device is able to send or receive information over a given distance.
		ii.	The device must use light or sound to communicate.
	b	Students use only the materials provided when building the device.	
3	Evaluating potential solutions		
	a	Students describe* whether the device:	
		i.	Has the expected or required features of the design solution.
		ii.	Provides a solution to the problem involving people communicating over a distance by using light or sound.
	b	Students describe* how communicating over long distances helps people.	

With how frequently "communicating" is mentioned, I would include communication in the CONCEPTS

(d)

CONCEPTS: (nouns)	COMPLEXITY: (verbs)
Investigations	Plan and conduct – relational thinking
Evidence	Use, provide, gather,and describe – relational thinking
Reasoning	Use and explain – relational thinking
Materials	Use and describe – – multistructural thinking
(Design)solutions	Test and design – abstract thinking
Problems	Test, describe, and solve – abstract thinking
Questions	Answer – relational thinking
Ideas	Supportor refute – relational thinking
Causes	Supportor refute – relational thinking
Fair tests	Design and conduct – relational thinking
Explanations	Supportand construct – relational thinking
Purpose of the investigation	Identify and describe – relational thinking
Investigation plan	Develop – relational thinking
Natural Phenomenon	Identify and describe – relational thinking
Relationship	Describe – relational thinking
Observations	Make, collect, record, and describe – relational thinking
Appearance	Describe – multistructural thinking
Lines of reasoning	Describe – relational thinking
Data	Describe – multistructural thinking
Evidence based account	Construct – relational thinking
Sound	Observe and describe – multistructural thinking
Matter	Observe and describe – multistructural thinking
Vibrating matter	Observe and describe – multistructural thinking
Materials	Identify and describe – multistructural thinking
Scientific idea	Articulate – relational thinking
Statement	Articulate – relational thinking
Light	Observe and describe – multistructural thinking
Objects (in darkness)	Observe and describe – multistructural thinking
Space(with light or with no light)	Describe – multistructural thinking
Effects	Describe – relational thinking
Beam of light	Identifyand describe – multistructural thinking
Shadow	Observe and describe – relational thinking
Surface	Describe – multistructural thinking
Background	Describe – multistructural thinking
Mirror (or object that changes direction of light)	Use, observe, and describe effects – relational thinking
Direction	Describe – relational thinking
Materials that allow all light through	Observe and describe – multistructural thinking
Materials that allow only some light through	Observe and describe – multistructural thinking
Materials that block all light	Observe and describe – multistructural thinking
Light source	Describe – multistructural thinking
Path of the light	Observe and describe – multistructural thinking
People	Know – multistructural thinking
Technologies	Know – multistructural thinking
Human life	Know – multistructural thinking
Communication*	Describe – multistructural thinking
Device	Describe, design, and build – abstract thinking
Long distances	Describe – multistructural thinking
Features	Describe – multistructural thinking

*The idea of communicating is referenced in 1-PS4-4 though the term communication itself is not used. This forms the crux of the problem solving task of the standard, therefore, it is included as a concept.

Second Grade

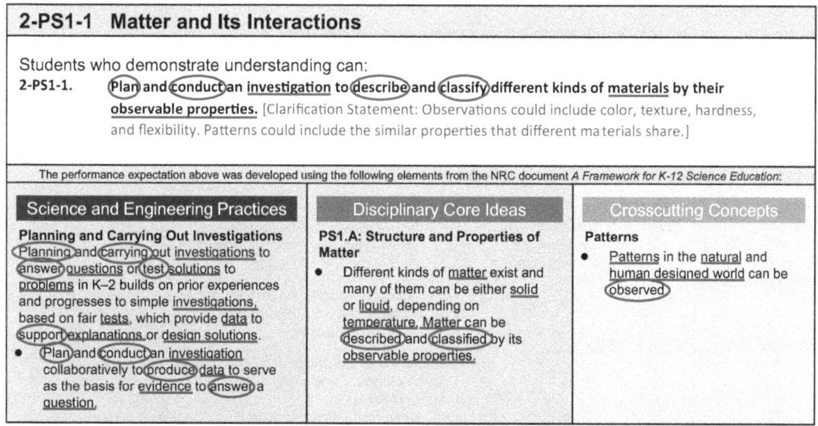

2-PS1-1 Matter and Its Interactions

Students who demonstrate understanding can:

2-PS1-1. **Plan and conduct an investigation to describe and classify different kinds of materials by their observable properties.** [Clarification Statement: Observations could include color, texture, hardness, and flexibility. Patterns could include the similar properties that different materials share.]

The performance expectation above was developed using the following elements from the NRC document *A Framework for K-12 Science Education*:

Science and Engineering Practices	Disciplinary Core Ideas	Crosscutting Concepts
Planning and Carrying Out Investigations Planning and carrying out investigations to answer questions or test solutions to problems in K–2 builds on prior experiences and progresses to simple investigations, based on fair tests, which provide data to support explanations or design solutions. • Plan and conduct an investigation collaboratively to produce data to serve as the basis for evidence to answer a question.	**PS1.A: Structure and Properties of Matter** • Different kinds of matter exist and many of them can be either solid or liquid, depending on temperature. Matter can be described and classified by its observable properties.	**Patterns** • Patterns in the natural and human designed world can be observed.

Observable features of the student performance by the end of the grade:			
1	Identifying the phenomenon under investigation		
	a	Students identify and describe* the phenomenon under investigation, which includes the following idea: different kinds of matter have different properties, and sometimes the same kind of matter has different properties depending on temperature.	
	b	Students identify and describe* the purpose of the investigation, which includes answering a question about the phenomenon under investigation by describing* and classifying different kinds of materials by their observable properties.	
2	Identifying the evidence to address the purpose of the investigation		
	a	Students collaboratively develop an investigation plan and describe* the evidence that will be collected including the properties of matter (e.g., color, texture, hardness, flexibility, whether is it a solid or a liquid) of the materials that would allow for classification, and the temperature at which those properties are observed.	
	b	Students individually describe* that:	
		i.	The observations of the materials provide evidence about the properties of different kinds of materials.
		ii.	Observable patterns in the properties of materials provide evidence to classify the different kinds of materials.
3	Planning the investigation		
	a	In the collaboratively developed investigation plan, students include:	
		i.	Which materials will be described* and classified (e.g., different kinds of metals, rocks, wood, soil, powders).
		ii.	Which materials will be observed at different temperatures, and how those temperatures will be determined (e.g., using ice to cool and a lamp to warm) and measured (e.g., qualitatively or quantitatively).
		iii.	How the properties of the materials will be determined.
		iv.	How the materials will be classified (i.e., sorted) by the pattern of the properties.
	b	Students individually describe* how the properties of materials, and the method for classifying them, are relevant to answering the question.	
4	Collecting the data		
	a	According to the developed investigation plan, students collaboratively collect and record data on the properties of the materials.	

Teacher Reflections: Important to note that 2a says to "collaboratively develop"...while developing an investigation plan is a cognitively complex task, students are doing it with the combined ideas of their peers and the guidance of the teacher. Whereas, 2b tasks students with individually describing their observations, so all studentsneed the vocabulary and scaffolding to complete that part of the task.

(a)

2-PS1-2 Matter and Its Interactions

Students who demonstrate understanding can:

2-PS1-2. Analyze data obtained from testing different materials to determine which materials have the properties that are best suited for an intended purpose.* [Clarification Statement: Examples of properties could include, strength, flexibility, hardness, texture, and absorbency.] [*Assessment Boundary: Assessment of quantitative measurements is limited to length.*]

The performance expectation above was developed using the following elements from the NRC document *A Framework for K-12 Science Education*:

Science and Engineering Practices	Disciplinary Core Ideas	Crosscutting Concepts
Analyzing and Interpreting Data Analyzing data in K–2 builds on prior experiences and progresses to collecting, recording, and sharing observations. • Analyze data from tests of an object or tool to determine if it works as intended.	**PS1.A: Structure and Properties of Matter** • Different properties are suited to different purposes.	**Cause and Effect** • Simple tests can be designed to gather evidence to support or refute student ideas about causes. - - - - - - - - - - ***Connections to Engineering, Technology, and Applications of Science*** **Influence of Engineering, Technology, and Science, on Society and the Natural World** • Every human-made product is designed by applying some knowledge of the natural world and is built using materials derived from the natural world.

Teacher Reflections: I have underlined the specified properties because I think they are concepts that are important to this unit, though not necessarily an all-inclusive list of the properties to explore. However, I did not underline the given examples (e.g. metal is strong).

Observable features of the student performance by the end of the grade:		
1	Organizing data	
	a	Using graphical displays (e.g., pictures, charts, grade-appropriate graphs), students use the given data from tests of different materials to organize those materials by their properties (e.g., strength, flexibility, hardness, texture, ability to absorb).
2	Identifying relationships	
	a	Students describe* relationships between materials and their properties (e.g., metal is strong, paper is absorbent, rocks are hard, sandpaper is rough).
	b	Students identify and describe* relationships between properties of materials and some potential uses purpose (e.g., hardness is good for breaking objects or supporting objects; roughness is good for keeping objects in place; flexibility is good to keep a materials from breaking, but not good for keeping materials rigidly in place).
3	Interpreting data	
	a	Students describe* which properties allow a material to be well suited for a given intended use (e.g., ability to absorb for cleaning up spills, strength for building material, hardness for breaking a nut).
	b	Students use their organized data to support or refute their ideas about which properties of materials allow the object or tool to be best suited for the given intended purpose relative to the other given objects/tools (e.g., students could support the idea that hardness allows a wooden shelf to be better suited for supporting materials placed on it than a sponge would be, based on the patterns relating property to a purpose; students could refute an idea that a thin piece of glass is better suited to be a shelf than a wooden plank would be because it is harder than the wood by using data from tests of hardness and strength to give evidence that the glass is less strong than the wood).
	c	Students describe* how the given data from the test provided evidence of the suitability of different materials for the intended purpose.

(b)

2-PS1-3 Matter and Its Interactions

Students who demonstrate understanding can:

2-PS1-3. **Make observations to construct an evidence-based account of how an object made of a small set of pieces can be disassembled and made into a new object.** [Clarification Statement: Examples of pieces could include blocks, building bricks, or other assorted small objects.]

The performance expectation above was developed using the following elements from the NRC document *A Framework for K-12 Science Education*:

Science and Engineering Practices	Disciplinary Core Ideas	Crosscutting Concepts
Constructing Explanations and Designing Solutions Constructing explanations and designing solutions in K–2 builds on prior experiences and progresses to the use of evidence and ideas in constructing evidence-based accounts of natural phenomena and designing solutions. • Make observations (firsthand or from media) to construct an evidence-based account for natural phenomena.	**PS1.A: Structure and Properties of Matter** • Different properties are suited to different purposes. • A great variety of objects can be built up from a small set of pieces.	**Energy and Matter** • Objects may break into smaller pieces and be put together into larger pieces, or change shapes.

Observable features of the student performance by the end of the grade:			
1	Articulating the explanation of phenomena		
	a	Students articulate a statement that relates the given phenomenon to a scientific idea, including that an object made of a small set of pieces can be disassembled and made into a new object.	
	b	Students use evidence and reasoning to construct an evidence-based account of the phenomenon.	
2	Evidence		
	a	Students describe* evidence from observations (firsthand or from media), including:	
		i.	The characteristics (e.g., size, shape, arrangement of parts) of the original object.
		ii.	That the original object was disassembled into pieces.
		iii.	That the pieces were reassembled into a new object or objects.
		iv.	The characteristics (e.g., size, shape, arrangement of parts) of the new object or objects.
3	Reasoning		
	a	Students use reasoning to connect the evidence to support an explanation. Students describe* a chain of reasoning that includes:	
		i.	The original object was disassembled into its pieces and is reassembled into a new object or objects.
		ii.	Many different objects can be built from the same set of pieces.
		iii.	Compared to the original object, the new object or objects can have different characteristics, even though they were made of the same set of pieces.

(c)

2-PS1-4 Matter and Its Interactions

Students who demonstrate understanding can:

2-PS1-4. **Construct an argument with evidence that some changes caused by heating or cooling can be reversed and some cannot.** [Clarification Statement: Examples of reversible changes could include materials such as water and butter at different temperatures. Examples of irreversible changes could include cooking an egg, freezing a plant leaf, and heating paper.]

The performance expectation above was developed using the following elements from the NRC document *A Framework for K-12 Science Education*:

Science and Engineering Practices	Disciplinary Core Ideas	Crosscutting Concepts
Engaging in Argument from Evidence Engaging in argument from evidence in K–2 builds on prior experiences and progresses to comparing ideas and representations about the natural and designed world(s). • Construct an argument with evidence to support a claim. - ***Connections to Nature of Science*** **Science Models, Laws, Mechanisms, and Theories Explain Natural Phenomena** • ~~Science~~ searches for cause and effect ~~relationships to explain natural events.~~	**PS1.B: Chemical Reactions** • Heating or cooling a substance may cause changes that can be observed. Sometimes these changes are reversible, and sometimes they are not.	**Cause and Effect** • Events have causes that generate observable patterns.

Observable features of the student performance by the end of the grade:			
1	Supported claims		
	a	Students make a claim to be supported about a phenomenon. In their claim, students include the idea that some changes caused by heating or cooling can be reversed and some cannot.	
2	Identifying scientific evidence		
	a	Students describe* the given evidence, including:	
		i.	The characteristics of the material before heating or cooling.
		ii.	The characteristics of the material after heating or cooling.
		iii.	The ~~characteristics~~ of the ~~material~~ when the ~~heating~~ or ~~cooling~~ is ~~reversed.~~
3	Evaluating and critiquing the evidence		
	a	Students evaluate the evidence to determine:	
		i.	The change in the material after heating (e.g., ice becomes water, an egg becomes solid, solid chocolate becomes liquid).
		ii.	Whether the change in the material after heating is reversible (e.g., water becomes ice again, a cooked egg remains a solid, liquid chocolate becomes solid but can be a different shape).
		iii.	The change in the material after cooling (e.g., when frozen, water becomes ice, a plant leaf dies).
		iv.	Whether the change in the material after cooling is reversible (e.g., ice becomes water again, a plant leaf does not return to normal).
	b	Students describe* whether the given evidence supports the claim and whether additional evidence is needed.	
4	Reasoning and synthesis		
	a	Students use reasoning to connect the evidence to the claim. Students describe* the following chain of reasoning:	
		i.	Some changes caused by heating or cooling can be reversed by cooling or heating (e.g., ice that is heated can melt into water, but the water can be cooled and can freeze back into ice [and vice versa]).
		ii.	Some changes caused by heating or cooling cannot be reversed by cooling or heating (e.g., a raw egg that is cooked by heating cannot be turned back into a raw egg by cooling the cooked egg, cookie dough that is baked does not return to its uncooked form when cooled, charcoal that is formed by heating wood does not return to its original form when cooled).

Teacher Reflections: I considered "reversed" a concept not a verb because we aren't using it as a skill or level of complexity.

(c)

CONCEPTS: (nouns)	COMPLEXITY: (verbs)
Investigation	Plan and conduct – relational thinking
Purpose of the Investigation	Identify and describe – relational thinking
Investigation plan	Develop – relational thinking
Materials	Describe, classify/organize, test – relational thinking
Observable properties	Describe and classify – relational thinking
Color	Describe – multistructural thinking
Texture	Describe – multistructural thinking
Hardness	Describe – multistructural thinking
Flexibility	Describe – multistructural thinking
Method of classification	Determineand describe – relational thinking
Observations	Describe, make/collect, record, and share – multistructural thinking
Questions	Answer – relational thinking
Solutions	Design, test,and support – abstract thinking
Problems	Test – relational thinking
Data	Collect, record, organize, and analyze – relational thinking
Object	Test, build, and compare* – relational thinking
Tool	Test and compare* – relational thinking
Explanations	Supportand construct – relational thinking
Evidence	Describeand connect – relational thinking
Matter	Describe and classify – relational thinking
Solid	Know – multistructural thinking
Liquid	Know – multistructural thinking
Temperature	Identify, describe, and measure – multistructural thinking
Changes	Describe – multistructural thinking
Heating	Describe – multistructural thinking
Cooling	Describe – multistructural thinking
Reversible	Know – multistructural thinking
Patterns	Observeand describe – relational thinking
Natural world	Observe – multistructural thinking
Human designed world	Observe – multistructural thinking
Phenomenon	Identify, describe, and relate – relational thinking
Idea	Identify, describe, compare, support/refute – relational thinking
Claim	Make and support – relational thinking
Causes	Support or refute – relational thinking
Intended purpose/use	Describe – multistructural thinking
Suitability	Determine and Describe – relational thinking
Test	Design – relational thinking
Human-made product	Design – relational thinking
Graphical displays	Create – relational thinking
Knowledge	Apply – abstract thinking
Relationships	Identify and describe – relational thinking
Evidence-based account	Construct – relational thinking
Set of pieces	Manipulate** – relational thinking
Shapes	Describe – multistructural thinking
Characteristics	Describe and compare – relational thinking
Statement	Articulate – relational thinking
Chain of Reasoning	Use and describe – relational thinking
Argument	Construct – relational thinking

*2-PS1-2 feature 3b "best suited for the given intended purpose relative to the other given objects/tools"= comparing

**2-PS1-3 "an object made of a small set of pieces can be disassembled and made into a new object" = manipulate

Third Grade

3-PS2-1 Motion and Stability: Forces and Interactions

Students who demonstrate understanding can:

3-PS2-1. **Plan and conduct an investigation to provide evidence of the effects of balanced and unbalanced forces on the motion of an object.** [Clarification Statement: Examples could include an unbalanced force on one side of a ball can make it start moving; and, balanced forces pushing on a box from both sides will not produce any motion at all.] [*Assessment Boundary: Assessment is limited to one variable at a time: number, size, or direction of forces. Assessment does not include quantitative force size, only qualitative and relative. Assessment is limited to gravity being addressed as a force that pulls objects down.]*

The performance expectation above was developed using the following elements from the NRC document *A Framework for K-12 Science Education*:

Science and Engineering Practices

Planning and Carrying Out Investigations

Planning and carrying out investigations to answer questions or test solutions to problems in 3–5 builds on K–2 experiences and progresses to include investigations that control variables and provide evidence to support explanations or design solutions.

- Plan and conduct an investigation collaboratively to produce data to serve as the basis for evidence, using fair tests in which variables are controlled and the number of trials considered.

Connections to Nature of Science

Scientific Investigations Use a Variety of Methods

- Science investigations use a variety of methods, tools, and techniques.

Disciplinary Core Ideas

PS2.A: Forces and Motion

- Each force acts on one particular object and has both strength and a direction. An object at rest typically has multiple forces acting on it, but they add to give zero net force on the object. Forces that do not sum to zero can cause changes in the object's speed or direction of motion. (Boundary: Qualitative and conceptual, but not quantitative addition of forces are used at this level.)

PS2.B: Types of Interactions

- Objects in contact exert forces on each other.

Crosscutting Concepts

Cause and Effect

- Cause and effect relationships are routinely identified.

Observable features of the student performance by the end of the grade:			
1	Identifying the phenomenon under investigation		
	a	Students identify and describe the phenomenon under investigation, which includes the effects of different forces on an object's motion (e.g., starting, stopping, or changing direction).	
	b	Students describe the purpose of the investigation, which includes producing data to serve as the basis for evidence for how balanced and unbalanced forces determine an object's motion.	
2	Identifying the evidence to address the purpose of the investigation		
	a	Students collaboratively develop an investigation plan. In the investigation plan, students describe* the data to be collected, including:	
		i.	The change in motion of an object at rest after:
			1. Different strengths and directions of balanced forces (forces that sum to zero) are applied to the object.
			2. Different strengths and directions of unbalanced forces (forces that do not sum to zero) are applied to the object (e.g., strong force on the right, weak force or the left).
		ii.	What causes the forces on the object.
	b	Students individually describe* how the evidence to be collected will be relevant to determining the effects of balanced and unbalanced forces on an object's motion.	
3	Planning the investigation		
	a	In the collaboratively developed investigation plan, students describe* how the motion of the object will be observed and recorded, including defining the following features:	
		i.	The object whose motion will be investigated.
		ii.	The objects in contact that exert forces on each other.
		iii.	Changing one variable at a time (e.g., control strength and vary the direction, or control direction and vary the strength).
		iv.	The number of trials that will be conducted in the investigation to produce sufficient data.
	b	Students individually describe* how their investigation plan will allow them to address the purpose of the investigation.	
4	Collecting the data		
	a	Students collaboratively collect and record data according to the investigation plan they developed, including data from observations and/or measurements of:	
		i.	An object at rest and the identification of the forces acting on the object.
		ii.	An object in motion and the identification of the forces acting on the object.

(a)

3-PS2-2 Motion and Stability: Forces and Interactions

Students who demonstrate understanding can:

3-PS2-2. **Make observations and/or measurements of an object's motion to provide evidence that a pattern can be used to predict future motion.** [Clarification Statement: Examples of motion with a predictable pattern could include a child swinging in a swing, a ball rolling back and forth in a bowl, and two children on a see-saw.] [*Assessment Boundary: Assessment does not include technical terms such as period and frequency.*]

The performance expectation above was developed using the following elements from the NRC document *A Framework for K-12 Science Education*:

Science and Engineering Practices	Disciplinary Core Ideas	Crosscutting Concepts
Planning and Carrying Out Investigations Planning and carrying out investigations to answer questions or test solutions to problems in 3–5 builds on K–2 experiences and progresses to include investigations that control variables and provide evidence to support explanations or design solutions. • Make observations and/or measurements to produce data to serve as the basis for evidence for an explanation of a phenomenon or test a design solution. - - - - - - - - - - ***Connections to Nature of Science*** **Science Knowledge is Based on Empirical Evidence** • Science findings are based on recognizing patterns.	**PS2.A: Forces and Motion** • The patterns of an object's motion in various situations can be observed and measured; when that past motion exhibits a regular pattern, future motion can be predicted from it. (Boundary: Technical terms, such as magnitude, velocity, momentum, and vector quantity, are not introduced at this level, but the concept that some quantities need both size and direction to be described is developed.)	**Patterns** • Patterns of change can be used to make predictions.

Observable features of the student performance by the end of the grade:		
1	Identifying the phenomenon under investigation	
	a	From the given investigation plan, students identify and describe the phenomenon under investigation, which includes observable patterns in the motion of an object.
	b	Students identify and describe* the purpose of the investigation, which includes providing evidence for an explanation of the phenomenon that includes the idea that patterns of motion can be used to predict future motion of an object.
2	Identifying the evidence to address the purpose of the investigation	
	a	Based on a given investigation plan, students identify and describe the data to be collected through observations and/or measurements, including data on the motion of the object as it repeats a pattern over time (e.g., a pendulum swinging , a ball moving on a curvedtrack, a magnet repelling another magnet).
	b	Students describe* how the data will serve as evidence of a pattern in the motion of an object and how that pattern can be used to predict future motion.
3	Planning the investigation	
	a	From the given investigation plan, students identify and describe how the data will be collected, including how:
		i. The motion of the object will be observed and measured
		ii. Evidence of a pattern in the motion of the object will be identified from the data on the motion of the object.
		iii. The pattern in the motion of the object can be used to predict future motion.
4	Collecting the data	
	a	Students make observations and/or measurements of the motion of the object, according to the given investigation plan, to identify a pattern that can be used to predict future motion.

(b)

3-PS2-3 Motion and Stability: Forces and Interactions

Students who demonstrate understanding can:

3-PS2-3. **Ask questions to determine cause and effect relationships of electric or magnetic interactions between two objects not in contact with each other.** [Clarification Statement: Examples of an electric force could include the force on hair from an electrically charged balloon and the electrical forces between a charged rod and pieces of paper; examples of a magnetic force could include the force between two permanent magnets, the force between an electromagnet and steel paperclips, and the force exerted by one magnet versus the force exerted by two magnets. Examples of cause and effect relationships could include how the distance between objects affects strength of the force and how the orientation of magnets affects the direction of the magnetic force.] [*Assessment Boundary: Assessment is limited to forces produced by objects that can be manipulated by students, and electrical interactions are limited to static electricity.*]

The performance expectation above was developed using the following elements from the NRC document *A Framework for K-12 Science Education*:

Science and Engineering Practices	Disciplinary Core Ideas	Crosscutting Concepts
Asking Questions and Defining Problems Asking questions and defining problems in grades 3–5 builds on grades K–2 experiences and progresses to specifying qualitative relationships. • Ask questions that can be investigated based on patterns such as cause and effect relationships.	**PS2.B: Types of Interactions** • Electric, and magnetic forces between a pair of objects do not require that the objects be in contact. The sizes of the forces in each situation depend on the properties of the objects and their distances apart and, for forces between two magnets, on their orientation relative to each other.	**Cause and Effect** • Cause and effect relationships are routinely identified, tested, and used to explain change.

Observable features of the student performance by the end of the grade:			
1	Addressing phenomena of the natural world		
	a	Students ask questions that arise from observations of two objects not in contact with each other interacting through electric or magnetic forces, the answers to which would clarify the cause-and-effect relationships between:	
		i.	The sizes of the forces on the two interacting objects due to the distance between the two objects.
		ii.	The relative orientation of two magnets and whether the force between the magnets is attractive or repulsive.
		iii.	The presence of a magnet and the force the magnet exerts on other objects.
		iv.	Electrically charged objects and an electric force.
2	Identifying the scientific nature of the question		
	a	Students' questions can be investigated within the scope of the classroom.	

Teacher Reflections: "Attractive" and "repulsive" are not nouns, but they are certainly two key concepts

(c)

3-PS2-4 Motion and Stability: Forces and Interactions

Students who demonstrate understanding can:

3-PS2-4. **Define a simple design problem that can be solved by applying scientific ideas about magnets.*** [Clarification Statement: Examples of problems could include constructing a latch to keep a door shut and creating a device to keep two moving objects from touching each other.]

The performance expectation above was developed using the following elements from the NRC document *A Framework for K-12 Science Education*

Science and Engineering Practices	Disciplinary Core Ideas	Crosscutting Concepts
Asking Questions and Defining Problems Asking questions and defining problems in grades 3–5 builds on grades K–2 experiences and progresses to specifying qualitative relationships. • Define a simple problem that can be solved through the development of a new or improved object or tool.	**PS2.B: Types of Interactions** • Electric, and magnetic forces between a pair of objects do not require that the objects be in contact. The sizes of the forces in each situation depend on the properties of the objects and their distances apart and, for forces between two magnets, on their orientation relative to each other.	- - - - - - - - - - - - - - - - ***Connections to Engineering, Technology, and Applications of Science*** **Interdependence of Science, Engineering, and Technology** • Scientific discoveries about the natural world can often lead to new and improved technologies, which are developed through the engineering design process.

Observable features of the student performance by the end of the grade:			
1	Identifying the problem to be solved		
	a	Students identify and describe a simple design problem that can be solved by applying a scientific understanding of the forces between interacting magnets.	
	b	Students identify and describe the scientific ideas necessary for solving the problem, including:	
		i.	Force between objects do not require that those objects be in contact with each other
		ii.	The size of the force depends on the properties of objects, distance between the objects, and orientation of magnetic objects relative to one another.
2	Defining the criteria and constraints		
	a	Students identify and describe the criteria (desirable features) for a successful solution to the problem.	
	b	Students identify and describe the constraints (limits) such as:	
		i.	Time.
		ii.	Cost.
		iii.	Materials.

(d)

CONCEPTS: (nouns)	COMPLEXITY: (verbs)
Investigation	Plan and conduct – relational thinking
Evidence	Identify and describe – relational thinking
Effects	Describe – relational thinking
Unbalanced forces	Describe and apply – multistructuralthinking
Balancedforces	Describe and apply – multistructural thinking
Net force	Know – multistructural thinking
Strength	Describe – multistructural thinking
Direction	Describe – multistructuralthinking
Speed	Describe – multistructural thinking
Motion	Predict, observe, describe, measure – relational thinking
Objectin motion	Describe – multistructural thinking
Objectat rest	Describe – multistructural thinking
Changes	Describe – multistructural thinking
Questions	Ask, investigate, and answer – relational thinking
Problems	Identify, define, anddescribe – relational thinking
Variables	Controland define – relational thinking
Number of trials	Consider and define – multistructural thinking
Explanations	Support – relational thinking
Data	Produce, collect, and describe – multistructural thinking
Pattern of change	Identify, observe, recognize,measure, predict – relational thinking
Phenomenon	Identify and describe – multistructural thinking
Purposeof the investigation	Identify and describe – multistructural thinking
Investigation plan	Develop – relational thinking
Features	Define – multistructural thinking
Observations	Makeand record – multistructural thinking
Measurements	Makeand record – multistructural thinking
Cause and effect relationships	Identify and clarify/specify – relational thinking
Electric interactions	Investigate – relational thinking
Magnetic interactions	Investigate – relational thinking
Size (of force)	Identify and describe* – multistructural thinking
Orientation	Identify and describe * – multistructural thinking
Magnets	Investigate and understand* – relational thinking
(Magnetic) Object	Observe and describe – multistructural thinking
Properties	Identify and describe* – multistructural thinking
Scientific idea/understanding	Apply – relational thinking
Tool	Develop – abstract thinking
Design solutions	Test – relational thinking
Design process	Apply – relational thinking
Criteria	Identify and describe – multistructural thinking
Constraints	Identify and describe – multistructural thinking
Time	Identify and describe – multistructural thinking
Cost	Identify and describe – multistructural thinking
Materials	Identify and describe – multistructural thinking
Discoveries	Make* – relational thinking
Natural world	Observe* – multistructural thinking
Technologies	Develop – abstract thinking

*Verbs determined by thinking about what the standard is asking rather than by the wording usedin the standard.

3 Mapping Out the Progression of What to Teach in Inclusive Early Childhood Science

Our next step toward the implementation of effective teaching and learning in the inclusive early childhood science classroom requires us to take what we teach and design learning experiences that consider the how, who, where, and when. For example, we have to decide how best to approach the learning based on the prior knowledge and experiences of our learners - the who. Then we have to decide where and when to introduce new learning and where to build upon prior learning. The where and when aspects of teaching and learning is our starting point for this chapter. Mapping out the progression of what to teach will involve

1. developing a learning progression for the standard;
2. creating big idea statements;
3. crafting driving questions;
4. identifying supporting standards from other content areas; and
5. constructing initial assessments to determine where to begin daily instruction.

Learning progressions are composed from big ideas. Big ideas lead to driving questions. Driving questions are answered through daily learning experiences (Figure 3.1).

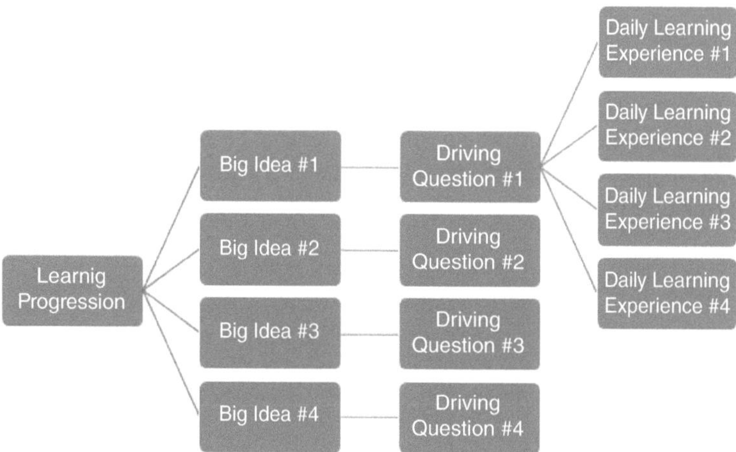

Figure 3.1 The Relationship between Learning Progressions, Big Ideas, Driving Questions, and Daily Learning Experiences.

Progression of Learning

Cheryl Lamb is a masterful early childhood teacher. Her learners engage in high-quality, high-impact learning the second they walk into her preschool classroom. When asked about her implementation of effective teaching and learning she responds, "Just be present. I dialogue with them, listen to them, and use that information to map out where we are going in their learning. They tell me when they are ready to move forward." However, Ms. Lamb has high expectations concerning their cognitive, social-emotional, psychomotor, and behavioral outcomes. "I map out a progression, but have clear indicators that I am looking for that help me decide where they are in their learning and when they are ready for something different." Ms. Lamb has used her unpacking of the early childhood standards for her school division and developed a learning progression for her students. Learning progressions provide the frame, plan, and design, and they implement high-quality, high-impact teaching and learning experiences for each standard. Learning progressions sequence the concepts and verbs in a way that promotes conceptual understanding, the development of skills, and the transfer or generalization of the learning. Learning progressions should support students in making meaning of the learning through (1) experiencing and constructing multiple representations of the learning, (2) seeking and finding patterns across concepts and skills, and (3) promoting emotional investment or buy-in to the learning (Medina, 2014). Learning progressions should move learners from simple to complex thinking and from concrete to abstract representations of the learning (Willingham, 2009).

For her Insects Unit, Ms. Lamb has mapped out the following progression that is scheduled to encompass approximately two weeks of time (Figure 3.2).

Looking over Ms. Lamb's insect learning progression likely sparks the question about how she decided on this. "After I unpack my standards and get a clear view of the expectations, I group concepts together that allow my students to build the background knowledge they need to move forward and then discover connections between the concepts." In addition, the development of the progression allows for her learners to continuously engage with the concepts of cycles, metamorphosis, head, thorax, abdomen, wings, and insects. At the same time, the progression promotes the seeking and finding patterns through a focus on insects within different contexts or environments (e.g., importance and impact, home and garden, and insects versus spiders). In addition, the topic of "bugs" is likely to invoke a visceral reaction, both positive and negative, for any young learner. Ms. Lamb also moves sets up a frame with this progression to engage her learners in complex thinking - the relationship between insects and the value they add to the environment. We will come back to Ms. Lamb's mapping, but for now, let's develop a learning progression from the unpacked standard in Chapter 2.

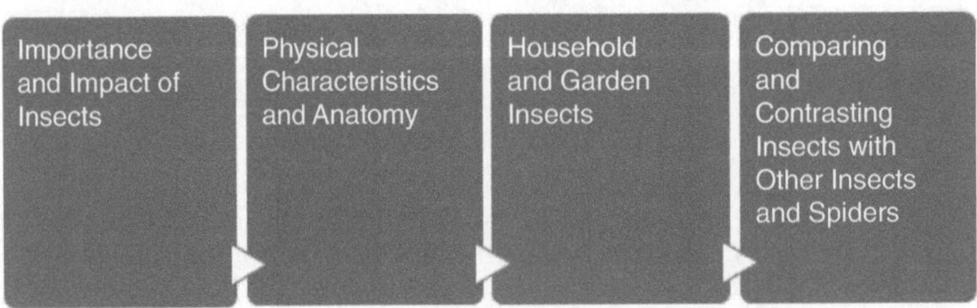

Figure 3.2 Insects Unit Learning Progression.

CONCEPTS: (nouns)	COMPLEXITY: (verbs)
Change	Claim – Relational Thinking
Argument	Present – Relational Thinking
Evidence	Support with – Relational Thinking
Plants	Identify and Describe – Multistructural Thinking
Animals	Identify and Describe – Multistructural Thinking
Humans	Identify and Describe – Multistructural Thinking
Environment	Identify and Describe – Multistructural Thinking
Needs	Identify and Describe – Multistructural Thinking
Ideas	Comparing – Relational Thinking
Representations	Comparing – Relational Thinking
Natural	Comparing – Relational Thinking
Designed	Comparing – Relational Thinking
Claim	Support – Relational Thinking
Phenomenon	Support – Relational Thinking
Impact	Know – Multistructural Thinking
Land	Know – Multistructural Thinking
Water	Know – Multistructural Thinking
Air	Know – Multistructural Thinking
Other Living Things	Know – Multistructural Thinking
Parts that work together	Know – Multistructural Thinking

Figure 3.3 Unpacking Concepts, Verbs, and Level of Complexity with SOLO.

As you may recall, we have analyzed K-ESS2-2, extracting the concepts and aligning those concepts with the level of complexity in the standard (Figure 3.3).

Opportunities for Reflective Practices

Before reading on, consider how you would cluster the concepts to develop a learning progression. How would you arrange these concepts so that learners can (1) experience and construct multiple representations, (2) seek and find patterns across concepts and skills, and (3) emotional invest or buy-in to the learning? What about progressing from simple to complex thinking and from concrete to abstract representations of the learning?

Learning progressions should and must engage us in critical conversations with our colleagues about when and where to introduce new learning and/or build upon prior learning. These conversations should reflect what we know about who we are teaching and how they grow, develop, and learning. A complete and thorough treatment of child development and how young children learn are beyond the scope of this book. Drawing from our understanding of these two important areas, we should take into consideraticn the developmental milestones of learners from birth to age eight. For example, what are the developmental trends across cognitive, social-emotional, psychomotor, and behavioral domains for early childhood and middle childhood (see McDevitt & Ormrod, 2013)?

Research to Classroom Practice Tasks

Take a moment and list important factors related to child development and how young children learn what must be considered in developing learning progressions.

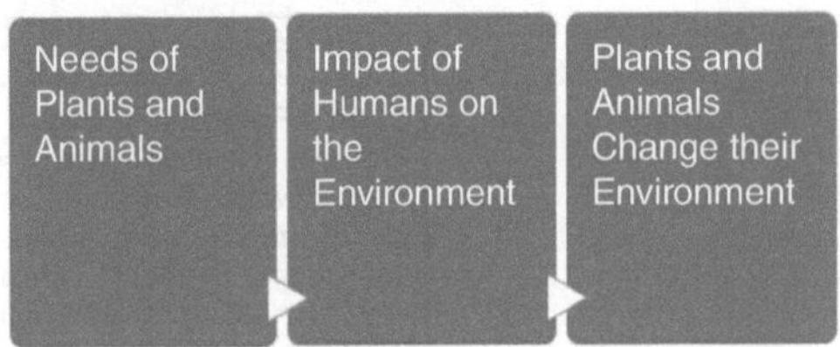

Figure 3.4 Earth's Systems Learning Progression.

In the end, there is no single progression that is "right" except the one that leads to the greatest learning gains in our young students. The critical conversations should continue once a learning progression is developed and implemented. Using evidence and feedback from progress monitoring, checks for understanding, and formative assessments, we can and should make adjustments to the learning progression during implementation. We will devote significant time to this topic in a later chapter. However, we must enter into our teaching and learning with a plan in place.

Returning to Ms. Cornish and her team's unpacking of K-ESS2-2, let's look at how they decided to arrange the concepts related to Earth's systems (Figure 3.4) into a learning progression for their kindergarteners. "We spent a lot of time discussing where to start with this unit. We wanted to make sure they had the vocabulary and background knowledge to make claims and identify or describe evidence. So we clustered those topics together and placed them at the beginning." (Figure 3.5).

Just like Ms. Lamb, Ms. Cornish and her team provide multiple ways for learners to engage in how plants and animals interact with their environment, seek and find patterns between the needs of plants and animals and how they change their environment, and emotionally engage in the learning by focusing on their own impact on the environment. Ms. Cornish also points out that "the content is the driver of our learning progression, but we will integrate representations, claims, arguments, and evidence at each point of the progression." What is not the driver of this learning progression are the verbs and levels of complexity. Engaging all learners in the highest level of complexity in their thinking, as early and frequently as possible, should be our expectation. In an inclusive early childhood science classroom, we scaffold this thinking to ensure equity of access and opportunity to the learning. For Ms. Rogers, Ms. Campbell, Ms. Cornish, and Ms. Lamb, they each engaged their learners in complex thinking from the very start. This thinking was embedded in content and part of the progression of learning developed by each of these teachers and their colleagues. What they teach is deliberately, purposefully, and intentionally mapped out for when and where learning will be introduced.

Big Ideas

As Ms. Lamb and Ms. Cornish join their colleagues in mapping out the progression of learning for the respective standards, they also begin to transition to how to make this learning relevant and authentic to their learners. That is, we are translating our work in analyzing the standard and establishing the learning progressions into student-friendly language that is accessible to all learners. What are the most relevant and essential content, skills, and understandings? How do we guide learners to focus on the most meaningful learning? The answer lies in the development of big ideas.

Big ideas are statements that articulate the key laws, principles, theories, and ideas, along with the essential processes and ways of knowing. These statements represent the big concepts

CONCEPTS: (nouns)	COMPLEXITY: (verbs)
Change Argument Evidence Plants Animals Humans Environment Needs Ideas Representations Natural Designed Claim Phenomenon Impact Land Water Air Other Living Things Parts that work together	Claim – Relational Thinking Construct – Relational Thinking Support with – Relational Thinking Identify and Describe – Multistructural Thinking Identify and Describe – Multistructural Thinking Identify and Describe – Multistructural Thinking Identify and Describe – Multistructural Thinking Identify and Describe – Multistructural Thinking Comparing – Relational Thinking Comparing – Relational Thinking Comparing – Relational Thinking Comparing – Relational Thinking Support – Relational Thinking Support – Relational Thinking Know – Multistructural Thinking Know – Multistructural Thinking Know – Multistructural Thinking Know – Multistructural Thinking Know – Multistructural Thinking Know – Multistructural Thinking

Figure 3.5 Clustering of Concepts.

within the standard and serve as anchors for the daily learning experiences, approaches, strategies, and tasks. Wiggins and McTighe (2005) refer to big ideas as conceptual Velcro that allow learners to see how specific content and skills fit together within a way of knowing in science. Ms. Anderson, a second-grade teacher, literally uses an umbrella to help learners anchor their thinking during daily learning experiences and see the relevancy of what they are learning.

> As we get started in our science learning, I Velcro the big idea to an umbrella that lives in the back corner of the classroom. As learners move through different parts of the day, the reading center, math block, and, of course, science block, we literally hook the things we learn on the metal stretchers of the umbrella. I ask the learners to explain to each other and then me how it is all connected.

The big ideas provide scaffolding and support for learners to see the purpose and relevancy of each learning experience. Finally, a big idea should be a statement that is not obvious to learners but something that requires them to make meaning, seek and find patterns, and motivates them to emotionally invest in the learning. Let's look at some examples and nonexamples of big ideas from Ms. Cornish and Ms. Lamb's classrooms. Each step of the learning progression is associated with a big idea (Figure 3.6).

LEARNING PROGRESSION FOR MS. LAMB'S LEARNERS	**NON-EXAMPLE**	**EXAMPLE**
IMPORTANCE AND IMPACT OF INSECTS	Insects are important and impact our environment.	Everything in our environment has an important role.
PHYSICAL CHARACTERISTICS AND ANATOMY	Insects have a head, thorax, and abdomen.	The parts of an organism work together to help it to survive.
HOUSEHOLD AND GARDEN INSECTS	There are insects that live in gardens and insects that live in houses.	Organisms thrive in an environment that meets their needs.
COMPARING AND CONTRASTING INSECTS WITH OTHER INSECTS AND SPIDERS	Insects are different from spiders.	Organisms are classified based on their characteristics.
LEARNING PROGRESSION FOR MS. CORNISH'S LEARNERS	**NON-EXAMPLE**	**EXAMPLE**
NEEDS OF PLANTS AND ANIMALS	Plants and animals have needs.	Living things have needs that are required for them to survive.
IMPACT OF HUMANS ON THE ENVIRONMENT	Humans impact the environment.	The decisions we make have an impact on the world around us.
PLANTS AND ANIMALS CHANGE THEIR ENVIRONMENT	Plants and animals change their environments.	Living things adjust their environments to meet their needs for survival.

Figure 3.6 Examples and Nonexamples of Big Ideas.

Notice that the big idea is not simply the restatement of a concept into a sentence. Instead, the big idea should represent an enduring understanding that extends beyond this particular standard, unit, or classroom (Wiggins & McTighe, 2005). Big ideas also aid us in being deliberate, purposeful, and intentional about the learning experiences we plan, design, and implement. Does each learning experience offer equity of access and opportunity to develop a deep understanding of the big idea? How would Ms. Lamb design learning experiences so that her preschoolers develop an understanding that organisms are classified based on their distinct characteristics? Likewise, how would Ms. Cornish design learning experiences so that her kindergarteners developed the understanding that our decisions impact the world around us?

Ms. Cornish and her team agree on the big ideas within their learning progression and add both of them to the unpacking template (see Appendix A; Figure 3.7).

Opportunities for Reflective Practices

Summarize your understanding of learning progressions and big ideas. What are they? What value do they have in the teaching and learning of inclusive early childhood science? In particular, what role do they play in supporting the inclusion of all learners?

LEARNING PROGRESSION: 1. Needs of plants and animals. 2. Impact of humans on the environment. 3. Plants and animals change their environment.
BIG IDEAS: 1. Living things have needs that are required for them to survive. 2. The decisions we make have an impact on the world around us. 3. Living things adjust their environments to meet their needs.

Figure 3.7 Big Ideas in the Unpacking Template.

Big ideas, by themselves, may not promote the emotional investment in science learning that we desire from our students. Big ideas are always accompanied by driving questions.

Driving Questions

Driving questions direct our learners' attention to the why behind their learning. In other words, the students in Ms. Lamb's and Ms. Cornish's classrooms are not just learning about insects and how plants and animals change their environment. Through driving questions, these students will make it clear why they are learning this content and these specific skills. Krajcik and Shin (2014) found that good driving questions have the following characteristics:

1. They are developmentally appropriate; learners can successfully answer the question in a supportive learning environment.
2. They incorporate science content, skills, and understandings into the answer.
3. They are authentic and relevant to individuals who would interact with the content and skill (e.g., insects-entomologists; plants-botanists).
4. They promote sustained engagement in learning.
5. They are ethical in nature (p. 281).

Lissa Pijanowski (2018) also identified several characteristics of driving questions that supported the planning, designing, and implementing of instruction that promotes deeper understanding. Driving questions should provide relevance and authenticity to the learning that promotes the emotional investing needed for learners to make meaning of their learning (Figure 3.8).

What really sets driving questions apart from other questions is the actionable nature of these questions (Pijanowski, 2018). Driving questions are introduced from the perspective of an individual or stakeholder, present a task that this individual or stakeholder would complete, and conclude with a clear identification of an audience (Pijanowski, 2018). Take for example Ms. Lamb's first driving question. In this case, learners are asked to take on the role of a scientist and create a way to share the value and importance of insects with their community. The role of the learners is a scientist. The audience is the community. The task is some product that presents the importance of insects. We will come back to the importance of choice in inclusive early childhood science. But for now, let's just focus on the features of a driving question (Figure 3.9).

Given them the opportunity to take on the role provides them with a specific example of why this information is important (i.e., relevant and authentic). Furthermore, as learners work to create the product that will "inform the community," the process will allow them to uncover why this

LEARNING PROGRESSION FOR MS. LAMB'S LEARNERS	BIG IDEA	DRIVING QUESTION
IMPORTANCE AND IMPACT OF INSECTS	Everything in our environment has an important role.	How can I, as a scientist, inform my community about the importance of insects?
PHYSICAL CHARACTERISTICS AND ANATOMY	The parts of an organism work together to help it to survive.	How could I, as a teacher, create a model of an insect that helps others understand the parts of an insect?
HOUSEHOLD AND GARDEN INSECTS	Organisms thrive in an environment that meets their needs.	Could I, as a horticulturalist, create a guide to help citizens identify insects that might be in their home or garden?
COMPARING AND CONTRASTING INSECTS WITH OTHER INSECTS AND SPIDERS	Organisms are classified based on their characteristics.	What can I do, as an artist, to help citizens understand the difference between insects and spiders?
LEARNING PROGRESSION FOR MS. CORNISH'S LEARNERS	**BIG IDEA**	**DRIVING QUESTION**
NEEDS OF PLANTS AND ANIMALS	Living things have needs that are required for them to survive.	How can I, as a scientist, discover what plants need to survive?
IMPACT OF HUMANS ON THE ENVIRONMENT	The decisions we make have an impact on the world around us.	What can I, as an environmental advocate, create to show my community how they impact the environment?
PLANTS AND ANIMALS CHANGE THEIR ENVIRONMENT	Living things adjust their environments to meet their needs for survival.	How can I, as a student, document the different ways plants and animals change their environment?

Figure 3.8 Big Ideas and Driving Questions.

Figure 3.9 Components of a Driving Question.
Source: Adapted from Pijanowski, L. (2018). Architects of deeper learning. Intentional design for high-impact instruction. Rexford, NY: International Center for Leadership in Education, Inc.

learning is relevant and authentic for them as individuals. Likewise, Ms. Cornish's learners take on the role of a scientist and must discover what plants need to survive. This will engage them in the design of an experiment that will help them "discover" the needs of plants. In both Ms. Lamb's and Ms. Cornish's classrooms, the driving question is anchored in the big idea and creates a culture of inquiry where learners generate their own questions (Weizman, Shwartz, & Fortus, 2008).

Essential questions can also be used in mapping out learning progressions and guiding learners toward the big ideas. Wiggins and McTighe (2005) assert that essential questions should be thought-provoking questions that infuse inquiry into any learning experience. These questions do not have a single right answer and require the acquisition of a considerable amount of knowledge and skills to infer an answer to the essential question. For example, how are insects different from other living things? Or, how are insects helpful to the environment? For Ms. Cornish, an essential question might be how do the characteristics of plants and animals help them to survive? Although essential questions promote inquiries about big ideas, they do not provide a context within which those big ideas exist. For this reason, learners may tend to embrace driving questions more than essential questions. With that being said, there are times when we primarily seek to engage our learners in guided inquiry. For those occasions, an essential question provides that platform. However, the content must be highly relevant and authentic in and of itself. Let's look at examples of essential questions alongside driving questions to get a better understanding of how these big idea questions are different and when one might be preferable to the other (Figure 3.10).

Whether we opt for an essential question over a driving question depends on our professional judgment and the role the question will play in our students' learning. If we are seeking to engage learners in guided inquiry, an essential question is appropriate. If we need to provide a stronger sense of relevance and authenticity to the learning, a driving question is appropriate.

Opportunities for Reflective Practices

Consider the similarities and differences between essential questions and driving questions. When would one approach be preferable over the other?

Essential Question	Driving Question
Are insects important to life on our planet?	How can I, as a scientist, inform my community about the importance of insects?
What do insects look like?	How could I, as a teacher, create a model of an insect that helps others understand the parts of an insect?
Where can I find different insects?	Could I, as a horticulturalist, create a guide to help citizens identify insects that might be in their home or garden?
How are insects and spiders different?	What can I do, as an artist, to help citizens understand the difference between insects and spiders?
What do plants need to survive?	How can I, as a scientist, discover what plants need to survive?
How do humans impact the environment?	What can I, as an environmental advocate, create to show my community how they impact the environment?
How do plants and animals change their environment?	How can I, as a journalist document the different ways plants and animals change their environment?

Figure 3.10 Driving Questions in the Unpacking Template.

LEARNING PROGRESSION: 1. Needs of plants and animals. 2. Impact of humans on the environment. 3. Plants and animals change their environment.
BIG IDEAS: 1. Living things have needs that are required for them to survive. 2. The decisions we make have an impact on the world around us. 3. Living things adjust their environments to meet their needs.
DRIVING QUESTIONS: 1. How can I, as a scientist, discover what plants need to survive? 2. What can I, as an environmental advocate, create to show my community how they impact the environment? 3. How can I, as a journalist, document the different ways plants and animals change their environment?

Figure 3.11 Driving Questions in the Unpacking Template.

As they have throughout this process, Ms. Cornish and her team work through the decision about using an essential question or a driving question and agree on driving questions. They add them to the unpacking template (see Appendix A; Figure 3.11).

The relationship between big ideas and driving questions is this: The big idea is the answer to the driving question. As learners engage and persist in learning experiences that seek to scaffold the development of their own answer to the driving question, they develop a deep understanding of the big idea.

As we have already mentioned, big ideas and driving questions provide opportunities for learners to see relationships between content and skills. These relationships often lead us beyond the content area of science. In other words, the big ideas and driving questions often lead us and our learners into mathematics, social studies, the visual and performing arts, and, without a doubt, literacy. One of the most effective ways to support learners in experiencing and constructing multiple representations of their learning, seeking, and finding patterns across concepts and skills and investing emotionally or buying into the learning is through the integration of supporting standards. Ms. Rogers integrated multiple content areas (e.g., literacy, mathematics, and art) into sinking and floating. Ms. Campbell decided to integrate literacy and reading standards into her teaching and learning on vibrations and sound. Let's see how this might unfold in Ms. Cornish's and Ms. Lamb's classrooms.

Identifying Supporting Standards

To support learners as they experience and construct multiple representations of the learning, we must look at ways to integrate science teaching and learning with other content areas. This also provides opportunities for learners to use certain skills in other contexts and begin to see patterns across content areas. For Ms. Lamb, she works through one final step before implementing her unit plan through daily instruction.

> I spend time identify other content areas that connect to my students learning about insects. The mapping out of a learning progression allows me to be more intentional about my teaching throughout the day and across different subject areas.

For Ms. Lamb, she decides to incorporate dramatic play, mathematics, literacy, and visual arts into this unit. "My thinking is that I can have a center where learners engage in dramatic play using camping props, plastic bugs, magnifying glasses, bug catcher jars, and sorting charts." The use of dramatic play will provide additional opportunities for learners to answer the driving question by role-playing - working with the concepts and doing the skills. In addition, Ms. Lamb chooses to incorporate beginning letter sounds, vocabulary, and writing tasks. The availability of insect books, digital texts, and storyboards works literacy into the learning experiences. Learners can work on sequencing with the life cycle of specific insects and one-to-one correspondence through counting insects,

Ms. Lamb does not simply pull these ideas out of thin air; she carefully looks at the other early learning guidelines and standards to see which ones naturally fit with her insect unit. This is similar to the process Ms. Cornish and her colleagues use with K-ESS2-2.

> We will certainly integrate dramatic play, visual arts, and mathematics into our learning. But we really want to focus on asking and answering questions about key details in a text. This is how we help learners construct arguments and make claims.

Ms. Cornish and her colleagues are using standards of learning from the school division's English language arts standards. "They are working on opinion pieces and informative/expository composition through drawing, dictating, or writing. This is something we should include in this unit as well."

This brings us to the implementation of effective teaching and learning in the inclusive early childhood science classroom. We have analyzed what mapped out the progression of learning. Now we have to take what we teach and design learning experiences that consider the how, who, where, and when. So where do we start? We have to decide how best to approach the learning based on the prior knowledge and experiences of our learners - the who. We do this through initial assessments that help us identify the background knowledge and prior experiences of our learners.

Initial Assessments

Just because we develop a learning progression, it does not mean we must explicitly teach each aspect of that progression. At first, this seems counterintuitive. If we take the time to analyze standards and map out a progression, why would we not start at the beginning of that progression and simply move through the big ideas and driving questions as a sequenced series of learning experiences? The answer lies in who we teach. The process we have engaged in over the past two chapters simply provides a road map for a learning journey within the context of the standard. Remember, standards tell us what to teach, not how. Ms. Lamb puts it this way:

> Once I know what the expectations are for learners, I have to figure out what they already know, understand, and are able to do with a high level of proficiency. This means taking into account what they bring to the learning experience. They may have specific background

knowledge and skills that allow them to move forward in their learning. They may need additional background knowledge to be successful and we have to go back and get those things. I don't want to just cover content and skills; I want to provide experiences that move them forward.

Initial assessments seek to gather information about three big questions:

1. What do my learners already know, understand (prior learning)?
2. What are my learners already able to do with that learning?
3. What experiences do they bring to the learning that will influence how they make meaning of this new learning?

Background Knowledge and Prior Learning. Gaining an understanding of background knowledge and prior learning involves content, skills, and understandings. Content knowledge, or the body of knowledge associated with science, includes facts, figures, theories, models, and scientific principles. This is the "stuff" within science like, for example, the metric system, life cycles and changes in organisms, the organization of our solar system, or laws of motion. Without this prior learning or background knowledge, learners may find it challenging to make meaning of the new learning. For example, they may not be able to identify what is relevant or irrelevant as they move into content related to insects or how plants and animals change their environment.

What is or is not necessarily prior learning and background knowledge depends on the content and the grade level. If learners are still working on phonemic awareness, one-to-one correspondence, this should not inhibit their learning about insects and the needs of plants and animals. Similarly, if they do not know that we inhabit Earth and that Earth goes around the Sun, this still does not inhibit new learning about insects or plants and animals. However, some learners do not know the difference between living and nonliving things, plants, and animals, or what an insect is or is not and that prior learning and background knowledge is essential in their moving forward and must be in place before doing so. We must ensure that we can separate what learners need to know from what is simply neat to know to move forward in their learning.

With regard to skills, having a clear understanding of where learners are in observing, classifying, sequencing, communicating, measuring, predicting, hypothesizing, inferring, using variables in experimentation, interpreting, analyzing, and evaluating data, designing, constructing, and interpreting models is important. Without this, learners may not have the set of processes necessary for actively engaging with what they are learning at the level of complexity articulated by the standard. In other words, we must explicitly teach the processes of science and engineering practices. As we pointed out in Chapter 1, learners do not naturally acquire these process skills.

The Virginia Department of Education (2012) created a guide for the progression of scientific processes. This progression shows the necessary prior learning and background knowledge necessary for students to engage in these processes. Let's look at observing as an example.

For each aspect of observation, there is a direct link to the Virginia Standards of Learning. Therefore, Ms. Campbell can identify not only what is expected of her first graders but also the prior learning and background knowledge from her learners' kindergarten year.

Opportunities for Reflective Practices

Looking at a standard or unit you will be teaching in the near future, what prior experiences and background knowledge are necessary for learners to make meaning of the new learning and move forward in their learning journeys?

When learners do not yet have the necessary prior learning and background knowledge, this can be a barrier to moving forward in their new learning and hinder their ability to develop a deep understanding of science. If we are to truly provide an inclusive early childhood science learning environment, we must use initial assessments to gather information about what learners know, understand, and are able to do. This ensures that all learners are actively engaged, valued as important members of the community, and provided the necessary supports to have an equal opportunity for success. We must gather information about where they are starting out in their learning journeys and what they bring to the learning experience. Learners may simply have had no prior experiences with insects or how plants change their environments to meet their needs. This prior learning and background knowledge is not due to ability but simply access to learning experiences.

Yet research on learners from disadvantaged backgrounds, speakers of other languages, and individuals with a disability guide us to be on the lookout for their unique abilities and thus ensure their inclusion and success in the learning journey (see Gelman & Brenneman, 2004; Mastropieri & Scruggs, 1994; McDevitt & Ormrod, 2013; Spooner et al., 2011). For example, students from disadvantaged backgrounds may not have had the same experiences as their peers and thus do not have the same level of prior knowledge or background knowledge. Similarly, English-language learners may not yet have the necessary vocabulary to engage in science learning at a deep level. Students with disabilities may need modifications, accommodations, skill building, or enrichment in order to have equal access and opportunity to move beyond snorkeling and engage in successful scuba diving.

Research to Classroom Practice Tasks

Take a moment and explore the research on what works best in the teaching and learning of science for learners from disadvantaged backgrounds, learners who are speakers of other languages, and learners with a disability. Keep this research handy, as we will refer to your findings across the next several chapters.

Our role in the classroom is to plan and implement educational experiences that represent conscious decisions about how to support learners, regardless of their background knowledge or prior learning, as they move through the learning progression. If initial assessments seek to gather information, let's close out this chapter by looking at how to develop those initial assessments.

Development of Initial Assessments

Let's start by addressing two misconceptions about initial assessments. First, initial assessments are not pretests. Pretests are assessments that establish a baseline for measuring growth at the end of a unit or grade level. For example, pretests compared with end-of-year assessments set up by the state or province provide us with much-needed information about student growth and achievement over the course of the year. While there is certainly a valid debate and argument for the developmental appropriateness of such testing (see Meador, 2020), and we certainly agree on the importance of measuring growth, this debate is above and beyond this particular discussion. Instead, we can advocate for the use of initial assessments and ongoing assessments that guide our decisions around teaching and learning in the inclusive early childhood science classroom. Within the context of analyzing and mapping out what to teach, the initial assessments of the specific content, skills, and understandings within a particular standard of our unit should provide information about what learners know, understand, and are able to do so that we can decide how to move forward in the learning progression.

Second, initial assessments are different from those assessments used for universal screening. Universal screening is an important and necessary component of tier systems of support. In districts and schools that successfully use a multitiered system of support, all students are initially assessed to determine who might need supplemental or intensive interventions right away. These screening tools should be quick and fairly easy to use because they are going to be administered to all students. As such, these tools are not expected to be diagnostic and might unintentionally identify students who really do not need an intervention. Keep in mind that a screening tool merely identifies students who are working below grade level; these tools cannot assess what has been tried in the past instructionally and whether it has been successful or not (Fisher et al., 2020).

Instead, initial assessments are "a way to gather evidence of students' readiness, interests, or learning profiles before beginning a lesson or unit and then using that evidence to plan instruction that will meet learners' needs" (Hockett & Doubet, 2014, p. 50). When learners engage in our initial assessments, they share their prior knowledge, skills, and understandings that help us see where they are in the established learning progression, and we use that to plan inclusive learning experiences that move all learners forward in that progression. Initial assessments can take the form of open-ended tasks, mini-laboratories, open-ended questions, and classroom dialogue. This evidence also serves as a reminder of why we do not have to start at the beginning of a progression simply because our learners are already proficient in the content and/or skills. To be clear, this does not mean that we do not have to use checks for understanding and progress monitoring to ensure retention.

Guskey and McTighe (2016) have provided guidelines that will help us design and implement initial assessments. First, initial assessments should have a clear purpose. This purpose should come directly from the analysis of the standard and the mapping out of a learning progression. Simply put, the purpose should be to figure out where in the progression we should start for this new learning. Ms. Lamb uses initial assessments to observe how learners interact with content, use skills, and share understandings.

> Before I start a unit, I provide multiple opportunities through morning meetings, centers, and hands-on experiences to see what they know, what they do, and what they understand. These experiences are a try-out, so to speak. And, during the entire experience, I am watching and listening.

Similarly,

Ms. Cornish starts introducing experiences to learners a week early.

> I ask questions, I bring in artifacts, I incorporate the concepts into my read aloud. Each of these actions is for the purpose of figuring out what experiences they have and what they already know about plants and animals. I record this information and we talk about this during planning to decide where to start.

The second guideline for designing and implementing initial assessments is to plan how to use the information generated by the initial assessment. Ms. Lamb documents what she sees and hears from her learners as they initially engage in open-ended tasks, mini-laboratories, open-ended questions, and classroom dialogue around insects.

> I keep informal notes about what my learners show me, what they show each other, during these experiences. This is the information that will help me decide what their prior experiences are and what they know. I, then, know where to start in their next learning journey.

The main point here is that if Ms. Lamb or Ms. Cornish plan on teaching as usual (e.g., per the district's or school's pacing guides), then the initial assessment is a waste of time, and evidence generated is not of value. Ms. Cornish points out that

> I need this information to ensure I know how to actively engage all of my learners, ensure they can leverage their backgrounds and prior experiences as an important member of the community, and for me to provide the necessary supports to give all learners an opportunity for success.

Finally, initial assessments should fit into the ebb and flow of the classroom environment. In other words, the initial assessment should not require teaching and learning to stop or draw on the limited resources of time that are already strained. We should not feel compelled to leave our learners to their own accord while we pull other learners aside for an initial assessment. Likewise, this should not be a situation where we announce the initial assessment and sit our young learners down for a formal pretest. Initial assessments should provide quick and readily accessible evidence to both teachers and students. If the initial assessment cannot inform the immediate next steps, we should reconsider the initial assessment. Initial assessments need to be used when "results cannot be predicted and when the exercise provides clear benefits to students" (Guskey & McTighe, 2016, p. 42). If initial assessments are created from the learning progression, with the big ideas and driving questions in mind, they provide us with information about what learners know, understand, and are able to do.

By engaging learners in initial assessments, we are making their thinking visible, and thus gathering information about what learners know, understand, and are able to do within the specific standard or unit of study. This allows us to make intentional, purposeful, and deliberate decisions about the daily learning experiences that will move learners toward answering the driving questions, gaining the enduring understandings represented by the big ideas, and meeting the expectations embedded in the standards of learning.

Now, let's start making the intentional, purposeful, and deliberate decisions about the daily learning experiences that will move learners forward.

There are additional examples at the end of this chapter on page 74 that build on the examples from Chapter 2 and will continue in Chapter 4. Again, these examples are available for you and your colleagues to critically examine the analysis of a vertical progression of an NGSS standard from kindergarten to third grade. These are merely examples and are not the only way to approach progressions, big ideas, and driving questions. The teachers also provided commentary and reflections about their process. As you critically examine each vertical progression, consider the following reflective questions:

1. Do we see how the learning progression was developed?
2. Is this how your colleagues would have sequenced the learning?
3. What about the big ideas? Do you agree or disagree? What would you have identified as the big ideas for the particular cluster or chunk of the standard? Do the big ideas have all of the characteristics presented in this chapter?
4. What about the driving questions? Do you agree or disagree? How would you have crafted the driving questions for the particular cluster or chunk of the standard? Do the driving questions have all of the characteristics presented in this chapter?
5. How does this example support your learning and understanding of big ideas and driving questions?

Professional Learning Tasks

1. Identify resources related to child development and science. What special consideration must be given to young children as they learn science? What does the research say about how young children learn science? Keep these resources handy as we move into planning, developing, and implementing daily learning experiences.
2. Returning to the science standard of learning you are unpacking, develop the big ideas and driving questions. Complete the template in Appendix A.
3. Design several initial assessments that will provide you with information about your learners' background knowledge and prior experiences. Make sure your initial assessments provide information for each of the big ideas of the learning progression. Along with the initial assessments, be sure to think through what you are looking for and how you will use the information generated by the initial assessment.
4. One of the ways to initially assess learners' background knowledge and prior experiences is through student conferences or one-on-one conversations. Using the "Misconceptions Interview Task" in Appendix D, develop an interview protocol for engaging your learners in student conferences or one-on-one interviews.

Engaging the Family and Community

1. **Share your story:** In the previous chapter, we talked about the importance of establishing common ground with families. Now, let's look at two specific strategies for establishing common ground and enticing families and the community to engage in our classrooms. Using Facebook, Twitter, Instagram, or a web page/blog, provide a short biography about yourself and your interests. Parents, guardians, and

community members seldom have opportunities to get to hear your story. In addition, during "drop-off" and "pickup" times, there is little time to converse. If you have experienced the car loop or bus loop during arrival or dismissal, you know how intense these moments can be and the lack of opportunity for chitchat. Instead, provide access to your story well before that first introduction. Talk about your interests in science and how that will shine through in your classroom. This helps families and the community get to know who is in the classroom.

When this is a common practice across a school division, district, or school, everyone has common ground. When going to the grocery store, you may have community members who speak to you and ask about something in your biography. In fact, you may have a community member donate things to your classroom based on something from your bio (e.g., local hardware store, grocery store). Sharing some particular details about your special talents and interests can lessen any "stranger" anxiety and make everyone feel more at ease.

2. **Family questionnaire:** Invite parents or guardians to complete a brief questionnaire that will help identify the interests and passions of their children. To avoid being perceived as intrusive or generating skepticism, be very clear with families about why this information is valuable and how it will help you provide better learning experiences for their children. In the questionnaire, provide examples of how you will use the information. Better yet, have your students explain the purpose of the survey and encourage them to complete the survey together with their parents or guardians. Not only can family members be an invaluable source of information about their own children, but they can also bring special interests and talents to share with the entire school community. You may want to ask parents to fill out a questionnaire on the first day of school or invite them to take it home and return it at a later date.

   To ensure that the survey is inclusive and does not inadvertently exclude families, meet with your school counselor, instructional coach, or administrator to see if the survey needs to be translated into different languages. If reading the survey is a problem, or if there is any doubt about sending a survey home, refer to the previous chapters and opt for a home visit or call home.

   Some questions to ask might include the following:

- What are your child's strengths?
- What does your child like to do in his or her spare time?
- What are two or three things you want me to know about your child?
- Would you be interested in being a "guest" in our classroom? Could you be a story reader? Teach a song? Help with an art project?
- Is there a special topic that you would like to see incorporated into the curriculum (e.g., adoption, new siblings, moving to a new home)?
- Is there a special interest or talent you would like to share with the children? The staff?
- What is the best way to reach you during the day?
- What is your availability during the day?

Additional Examples of Mapping Out the Progression of What to Teach in Inclusive Early Childhood Science

Kindergarten

K-PS2-1 Motion and Stability: Forces and Interactions

Students who demonstrate understanding can:

K-PS2-1. **Plan and conduct an investigation to compare the effects of different strengths or different directions of pushes and pulls on the motion of an object.** [Clarification Statement: Examples of pushes or pulls could include a string attached to an object being pulled, a person pushing an object, a person stopping a rolling ball, and two objects colliding and pushing on each other.] [*Assessment Boundary: Assessment is limited to different relative strengths or different directions, but not both at the same time. Assessment does not include non-contact pushes or pulls such as those produced by magnets.*]

The performance expectation above was developed using the following elements from the NRC document *A Framework for K-12 Science Education*:

Science and Engineering Practices

Planning and Carrying Out Investigations
Planning and carrying out investigations to answer questions or test solutions to problems in K–2 builds on prior experiences and progresses to simple investigations, based on fair tests, which provide data to support explanations or design solutions.

- With guidance, plan and conduct an investigation in collaboration with peers.

Connections to the Nature of Science

Scientific Investigations Use a Variety of Methods

- Scientists use different ways to stud y the world.

Disciplinary Core Ideas

PS2.A: Forces and Motion

- Pushes and pulls can have different strengths and directions.
- Pushing or pulling on an object can change the speed or direction of its motion and can start or stop it.

PS2.B: Types of Interactions

- When objects touch or collide, they push on one another and can change motion.

PS3.C: Relationship Between Energy and Forces

- A bigger push or pull makes things speed up or slow down more quickly. *(secondary)*

Crosscutting Concepts

Cause and Effect

- Simple tests can be designed to gather evidence to support or refute student ideas about causes.

PS2.B and PS3.C are conclusions students will draw as part of the investigations they conduct (inquiry)

Observable features of the student performance by the end of the grade:			
1	Identifying the phenomenon to be investigated		
	a	With guidance, students collaboratively identify the phenomenon under investigation, which includes the following idea: the effect caused by different strengths and directions of pushes and pulls on the motion of an object.	
	b	With guidance, students collaboratively identify the purpose of the investigation, which includes gathering evidence to support or refute student ideas about causes of the phenomenon by comparing the effects of different strengths of pushes and pulls on the motion of an object.	
2	Identifying the evidence to address this purpose of the investigation		
	a	With guidance, students collaboratively develop an investigation plan to investigate the relationship between the strength and direction of pushes and pulls and the motion of an object (i.e., qualitative measures or expressions of strength and direction; e.g., harder, softer, descriptions* of "which way").	
	b	Students describe* how the observations they make connect to the purpose of the investigation, including how the observations of the effects on object motion allow causal relationships between pushes and pulls and object motion to be determined	
	c	Students predict the effect of the push of pull on the motion of the object, based on prior experiences.	
3	Planning the investigation		
	a	In the collaboratively developed investigation plan, students describe*:	
		i.	The object whose motion will be investigated.
		ii.	What will be in contact with the object to cause the push or pull.
		iii.	The relative strengths of the push or pull that will be applied to the object to start or stop its motion or change its speed.
		iv.	The relative directions of the push or pull that will be applied to the object.
		v.	How the motion of the object will be observed and recorded.
		vi.	How the push or pull will be applied to vary strength or direction.
4	Collecting the data		
	a	According to the investigation plan they developed, and with guidance, students collaboratively make observations that would allow them to compare the effect on the motion of the object caused by changes in the strength or direction of the pushes and pulls and record their data.	

K-PS2-2 Motion and Stability: Forces and Interactions

Students who demonstrate understanding can:

K-PS2-2. **Analyze data to determine if a design solution works as intended to change the speed or direction of an object with a push or a pull.*** [Clarification Statement: Examples of problems requiring a solution could include having a marble or other object move a certain distance, follow a particular path, and knock down other objects. Examples of solutions could include tools such as a ramp to increase the speed of the object and a structure that would cause an object such as a marble or ball to turn.] [*Assessment Boundary: Assessment does not include friction as a mechanism for change in speed.*]

The performance expectation above was developed using the following elements from the NRC document *A Framework for K-12 Science Education*:

Science and Engineering Practices	Disciplinary Core Ideas	Crosscutting Concepts
Analyzing and Interpreting Data Analyzing data in K–2 builds on prior experiences and progresses to collecting, recording, and sharing observations. • Analyze data from tests of an object or tool to determine if it works as intended.	**PS2.A: Forces and Motion** • Pushes and pulls can have different strengths and directions. • Pushing or pulling on an object can change the speed or direction of its motion and can start or stop it. **ETS1.A: Defining Engineering Problems** • A situation that people want to change or create can be approached as a problem to be solved through engineering. Such problems may have many acceptable solutions. *(secondary)*	**Cause and Effect** • Simple tests can be designed to gather evidence to support or refute student ideas about causes.

Observable features of the student performance by the end of the grade:			
1	Organizing data		
	a	With guidance, students organize given information using graphical or visual displays (e.g., pictures, pictographs, drawings, written observations, tables, charts). The given information students organize includes:	
		i.	The relative speed or direction of the object before a push or pull is applied (i.e., qualitative measures and expressions of speed and direction; e.g., faster, slower, descriptions* of "which way").
		ii.	The relative speed or direction of the object after a push or pull is applied.
		iii.	How the relative strength of a push or pull affects the speed or direction of an object (i.e., qualitative measures or expressions of strength; e.g., harder, softer).
2	Identifying relationships		
	a	Using their organization of the given information, students describe* relative changes in the speed or direction of the object caused by pushes or pulls from the design solution.	
3	Interpreting data		
	a	Students describe* the goal of the design solution.	
	b	Students describe* their ideas about how the push or pull from the design solution causes the change in the object's motion.	
	c	Based on the relationships they observed in the data, students describe* whether the push or pull from the design solution causes the intended change in speed or direction of motion of the object.	

CONCEPTS: (nouns)	COMPLEXITY: (verbs)
Investigation	Plan and conduct – relational thinking
Investigation plan	Develop – relational thinking
Strength (relative strength)	Describe and compare – relational thinking
Direction (relative direction)	Describe and compare – relational thinking
Speed(relative speed)	Describe and compare – relational thinking
Motion(include start and stop)	Describe and observe – multistructural thinking
Object	Describe – multistructural thinking
Changes (in speed, direction, motion)	Describe – relational thinking
Push	Describe – multistructural thinking
Pull	Describe – multistructural thinking
Question	Answer – relational thinking
Goal	Describe – multistructural thinking
Explanation	Support – relational thinking
Tests	Design – relational thinking
Evidence	Gather – relational thinking
Ideas	Describe, support or refute – relational thinking
Causes	Support or refute – relational thinking
Phenomenon	Identify – multistructural thinking
Purpose of the investigation	Identify – multistructural thinking
Effects(on object motion)	Identify, describe, predict, and compare – relational thinking
Causal relationships	Investigate and connect – relational thinking
Observations	Describe and connect – relational thinking
Data	Recordandanalyze – relational thinking
Information	Organize – relational thinking
Design solution	Describe, determine, test – relational thinking
Graphic and visual displays	Create – relational thinking

There are a couple of spots in which “describe” has a different level of complexity based on the concept it is aligned with, hence it sometimes being listed as multistructural thinking and others as relational thinking.

Also, it is important to note that on the NGSS there is a qualification statement that reads “unless otherwise specified, “descriptions” referenced in the evidence statements could include but are not limited to written, oral, pictorial, and kinesthetic descriptions.”

Progression

Big Ideas

1. Objects move in different ways.
2. Forces can cause or change movement.
3. People or objects can create and use forces to impact the motion of objects in our environment.

Driving Questions

1. How can I, as a scientist, describe the movement of objects aroundme?
2. In what ways can I, as a physicist, change the motion of objects around me?
3. Can I, as an engineer, create a visual or graphic display that showsothersthe way pushes and pulls change object motion?

Teacher Reflections: In my mind, I would start with what is familiar to students: describing how things move. This is something they have been doing since toddlerhood, but we could use that as a starting point for understanding what causes object movement. I would expect them to know the terms speed, strength, and direction and be able to use those to describe movement (i.e. this one is slower, it’s moving in a circle, etc.) Then, we would introduce the vocabulary of push and pull and relate that to being the cause of movement (including start and stop) and how the strength or direction of a push or pull impacts speed and direction of object motion. This would help students draw conclusions to learn the DCI’s for PS2. Lastly, we would collaborativelytackle the problem solving task and create a way to organize the information into a graphical or visual display.

First Grade

1-PS4-1 Waves and Their Applications in Technologies for Information Transfer

Students who demonstrate understanding can:

1-PS4-1. **Plan and conduct investigations to provide evidence that vibrating materials can make sound and that sound can make materials vibrate.** [Clarification Statement: Examples of vibrating materials that make sound could include tuning forks and plucking a stretched string. Examples of how sound can make matter vibrate could include holding a piece of paper near a speaker making sound and holding an object near a vibrating tuning fork.]

The performance expectation above was developed using the following elements from the NRC document *A Framework for K-12 Science Education*:

Science and Engineering Practices	Disciplinary Core Ideas	Crosscutting Concepts
Planning and Carrying Out Investigations Planning and carrying out investigations to answer questions or test solutions to problems in K–2 builds on prior experiences and progresses to simple investigations, based on fair tests, which provide data to support explanations or design solutions. • Plan and conduct investigations collaboratively to produce evidence to answer a question. - - - - - - - - - - ***Connections to Nature of Science*** **Scientific Investigations Use a Variety of Methods** • Science investigations begin with a question. • Scientists use different ways to study the world.	**PS4.A: Wave Properties** • Sound can make matter vibrate, and vibrating matter can make sound.	**Cause and Effect** • Simple tests can be designed to gather evidence to support or refute student ideas about causes.

Observable features of the student performance by the end of the grade:			
1	Identifying the phenomenon under investigation		
	a	Students identify and describe* the phenomenon and purpose of the investigation, which include providing evidence to answer questions about the relationship between vibrating materials and sound.	
2	Identifying the evidence to address the purpose of the investigation		
	a	Students collaboratively develop an investigation plan and describe* the evidence that will result from the investigation, including:	
		i.	Observations that sounds can cause materials to vibrate.
		ii.	Observations that vibrating materials can cause sounds.
		iii.	How the data will provide evidence to support or refute ideas about the relationship between vibrating materials and sound.
	b	Students individually describe* (with support) how the evidence will address the purpose of the investigation.	
3	Planning the investigation		
	a	In the collaboratively developed investigation plan, students individually identify and describe*:	
		i.	The materials to be used.
		ii.	How the materials will be made to vibrate to make sound.
		iii.	How resulting sounds will be observed and described*.
		iv.	What sounds will be used to make materials vibrate.
		v.	How it will be determined that a material is vibrating.
4	Collecting the data		
	a	According to the investigation plan they develop, students collaboratively collect and record observations about:	
		i.	Sounds causing materials to vibrate.
		ii.	Vibrating materials causing sounds.

1-PS4-2 Waves and Their Applications in Technologies for Information Transfer

Students who demonstrate understanding can:

1-PS4-2. **Make observations to construct an evidence-based account that objects in darkness can be seen only when illuminated.** [Clarification Statement: Examples of observations could include those made in a completely dark room, a pinhole box, and a video of a cave explorer with a flashlight. Illumination could be from an external light source or by an object giving off its own light.]

The performance expectation above was developed using the following elements from the NRC document *A Framework for K-12 Science Education*:

Science and Engineering Practices	Disciplinary Core Ideas	Crosscutting Concepts
Constructing Explanations and Designing Solutions Constructing explanations and designing solutions in K–2 builds on prior experiences and progresses to the use of evidence and ideas in constructing evidence-based accounts of natural phenomena and designing solutions. • Make observations (firsthand or from media) to construct an evidence-based account for natural phenomena.	**PS4.B: Electromagnetic Radiation** • Objects can be seen if light is available to illuminate them or if they give off their own light.	**Cause and Effect** • Simple tests can be designed to gather evidence to support or refute student ideas about causes.

Observable features of the student performance by the end of the grade:			
1	Articulating the explanation of phenomena		
	a	Students articulate a statement that relates the given phenomenon to a scientific idea, including that when an object in the dark is lit (e.g., turning on a light in the dark space or from light the object itself gives off), it can be seen.	
	b	Students use evidence and reasoning to construct an evidence-based account of the phenomenon.	
2	Evidence		
	a	Students make observations (firsthand or from media) to serve as the basis for evidence, including:	
		i.	The appearance (e.g., visible, not visible, somewhat visible but difficult to see) of objects in a space with no light.
		ii.	The appearance (e.g., visible, not visible, somewhat visible but difficult to see) of objects in a space with light.
		iii.	The appearance (e.g., visible, not visible, somewhat visible but difficult to see) of objects (e.g., light bulbs, glow sticks) that give off light in a space with no other light.
	b	Students describe how their observations provide evidence to support their explanation.	
3	Reasoning		
	a	Students logically connect the evidence to support the evidence-based account of the phenomenon. Students describe lines of reasoning that include:	
		i.	The presence of light in a space causes objects to be able to be seen in that space.
		ii.	Objects cannot be seen if there is no light to illuminate them, but the same object in the same space can be seen if a light source is introduced.
		iii.	The ability of an object to give off its own light causes the object to be seen in a space where there is no other light.

1-PS4-3 Waves and Their Applications in Technologies for Information Transfer
Students who demonstrate understanding can: **1-PS4-3. Plan and conduct investigations to determine the effect of placing objects made with different materials in the path of a beam of light.** [Clarification Statement: Examples of materials could include those that are transparent (such as clear plastic), translucent (such as wax paper), opaque (such as cardboard), and reflective (such as a mirror).] [*Assessment Boundary: Assessment does not include the speed of light.*]

The performance expectation above was developed using the following elements from the NRC document *A Framework for K-12 Science Education*:

Science and Engineering Practices	Disciplinary Core Ideas	Crosscutting Concepts
Planning and Carrying Out Investigations Planning and carrying out investigations to answer questions or test solutions to problems in K–2 builds on prior experiences and progresses to simple investigations, based on fair tests, which provide data to support explanations or design solutions. • Plan and conduct investigations collaboratively to produce evidence to answer a question.	**PS4.B: Electromagnetic Radiation** • Some materials allow light to pass through them, others allow only some light through and others block all the light and create a dark shadow on any surface beyond them, where the light cannot reach. Mirrors can be used to redirect a light beam. (Boundary: The idea that light travels from place to place is developed through experiences with light sources, mirrors, and shadows, but no attempt is made to discuss the speed of light.)	**Cause and Effect** • Simple tests can be designed to gather evidence to support or refute student ideas about causes.

Observable features of the student performance by the end of the grade:			
1	Identifying the phenomenon under investigation		
	a	Students identify and describe* the phenomenon and purpose of the investigation, which include:	
		i.	Answering a question about what happens when objects made of different materials (that allow light to pass through them in different ways) are placed in the path of a beam of light.
		ii.	Designing and conducting an investigation to gather evidence to support or refute student ideas about putting objects made of different materials in the path of a beam of light.
2	Identifying evidence to address the purpose of the investigation		
	a	Students collaboratively develop an investigation plan and describe* the data that will result from the investigation, including:	
		i.	Observations of the effect of placing objects made of different materials in a beam of light, including:
			1. A material that allows all light through results in the background lighting up.
			2. A material that allows only some light through results in the background lighting up, but looking darker than when the material allows all light in.
			3. A material that blocks all of the light will create a shadow.
			4. A material that changes the direction of the light will light up the surrounding space in a different direction.
	b	Students individually describe* how these observations provide evidence to answer the question under investigation.	
3	Planning the investigation		
	a	In the collaboratively developed investigation plan, students individually describe* (with support):	
		i.	The materials to be placed in the beam of light, including:
			1. A material that allows all light through (e.g., clear plastic, clear glass).
			2. A material that allows only some light through (e.g., clouded plastic, wax paper).
			3. A material that blocks all of the light (e.g., cardboard, wood).
			4. A material that changes the direction of the light (e.g., mirror, aluminum foil).
		ii.	How the effect of placing different materials in the beam of light will be observed and recorded.
		iii.	The light source used to produce the beam of light.
4	Collecting the data		
	a	Students collaboratively collect and record observations about what happens when objects made of materials that allow light to pass through them in different ways are placed in the path of a beam of light, according to the developed investigation plan.	

1-PS4-4 Waves and Their Applications in Technologies for Information Transfer

Students who demonstrate understanding can:

1-PS4-4. **Use tools and materials to design and build a device that uses light or sound to solve the problem of communicating over a distance.*** [Clarification Statement: Examples of devices could include a light source to send signals, paper cup and string "telephones," and a pattern of drum beats.] [*Assessment Boundary: Assessment does not include technological details for how communication devices work.*]

The performance expectation above was developed using the following elements from the NRC document *A Framework for K-12 Science Education*:

Science and Engineering Practices

Constructing Explanations and Designing Solutions

Constructing explanations and designing solutions in K–2 builds on prior experiences and progresses to the use of evidence and ideas in constructing evidence-based accounts of natural phenomena and designing solutions.

- Use tools and materials provided to design a device that solves a specific problem.

Disciplinary Core Ideas

PS4.C: Information Technologies and Instrumentation

- People also use a variety of devices to communicate (send and receive information) over long distances.

Crosscutting Concepts

Connections to Engineering, Technology, and Applications of Science

Influence of Engineering, Technology, and Science, on Society and the Natural World

- People depend on various technologies in their lives; human life would be very different without technology.

Observable features of the student performance by the end of the grade:			
1	Using scientific knowledge to generate design solutions		
	a	Students describe a given problem involving people communicating over long distances.	
	b	With guidance, students design and build a device that uses light or sound to solve the given problem.	
	c	With guidance, students describe the scientific information they use to design the solution.	
2	Describing* specific features of the design solution, including quantification when appropriate		
	a	Students describe that specific expected or required features of the design solution should include:	
		i.	The device is able to send or receive information over a given distance.
		ii.	The device must use light or sound to communicate.
	b	Students use only the materials provided when building the device.	
3	Evaluating potential solutions		
	a	Students describe whether the device:	
		i.	Has the expected or required features of the design solution,
		ii.	Provides a solution to the problem involving people communicating over a distance by using light or sound.
	b	Students describe how communicating over long distances helps people.	

With how frequently "communicating" is mentioned, I would include communication in the CONCEPTS

CONCEPTS: (nouns)	COMPLEXITY: (verbs)
Investigations	Plan and conduct – relational thinking
Evidence	Use, provide, gather,and describe – relational thinking
Reasoning	Use and explain – relational thinking
Materials	Use and describe – – multistructural thinking
(Design)solutions	Test and design – abstract thinking
Problems	Test, describe,and solve – abstract thinking
Questions	Answer – relational thinking
Ideas	Supportor refute – relational thinking
Causes	Supportor refute – relational thinking
Fair tests	Design and conduct – relational thinking
Explanations	Supportand construct – relational thinking
Purpose of the investigation	Identify and describe – relational thinking
Investigation plan	Develop – relational thinking
Natural Phenomenon	Identify and describe – relational thinking
Relationship	Describe – relational thinking
Observations	Make, collect, record, and describe – relational thinking
Appearance	Describe – multistructural thinking
Lines of reasoning	Describe – relational thinking
Data	Describe – multistructural thinking
Evidence based account	Construct – relational thinking
Sound	Observe and describe – multistructural thinking
Matter	Observe and describe – multistructural thinking
Vibrating matter	Observe and describe – multistructural thinking
Materials	Identify and describe – multistructural thinking
Scientific idea	Articulate – relational thinking
Statement	Articulate – relational thinking
Light	Observe and describe – multistructural thinking
Objects (in darkness)	Observe and describe – multistructural thinking
Space(with light or with no light)	Describe – multistructural thinking
Effects	Describe – relational thinking
Beam of light	Identifyand describe – multistructural thinking
Shadow	Observe and describe – relational thinking
Surface	Describe – multistructural thinking
Background	Describe – multistructural thinking
Mirror (or object that changes direction of light)	Use, observe, and describe effects – relational thinking
Direction	Describe – relational thinking
Materials that allow all light through	Observe and describe – multistructural thinking
Materials that allow only some light through	Observe and describe – multistructural thinking
Materials that block all light	Observe and describe – multistructural thinking
Light source	Describe – multistructural thinking
Path of the light	Observe and describe – multistructural thinking
People	Know – multistructural thinking
Technologies	Know – multistructural thinking
Human life	Know – multistructural thinking
Communication*	Describe – multistructural thinking
Device	Describe, design, and build – abstract thinking
Long distances	Describe – multistructural thinking
Features	Describe – multistructural thinking

*The idea of communicating is referenced in 1-PS4-4 though the term communication itself is not used. This forms the crux of the problem solving task of the standard, therefore, it is included as a concept.

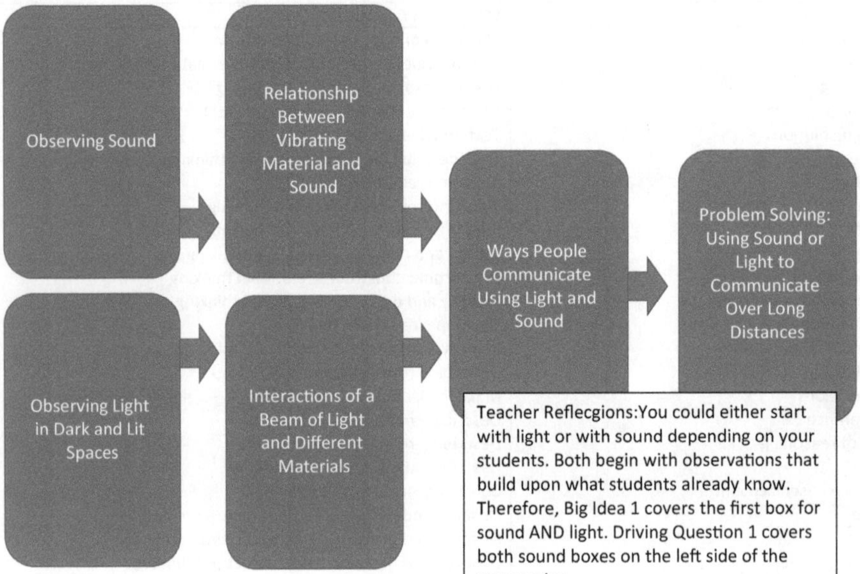

Observing Sound → Relationship Between Vibrating Material and Sound → Ways People Communicate Using Light and Sound → Problem Solving: Using Sound or Light to Communicate Over Long Distances

Observing Light in Dark and Lit Spaces → Interactions of a Beam of Light and Different Materials → Ways People Communicate Using Light and Sound

Teacher Reflecgions:You could either start with light or with sound depending on your students. Both begin with observations that build upon what students already know. Therefore, Big Idea 1 covers the first box for sound AND light. Driving Question 1 covers both sound boxes on the left side of the progression.

Big Ideas:

1. Observations help us understand the world around us.
2. Matter and energy interact in different ways. (I am stuck on how to word this one because matter and energy aren't mentioned inthe standard, but a study of light and sound is a study of how matter relates to energy and how its interactions can cause energy to be observable)
3. People can communicate using different technologies.
4. People develop new technologies to solve problems.

Driving Questions:

1. How could I, as the teacher, provide a way for my students to discover the relationship between vibrating material and sound?
2. How could I, as a scientist, articulate to someone else what makes an object visible in a dark space?
3. How could I, as a scientist, demonstrate and describe the way a beam of light interacts with different materials?
4. In what ways can I, as a member of a community, communicate with the people around me?
5. How could I, as an engineer, develop a device using light or soundto allow people to communicate over long distances?

Second Grade

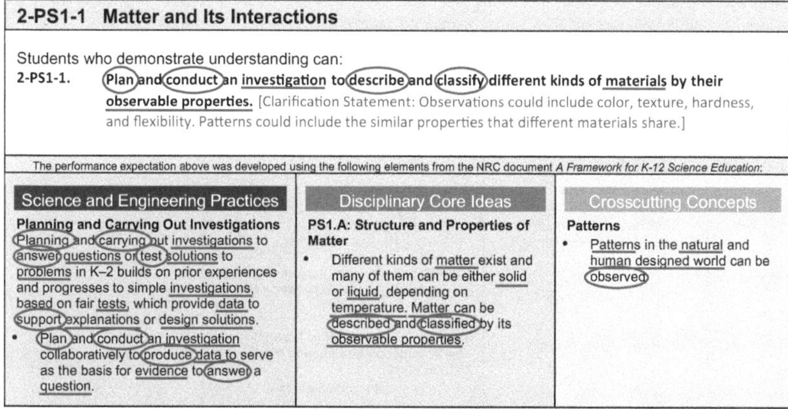

2-PS1-1 Matter and Its Interactions

Students who demonstrate understanding can:

2-PS1-1. **Plan and conduct an investigation to describe and classify different kinds of materials by their observable properties.** [Clarification Statement: Observations could include color, texture, hardness, and flexibility. Patterns could include the similar properties that different materials share.]

The performance expectation above was developed using the following elements from the NRC document *A Framework for K-12 Science Education*:

Science and Engineering Practices	Disciplinary Core Ideas	Crosscutting Concepts
Planning and Carrying Out Investigations Planning and carrying out investigations to answer questions or test solutions to problems in K–2 builds on prior experiences and progresses to simple investigations, based on fair tests, which provide data to support explanations or design solutions. • Plan and conduct an investigation collaboratively to produce data to serve as the basis for evidence to answer a question.	**PS1.A: Structure and Properties of Matter** • Different kinds of matter exist and many of them can be either solid or liquid, depending on temperature. Matter can be described and classified by its observable properties.	**Patterns** • Patterns in the natural and human designed world can be observed.

Observable features of the student performance by the end of the grade:			
1	Identifying the phenomenon under investigation		
	a	Students identify and describe the phenomenon under investigation, which includes the following idea: different kinds of matter have different properties, and sometimes the same kind of matter has different properties depending on temperature.	
	b	Students identify and describe the purpose of the investigation, which includes answering a question about the phenomenon under investigation by describing and classifying different kinds of materials by their observable properties.	
2	Identifying the evidence to address the purpose of the investigation		
	a	Students collaboratively develop an investigation plan and describe the evidence that will be collected, including the properties of matter (e.g., color, texture, hardness, flexibility, whether is it a solid or a liquid) of the materials that would allow for classification, and the temperature at which those properties are observed.	
	b	Students individually describe that:	
		i.	The observations of the materials provide evidence about the properties of different kinds of materials.
		ii.	Observable patterns in the properties of materials provide evidence to classify the different kinds of materials.
3	Planning the investigation		
	a	In the collaboratively developed investigation plan, students include:	
		i.	Which materials will be described and classified (e.g., different kinds of metals, rocks, wood, soil, powders).
		ii.	Which materials will be observed at different temperatures, and how those temperatures will be determined (e.g., using ice to cool and a lamp to warm) and measured (e.g., qualitatively or quantitatively).
		iii.	How the properties of the materials will be determined.
		iv.	How the materials will be classified (i.e., sorted) by the pattern of the properties.
	b	Students individually describe how the properties of materials, and the method for classifying them, are relevant to answering the question.	
4	Collecting the data		
	a	According to the developed investigation plan, students collaboratively collect and record data on the properties of the materials.	

Teacher Reflections: Important to note that 2a says to "collaboratively develop"... while developing an investigation plan is a cognitively complex task, students are doing it with the combined ideas of their peers and the guidance of the teacher. Whereas, 2b tasks students with individually describing their observations, so all students need the vocabulary and scaffolding to complete that part of the task.

2-PS1-2 Matter and Its Interactions

Students who demonstrate understanding can:

2-PS1-2. Analyze data obtained from testing different materials to determine which materials have the properties that are best suited for an intended purpose.* [Clarification Statement: Examples of properties could include, strength, flexibility, hardness, texture, and absorbency.] [*Assessment Boundary: Assessment of quantitative measurements is limited to length.*]

The performance expectation above was developed using the following elements from the NRC document *A Framework for K-12 Science Education*:

Science and Engineering Practices	Disciplinary Core Ideas	Crosscutting Concepts
Analyzing and Interpreting Data Analyzing data in K–2 builds on prior experiences and progresses to collecting, recording, and sharing observations. • Analyze data from tests of an object or tool to determine if it works as intended.	**PS1.A: Structure and Properties of Matter** • Different properties are suited to different purposes.	**Cause and Effect** • Simple tests can be designed to gather evidence to support or refute student ideas about causes. - - - - - - - - - - ***Connections to Engineering, Technology, and Applications of Science*** **Influence of Engineering, Technology, and Science, on Society and the Natural World** • Every human-made product is designed by applying some knowledge of the natural world and is built using materials derived from the natural world.

Observable features of the student performance by the end of the grade:		
1	Organizing data	
	a	Using graphical displays (e.g., pictures, charts, grade-appropriate graphs), students use the given data from tests of different materials to organize those materials by their properties (e.g., strength, flexibility, hardness, texture, ability to absorb).
2	Identifying relationships	
	a	Students describe relationships between materials and their properties (e.g., metal is strong, paper is absorbent, rocks are hard, sandpaper is rough).
	b	Students identify and describe relationships between properties of materials and some potential uses purpose (e.g., hardness is good for breaking objects or supporting objects; roughness is good for keeping objects in place; flexibility is good to keep a materials from breaking, but not good for keeping materials rigidly in place).
3	Interpreting data	
	a	Students describe which properties allow a material to be well suited for a given intended use (e.g., ability to absorb for cleaning up spills, strength for building material, hardness for breaking a nut).
	b	Students use their organized data to support or refute their ideas about which properties of materials allow the object or tool to be best suited for the given intended purpose relative to the other given objects/tools (e.g., students could support the idea that hardness allows a wooden shelf to be better suited for supporting materials placed on it than a sponge would be, based on the patterns relating property to a purpose; students could refute an idea that a thin piece of glass is better suited to be a shelf than a wooden plank would be because it is harder than the wood by using data from tests of hardness and strength to give evidence that the glass is less strong than the wood) .
	c	Students describe how the given data from the test provided evidence of the suitability of different materials for the intended purpose.

Teacher Reflections: I have underlined the specified properties because I think they are concepts that are important to this unit, though not necessarily an all-inclusive list of the properties to explore. However, I did not underline the given examples (e.g. metal is strong).

2-PS1-3 Matter and Its Interactions

Students who demonstrate understanding can:

2-PS1-3. **Make observations to construct an evidence-based account of how an object made of a small set of pieces can be disassembled and made into a new object.** [Clarification Statement: Examples of pieces could include blocks, building bricks, or other assorted small objects.]

The performance expectation above was developed using the following elements from the NRC document *A Framework for K-12 Science Education:*

Science and Engineering Practices	Disciplinary Core Ideas	Crosscutting Concepts
Constructing Explanations and Designing Solutions Constructing explanations and designing solutions in K–2 builds on prior experiences and progresses to the use of evidence and ideas in constructing evidence-based accounts of natural phenomena and designing solutions. • Make observations (firsthand or from media) to construct an evidence-based account for natural phenomena.	**PS1.A: Structure and Properties of Matter** • Different properties are suited to different purposes. • A great variety of objects can be built up from a small set of pieces.	**Energy and Matter** • Objects may break into smaller pieces and be put together into larger pieces, or change shapes.

Observable features of the student performance by the end of the grade:			
1	Articulating the explanation of phenomena		
	a	Students articulate a statement that relates the given phenomenon to a scientific idea, including that an object made of a small set of pieces can be disassembled and made into a new object.	
	b	Students use evidence and reasoning to construct an evidence-based account of the phenomenon.	
2	Evidence		
	a	Students describe* evidence from observations (firsthand or from media), including:	
		i.	The characteristics (e.g., size, shape, arrangement of parts) of the original object.
		ii.	That the original object was disassembled into pieces.
		iii.	That the pieces were reassembled into a new object or objects.
		Iv.	The characteristics (e.g., size, shape, arrangement of parts) of the new object or objects.
3	Reasoning		
	a	Students use reasoning to connect the evidence to support an explanation. Students describe* a chain of reasoning that includes:	
		i.	The original object was disassembled into its pieces and is reassembled into a new object or objects.
		ii.	Many different objects can be built from the same set of pieces.
		iii.	Compared to the original object, the new object or objects can have different characteristics, even though they were made of the same set of pieces.

2-PS1-4 Matter and Its Interactions		
Students who demonstrate understanding can: **2-PS1-4. Construct an argument with evidence that some changes caused by heating or cooling can be reversed and some cannot.** [Clarification Statement: Examples of reversible changes could include materials such as water and butter at different temperatures. Examples of irreversible changes could include cooking an egg, freezing a plant leaf, and heating paper.]		
The performance expectation above was developed using the following elements from the NRC document *A Framework for K-12 Science Education:*		
Science and Engineering Practices	**Disciplinary Core Ideas**	**Crosscutting Concepts**
Engaging in Argument from Evidence Engaging in argument from evidence in K–2 builds on prior experiences and progresses to comparing ideas and representations about the natural and designed world(s). • Construct an argument with evidence to support a claim. - ***Connections to Nature of Science*** **Science Models, Laws, Mechanisms, and Theories Explain Natural Phenomena** • Science searches for cause and effect relationships to explain natural events.	**PS1.B: Chemical Reactions** • Heating or cooling a substance may cause changes that can be observed. Sometimes these changes are reversible, and sometimes they are not.	**Cause and Effect** • Events have causes that generate observable patterns.

Observable features of the student performance by the end of the grade:			
1	Supported claims		
	a	Students make a claim to be supported about a phenomenon. In their claim, students include the idea that some changes caused by heating or cooling can be reversed and some cannot.	
2	Identifying scientific evidence		
	a	Students describe the given evidence, including:	
		i.	The characteristics of the material before heating or cooling.
		ii.	The characteristics of the material after heating or cooling.
		iii.	The characteristics of the material when the heating or cooling is reversed.
3	Evaluating and critiquing the evidence		
	a	Students evaluate the evidence to determine:	
		i.	The change in the material after heating (e.g., ice becomes water, an egg becomes solid, solid chocolate becomes liquid).
		ii.	Whether the change in the material after heating is reversible (e.g., water becomes ice again, a cooked egg remains a solid, liquid chocolate becomes solid but can be a different shape).
		iii.	The change in the material after cooling (e.g., when frozen, water becomes ice, a plant leaf dies).
		iv.	Whether the change in the material after cooling is reversible (e.g., ice becomes water again, a plant leaf does not return to normal).
	b	Students describe whether the given evidence supports the claim and whether additional evidence is needed.	
4	Reasoning and synthesis		
	a	Students use reasoning to connect the evidence to the claim. Students describe the following chain of reasoning:	
		i.	Some changes caused by heating or cooling can be reversed by cooling or heating (e.g., ice that is heated can melt into water, but the water can be cooled and can freeze back into ice [and vice versa]).
		ii.	Some changes caused by heating or cooling cannot be reversed by cooling or heating (e.g., a raw egg that is cooked by heating cannot be turned back into a raw egg by cooling the cooked egg, cookie dough that is baked does not return to its uncooked form when cooled, charcoal that is formed by heating wood does not return to its original form when cooled).

Teacher Reflections: I considered "reversed" a concept not a verb because we aren't using it as a skill or level of complexity.

CONCEPTS: (nouns)	COMPLEXITY: (verbs)
Investigation	Plan and conduct – relational thinking
Purpose of the Investigation	Identify and describe – relational thinking
Investigation plan	Develop – relational thinking
Materials	Describe, classify/organize, test – relational thinking
Observable properties	Describe and classify – relational thinking
Color	Describe – multistructural thinking
Texture	Describe – multistructural thinking
Hardness	Describe – multistructural thinking
Flexibility	Describe – multistructural thinking
Method of classification	Determineand describe – relational thinking
Observations	Describe, make/collect, record, and share – multistructural thinking
Questions	Answer – relational thinking
Solutions	Design, test,and support – abstract thinking
Problems	Test – relational thinking
Data	Collect, record, organize, and analyze – relational thinking
Object	Test, build, and compare* – relational thinking
Tool	Test and compare* – relational thinking
Explanations	Supportand construct – relational thinking
Evidence	Describeand connect – relational thinking
Matter	Describe and classify – relational thinking
Solid	Know – multistructural thinking
Liquid	Know – multistructural thinking
Temperature	Identify, describe, and measure – multistructural thinking
Changes	Describe – multistructural thinking
Heating	Describe – multistructural thinking
Cooling	Describe – multistructural thinking
Reversible	Know – multistructural thinking
Patterns	Observeand describe – relational thinking
Natural world	Observe – multistructural thinking
Human designed world	Observe – multistructural thinking
Phenomenon	Identify, describe, and relate – relational thinking
Idea	Identify, describe, compare, support/refute – relational thinking
Claim	Make and support – relational thinking
Causes	Support or refute – relational thinking
Intended purpose/use	Describe – multistructural thinking
Suitability	Determine and Describe – relational thinking
Test	Design – relational thinking
Human-made product	Design – relational thinking
Graphical displays	Create – relational thinking
Knowledge	Apply – abstract thinking
Relationships	Identify and describe – relational thinking
Evidence-based account	Construct – relational thinking
Set of pieces	Manipulate** – relational thinking
Shapes	Describe – multistructural thinking
Characteristics	Describe and compare – relational thinking
Statement	Articulate – relational thinking
Chain of Reasoning	Use and describe – relational thinking
Argument	Construct – relational thinking

*2-PS1-2 feature 3b "best suited for the given intended purpose relative to the other given objects/tools"= comparing
**2-PS1-3 "an object made of a small set of pieces can be disassembled and made into a new object" = manipulate

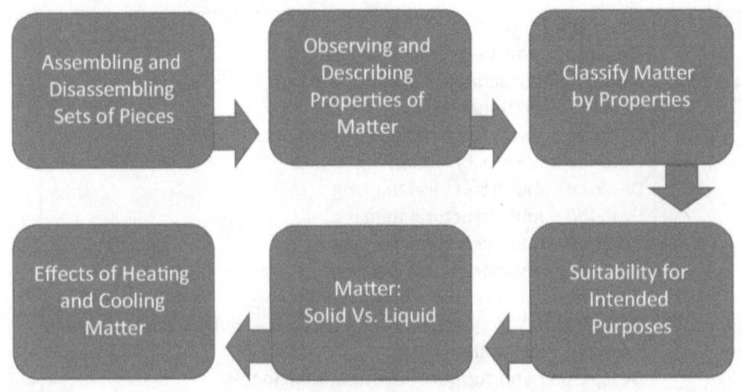

Teacher Reflections: My thinking: I began with 2-PS1-3 because it is something kids explore through play beginning in toddlerhood... they make towers of blocks that use the same pieces but are different each time. Plus, this concept involved a less complex level of thinking. Then, movingto observing the properties (2-PS1-1) allows the teacher to guide students in building the vocabulary to describe properties using academic language so they can compare objects and later classify matter by its properties. Once they have created a classification system, they can use it to help them evaluate the suitability of an object for an intended purpose based on its properties (2-PS1-2). Based on my evaluation of the vertical alignment of the physical science strand, this is the first time solid and liquid are explicitly covered, so some time should be devoted to developing definitions that clarify common misconceptions, such as that "all solids are hard," which is false. Then, with a firm understanding of the difference between solids and liquids as well as their exploration of properties, students are ready to investigate how heating and cooling changes objects and can change their characteristics, which is just another word for properties.

Big Ideas:

1. Many different objects can be built from the same setof pieces.
2. Matter can be described by properties, which then allow us to classify and compare those objects.(covers 2 parts of the progression: top middle and top right)
3. Choosing the best material for a task or design helps it to be successful or effective.
4. Matter exists in different forms with different properties. **This may be somewhat redundant to #2?
5. Physical or chemical changes to matter can change its properties, sometimes in ways that cannot be reversed.

Driving Questions:

1. How can I, as an engineer, create different designs from the same set of pieces that will allow others to use itin different ways?
2. How can I, as a scientist, create a classification system that will help others compare and describe objects by their observable properties?
3. How could I, as an engineer, evaluate the suitability of materials for different purposes and communicate my findings to prospective builders with evidence?
4. How will I, as a teacher, help my students determine the properties of solids and liquids?
5. How can I, as a student, use evidence to support my claim about how heating or cooling an object changes its properties and whether or not those changes are reversible?

Third Grade

3-PS2-1 Motion and Stability: Forces and Interactions

Students who demonstrate understanding can:

3-PS2-1. **Plan and conduct an investigation to provide evidence of the effects of balanced and unbalanced forces on the motion of an object.** [Clarification Statement: Examples could include an unbalanced force on one side of a ball can make it start moving; and, balanced forces pushing on a box from both sides will not produce any motion at all.] [*Assessment Boundary: Assessment is limited to one variable at a time: number, size, or direction of forces. Assessment does not include quantitative force size, only qualitative and relative. Assessment is limited to gravity being addressed as a force that pulls objects down.*]

The performance expectation above was developed using the following elements from the NRC document *A Framework for K-12 Science Education:*

Science and Engineering Practices	Disciplinary Core Ideas	Crosscutting Concepts
Planning and Carrying Out Investigations Planning and carrying out investigations to answer questions or test solutions to problems in 3–5 builds on K–2 experiences and progresses to include investigations that control variables and provide evidence to support explanations or design solutions. • Plan and conduct an investigation collaboratively to produce data to serve as the basis for evidence, using fair tests in which variables are controlled and the number of trials considered. - ***Connections to Nature of Science*** **Scientific Investigations Use a Variety of Methods** • Science investigations use a variety of methods, tools, and techniques.	**PS2.A: Forces and Motion** • Each force acts on one particular object and has both strength and a direction. An object at rest typically has multiple forces acting on it, but they add to give zero net force on the object. Forces that do not sum to zero can cause changes in the object's speed or direction of motion. (Boundary: Qualitative and conceptual, but not quantitative addition of forces are used at this level.) **PS2.B: Types of Interactions** • Objects in contact exert forces on each other.	**Cause and Effect** • Cause and effect relationships are routinely identified.

Observable features of the student performance by the end of the grade:		
1	Identifying the phenomenon under investigation	
	a	Students identify and describe the phenomenon under investigation, which includes the effects of different forces on an object's motion (e.g., starting, stopping, or changing direction).
	b	Students describe the purpose of the investigation, which includes producing data to serve as the basis for evidence for how balanced and unbalanced forces determine an object's motion.
2	Identifying the evidence to address the purpose of the investigation	
	a	Students collaboratively develop an investigation plan. In the investigation plan, students describe the data to be collected, including:
		i. The change in motion of an object at rest after:
		1. Different strengths and directions of balanced forces (forces that sum to zero) are applied to the object.
		2. Different strengths and directions of unbalanced forces (forces that do not sum to zero) are applied to the object (e.g., strong force on the right, weak force or the left).
		ii. What causes the forces on the object.
	b	Students individually describe how the evidence to be collected will be relevant to determining the effects of balanced and unbalanced forces on an object's motion.
3	Planning the investigation	
	a	In the collaboratively developed investigation plan, students describe how the motion of the object will be observed and recorded, including defining the following features:
		i. The object whose motion will be investigated.
		ii. The objects in contact that exert forces on each other.
		iii. Changing one variable at a time (e.g., control strength and vary the direction, or control direction and vary the strength).
		iv. The number of trials that will be conducted in the investigation to produce sufficient data.
	b	Students individually describe how their investigation plan will allow them to address the purpose of the investigation.
4	Collecting the data	
	a	Students collaboratively collect and record data according to the investigation plan they developed, including data from observations and/or measurements of:
		i. An object at rest and the identification of the forces acting on the object.
		ii. An object in motion and the identification of the forces acting on the object.

3-PS2-2 Motion and Stability: Forces and Interactions

Students who demonstrate understanding can:

3-PS2-2. **Make observations and/or measurements of an object's motion to provide evidence that a pattern can be used to predict future motion.** [Clarification Statement: Examples of motion with a predictable pattern could include a child swinging in a swing, a ball rolling back and forth in a bowl, and two children on a see-saw.] [Assessment Boundary: Assessment does not include technical terms such as period and frequency.]

The performance expectation above was developed using the following elements from the NRC document *A Framework for K-12 Science Education*:

Science and Engineering Practices	Disciplinary Core Ideas	Crosscutting Concepts
Planning and Carrying Out Investigations Planning and carrying out investigations to answer questions or test solutions to problems in 3–5 builds on K–2 experiences and progresses to include investigations that control variables and provide evidence to support explanations or design solutions. • Make observations and/or measurements to produce data to serve as the basis for evidence for an explanation of a phenomenon or test a design solution. - - - - - - - - - - - - - - - - ***Connections to Nature of Science*** **Science Knowledge is Based on Empirical Evidence** • Science findings are based on recognizing patterns.	**PS2.A: Forces and Motion** • The patterns of an object's motion in various situations can be observed and measured; when that past motion exhibits a regular pattern, future motion can be predicted from it. (Boundary: Technical terms, such as magnitude, velocity, momentum, and vector quantity, are not introduced at this level, but the concept that some quantities need both size and direction to be described is developed.)	**Patterns** • Patterns of change can be used to make predictions.

Observable features of the student performance by the end of the grade:		
1	Identifying the phenomenon under investigation	
	a	From the given investigation plan, students identify and describe* the phenomenon under investigation, which includes observable patterns in the motion of an object.
	b	Students identify and describe* the purpose of the investigation, which includes providing evidence for an explanation of the phenomenon that includes the idea that patterns of motion can be used to predict future motion of an object.
2	Identifying the evidence to address the purpose of the investigation	
	a	Based on a given investigation plan, students identify and describe* the data to be collected through observations and/or measurements, including data on the motion of the object as it repeats a pattern over time (e.g., a pendulum swinging, a ball moving on a curved track, a magnet repelling another magnet).
	b	Students describe* how the data will serve as evidence of a pattern in the motion of an object and how that pattern can be used to predict future motion.
3	Planning the investigation	
	a	From the given investigation plan, students identify and describe* how the data will be collected, including how:
		i. The motion of the object will be observed and measured.
		ii. Evidence of a pattern in the motion of the object will be identified from the data on the motion of the object.
		iii. The pattern in the motion of the object can be used to predict future motion.
4	Collecting the data	
	a	Students make observations and/or measurements of the motion of the object, according to the given investigation plan, to identify a pattern that can be used to predict future motion.

3-PS2-3 Motion and Stability: Forces and Interactions
Students who demonstrate understanding can: **3-PS2-3. Ask questions to determine cause and effect relationships of electric or magnetic interactions between two objects not in contact with each other.** [Clarification Statement: Examples of an electric force could include the force on hair from an electrically charged balloon and the electrical forces between a charged rod and pieces of paper; examples of a magnetic force could include the force between two permanent magnets, the force between an electromagnet and steel paperclips, and the force exerted by one magnet versus the force exerted by two magnets. Examples of cause and effect relationships could include how the distance between objects affects strength of the force and how the orientation of magnets affects the direction of the magnetic force.] [*Assessment Boundary: Assessment is limited to forces produced by objects that can be manipulated by students, and electrical interactions are limited to static electricity.*]

The performance expectation above was developed using the following elements from the NRC document *A Framework for K-12 Science Education*:

Science and Engineering Practices	Disciplinary Core Ideas	Crosscutting Concepts
Asking Questions and Defining Problems Asking questions and defining problems in grades 3–5 builds on grades K–2 experiences and progresses to specifying qualitative relationships. • Ask questions that can be investigated based on patterns such as cause and effect relationships.	**PS2.B: Types of Interactions** • Electric, and magnetic forces between a pair of objects do not require that the objects be in contact. The sizes of the forces in each situation depend on the properties of the objects and their distances apart and, for forces between two magnets, on their orientation relative to each other.	**Cause and Effect** • Cause and effect relationships are routinely identified, tested, and used to explain change.

Observable features of the student performance by the end of the grade:			
1	Addressing phenomena of the natural world		
	a	Students ask questions that arise from observations of two objects not in contact with each other interacting through electric or magnetic forces, the answers to which would clarify the cause-and-effect relationships between:	
		i.	The sizes of the forces on the two interacting objects due to the distance between the two objects.
		ii.	The relative orientation of two magnets and whether the force between the magnets is attractive or repulsive.
		iii.	The presence of a magnet and the force the magnet exerts on other objects.
		iv.	Electrically charged objects and an electric force.
2	Identifying the scientific nature of the question		
	a	Students' questions can be investigated within the scope of the classroom.	

Teacher Reflections: "Attractive" and "repulsive" are not nouns, but they are certainly two key concepts

3-PS2-4 Motion and Stability: Forces and Interactions

Students who demonstrate understanding can:

3-PS2-4. Define a simple design problem that can be solved by applying scientific ideas about magnets.* [Clarification Statement: Examples of problems could include constructing a latch to keep a door shut and creating a device to keep two moving objects from touching each other.]

The performance expectation above was developed using the following elements from the NRC document *A Framework for K-12 Science Education*:

Science and Engineering Practices	Disciplinary Core Ideas	Crosscutting Concepts
Asking Questions and Defining Problems Asking questions and defining problems in grades 3–5 builds on grades K–2 experiences and progresses to specifying qualitative relationships. • Define a simple problem that can be solved through the development of a new or improved object or tool.	**PS2.B: Types of Interactions** • Electric, and magnetic forces between a pair of objects do not require that the objects be in contact. The sizes of the forces in each situation depend on the properties of the objects and their distances apart and, for forces between two magnets, on their orientation relative to each other.	- - - - - - - - - - - - - - - - - ***Connections to Engineering, Technology, and Applications of Science*** **Interdependence of Science, Engineering, and Technology** • Scientific discoveries about the natural world can often lead to new and improved technologies, which are developed through the engineering design process.

Observable features of the student performance by the end of the grade:			
1	Identifying the problem to be solved		
	a	Students identify and describe a simple design problem that can be solved by applying a scientific understanding of the forces between interacting magnets.	
	b	Students identify and describe the scientific ideas necessary for solving the problem, including:	
		i.	Force between objects do not require that those objects be in contact with each other
		ii.	The size of the force depends on the properties of objects, distance between the objects, and orientation of magnetic objects relative to one another.
2	Defining the criteria and constraints		
	a	Students identify and describe the criteria (desirable features) for a successful solution to the problem.	
	b	Students identify and describe the constraints (limits) such as:	
		i.	Time.
		ii.	Cost.
		iii.	Materials.

CONCEPTS: (nouns)	COMPLEXITY: (verbs)
Investigation	Plan and conduct – relational thinking
Evidence	Identify and describe – relational thinking
Effects	Describe – relational thinking
Unbalanced forces	Describe and apply – multistructuralthinking
Balancedforces	Describe and apply – multistructural thinking
Net force	Know – multistructural thinking
Strength	Describe – multistructural thinking
Direction	Describe – multistructuralthinking
Speed	Describe – multistructural thinking
Motion	Predict, observe, describe, measure – relational thinking
Objectin motion	Describe – multistructural thinking
Objectat rest	Describe – multistructural thinking
Changes	Describe – multistructural thinking
Questions	Ask, investigate, and answer – relational thinking
Problems	Identify, define, anddescribe – relational thinking
Variables	Controland define – relational thinking
Number of trials	Consider and define – multistructural thinking
Explanations	Support – relational thinking
Data	Produce, collect, and describe – multistructural thinking
Pattern of change	Identify, observe, recognize, measure, predict – relational thinking
Phenomenon	Identify and describe – multistructural thinking
Purposeof the investigation	Identify and describe – multistructural thinking
Investigation plan	Develop – relational thinking
Features	Define – multistructural thinking
Observations	Makeand record – multistructural thinking
Measurements	Makeand record – multistructural thinking
Cause and effect relationships	Identify and clarify/specify – relational thinking
Electric interactions	Investigate – relational thinking
Magnetic interactions	Investigate – relational thinking
Size (of force)	Identify and describe* – multistructural thinking
Orientation	Identify and describe * – multistructural thinking
Magnets	Investigate and understand* – relational thinking
(Magnetic) Object	Observe and describe – multistructural thinking
Properties	Identify and describe* – multistructural thinking
Scientific idea/understanding	Apply – relational thinking
Tool	Develop – abstract thinking
Design solutions	Test – relational thinking
Design process	Apply – relational thinking
Criteria	Identify and describe – multistructural thinking
Constraints	Identify and describe – multistructural thinking
Time	Identify and describe – multistructural thinking
Cost	Identify and describe – multistructural thinking
Materials	Identify and describe – multistructural thinking
Discoveries	Make* – relational thinking
Natural world	Observe* – multistructural thinking
Technologies	Develop – abstract thinking

*Verbs determined by thinking about what the standard is asking rather than by the wording used

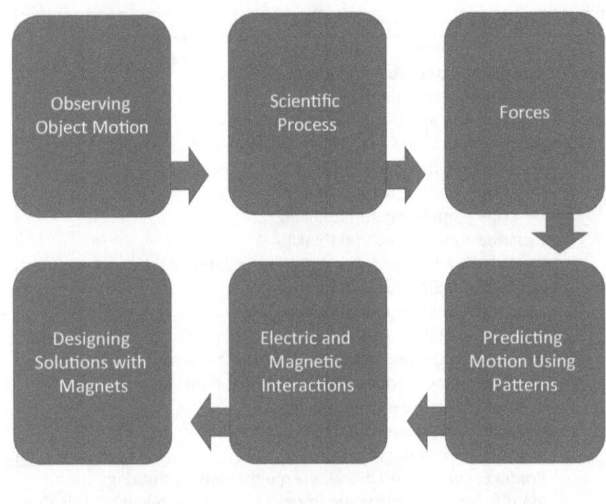

Teacher Reflections: I chose to start with something familiar to students from previous learning (K-PS2). Depending on where a class is in their year, taking a look at the scientific process to introduce the idea of variables and repeated trials may not be necessary, but giventhis is the first mention of it in the physical science strand K-3, I included time to introduce those concepts. Then, building on students' background knowledge and experiences with pushes and pulls, the concepts of balanced forces, unbalanced forces, and net force could be introduced and explored through inquiry. All of that knowledge would come together for students to apply when prediction motion using patterns of change they observed. Electric and magnetic forces are late in this unit because they area more abstract concept and require knowledge of forces as background.

Big Ideas:

1. Many factors can change, start, or stop the motion of an object.
2. Scientists use a series of steps to answer questions with accurate data.
3. Motion is the result of forces.
4. Observing patterns of change in the world around us helps us make predictions.
5. Objects can interact in many different ways.
6. Engineers work within constraints when designing solutions to problems.

Driving Questions:

1. In what ways can I, as a physicist, describe to someone younger than me changes in motion and the factors causing it?
2. How can I, as a scientist, apply the design process to conduct investigations on object motion and share my conclusions with evidence?
3. How can I, as a physicist, discoverthe effects offorces on the motion of objects?
4. How can I, as a scientist, use evidence from patterns of change to predict to my peers the future motion of an object?
5. How can I, as a physicist, discover the ways electric and magnetic forces interact with objects?
6. How can I, as an engineer, apply scientific ideas to design a solution to a problem using magnets that will help others?

Teacher Reflections: I hope that once teachers are comfortable with the process, they would revisit these standards with their teams to evaluate the progressions, big ideas, and driving questions for themselves.The longer I teach a set of standards, the more familiar with it I become, which leads me to better determine these aspects of my planning process. Reflective and responsive teaching are critical to the growth of our students. Unwrapping thestandards once is not enough...they must be revisited annually at minimum, but better yet, revisit throughout the unit and leave notes reflecting on what did or didn't work, whether students had sufficient supports to grapple with a concept, and thoughts onhow to extend student learning.

4 Implementing Daily Learning Experiences

Establishing and Sharing Learning Intentions and Success Criteria

At this point in our learning journey, we have arrived at the transition from analyzing and mapping out the big ideas or learning progressions to the planning and implementation of high-quality, high-impact daily learning experiences that move all learners toward an understanding of the big ideas, mastery of the standards, and success in cognitive, social-emotional, psychomotor, and behavioral outcomes. We should take a few moments and place our next steps into the broader context of teaching and learning in the inclusive early childhood science classroom. The metaphor of an umbrella provides us with a way of looking at the relationship between learning progressions, big ideas, and driving questions. We mentioned the use of an umbrella in the previous chapter by looking in on Ms. Anderson's classroom. Just as she used Velcro to attach big ideas and driving questions to an umbrella and hooked learning experiences on the metal stretchers, our high-quality, high-impact daily learning experiences should link directly to specific locations on the learning progression, lead learners toward the understandings represented by the big ideas, and build capacity in our learners to answer the driving questions.

Opportunities for Reflective Practices

What do you believe is involved in the transition from analyzing and mapping out the big ideas or learning progressions to the planning and implementation of high-quality, high-impact daily learning experiences?

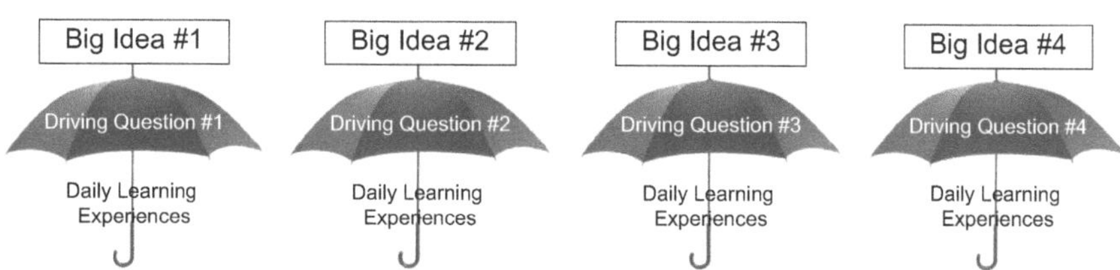

Figure 4.1 The Relationship between Daily Learning Experiences and Analyzing Standards.
Source: Author created.

When planning and implementing what works best in daily learning experiences, we must pull together the most recent research on evidence-based practices and then be deliberate, intentional, and purposeful in how we implement them in our classrooms. This involves the following:

1. Establishing and sharing learning intentions and success criteria
2. Selecting the model of instruction that best aligns with the learning intention and success criteria
3. Designing formative assessments and checks for understanding to monitor student learning
4. Creating rigorous tasks within the particular model of instruction that allows learners to engage in authentic learning across all domains
5. Evaluating the progress learners have made toward the learning intention and success criteria

As you recall from Chapter 1, we can access John Hattie's Visible Learning database (Visible Learning Meta X, 2020) to begin identifying evidence-based practices. These effect sizes help us look at a particular influence and see its relative impact compared to other influences (e.g., learning intentions, success criteria, models of instruction, task relevance, formative assessment, and feedback). Each of these practices will play a central role in the planning and implementation of high-quality, high-impact daily learning experiences that move all learners toward an understanding of the big ideas, mastery of the standards, and success in cognitive, social-emotional, psychomotor, and behavioral outcomes. In this chapter, we will focus on establishing and sharing learning intentions and success criteria.

Establishing and Sharing Learning Intentions and Success Criteria

To move forward in crafting daily learning experiences, we have to, again, refer to an early discussion. This time, we need to revisit the characteristics of assessment-capable visible science learners (Table 4.1).

Table 4.1 Characteristics of Assessment-Capable Visible Science Learners

- Assessment-capable visible science learners know their current level of understanding in science content, skills, and understandings.
- Assessment-capable visible science learners know where they are going next in their science learning and are confident to take on the challenge.
- Assessment-capable visible science learners have the tools to move learning forward and know when and how to use them.
- Assessment-capable visible science learners recognize that errors are learning opportunities and seek feedback.
- Assessment-capable visible science learners monitor their learning and make adjustments when necessary.
- Assessment-capable visible science learners recognize when they have learned something and act as teachers to others.

Source: Adapted from: Frey, N., Hattie, J., & Fisher, D. (2018). *Developing assessment-capable visible learners*. Thousand Oaks, CA: Corwin.

When our students build and leverage these characteristics in their learning, research indicates that this triples the rate of learning for our students. Yes, triple the rate of learning as indicated by an effect size 1.29 (see Visible Learning Meta X, 2020). Looking at the first two characteristics, for learners to know their current level of understanding and where they are going next in their learning, we must ensure that they have a clear understanding of the learning intentions and success criteria each and every day. More specifically, alongside our learners, we must ensure that all members of our classroom community know the focus of our learning, why this particular learning is important to us, what this learning will help us do, and what successful learning looks like (adapted from Frey, Hattie, & Fisher, 2018).

Ms. Shay, a kindergarten teacher, ensures that all of her learners build their capacity as self-directed learners by ensuring that they begin to acquire the academic language to talk about their learning, develop the social-emotional skills to self-monitor and self-regulate their instructional time, and make decisions about how to engage with their peers and the learning. "This is a year-long process, but I want my learners to talk about what they are learning and then explain what they understand and do not understand about their learning. For example, I want for them to talk about what they are learning throughout the day and not so much about completing a task."

When you talk to Ms. Shay's learners, they are quick to tell you what they are learning. For example, Javier tells us, "I am learning how to make a plant. See. My plant needs soil, water, and the sun." Although he is still working on the precise academic language, his answer focuses on learning.

Across the room, Samantha explains, "I need to write in my science journal. I still have trouble with my words, so I go to the word wall to help me write my words. Then I use pictures, see."

When you ask either learner about why this particular learning is important or what this learning will help them do, they are fast to point out, "so we can grow plants and remember what we did."

Samantha sees her writing in the journal as a way to record her thinking and learning. Ms. Shay then mentions, "I provide them with pictures and examples so that they can see success." So how did she get to this point with her young learners? "I make sure that I establish and share the learning intentions and success criteria with my students, each and every day."

Opportunities for Reflective Practices

What do you already know about learning intentions and success criteria? If these are new concepts for you, what do you think they are, and what is their role in inclusive early childhood science teaching and learning?

Establishing and Sharing Learning Intentions

Learning intentions are statements about what we intend for our students to learn today (Ainsworth & Donovan, 2019). This learning is tied to the understandings of the big ideas, mastering the standards, and framing success in cognitive, social-emotional, psychomotor, and behavioral outcomes. Learning intentions also convey why the learning is important and what it will help us do. Consider the following two statements. One of them is an example of a learning intention, while the other serves as a nonexample.

> Statement #1: Today, we are doing centers related to plants.
> Statement #2: Today, we are learning that plants have parts so that we understand how those parts help them to survive.

Statement #2 is an example of a learning intention. This statement is about learning and conveys a high level of relevancy for this learning. What are these students learning? The parts of a plant. Why are they learning the parts of a plant? To better understand how the parts help plants to survive. Statement #1 is simply an agenda item, not about the learning, and it is more focused on "doing." Let's look at two more examples through the same lens of learning versus doing and the relevancy of the learning.

> Statement #1: I am learning that animals adapt to their habitats so that they can survive.
> Statement #2: Today, I am completing a WebQuest on habitats.

Again, one of these statements focuses on learning and establishing relevancy while the other statement is simply an agenda item, void of a reason for why beyond "the teacher told me to do it."

Yet we do not have to limit ourselves to content learning intentions. As we have acknowledged several times, there are learning outcomes beyond cognitive outcomes. Ms. Shay pointed this out when she shared with us that self-monitoring and self-regulating were part of her learning expectations. Therefore, learning intentions can focus on social-emotional learning outcomes, as well as psychomotor outcomes. Let's look at several examples.

Mr. Reinhart, a first-grade teacher, and his team are working on their daily learning intentions for Monday. They have analyzed the standard 1-LS3-1, developed a learning progression, created big ideas, crafted driving questions, identified supporting standards, and used data generated from initial assessments to know where to start his daily instruction. Now, they are ready to establish learning intentions for today.

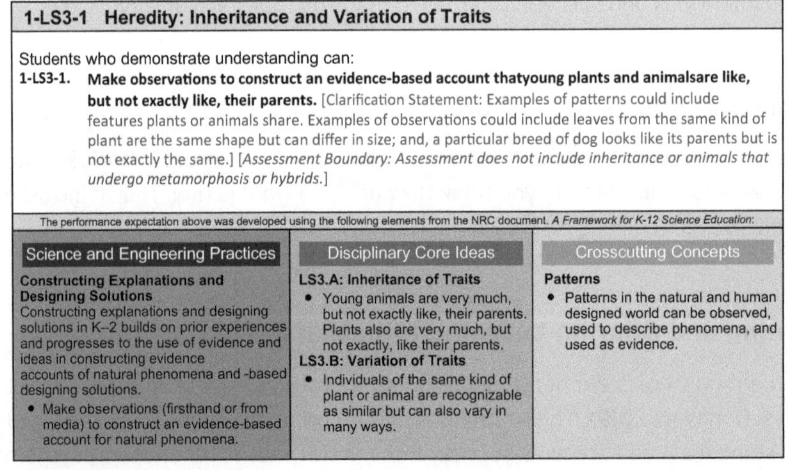

1-LS3-1 Heredity: Inheritance and Variation of Traits

Students who demonstrate understanding can:
1-LS3-1. Make observations to construct an evidence-based account thatyoung plants and animalsare like, but not exactly like, their parents. [Clarification Statement: Examples of patterns could include features plants or animals share. Examples of observations could include leaves from the same kind of plant are the same shape but can differ in size; and, a particular breed of dog looks like its parents but is not exactly the same.] [*Assessment Boundary: Assessment does not include inheritance or animals that undergo metamorphosis or hybrids.*]

The performance expectation above was developed using the following elements from the NRC document. *A Framework for K-12 Science Education*:

Science and Engineering Practices	Disciplinary Core Ideas	Crosscutting Concepts
Constructing Explanations and Designing Solutions Constructing explanations and designing solutions in K–2 builds on prior experiences and progresses to the use of evidence and ideas in constructing evidence accounts of natural phenomena and -based designing solutions. • Make observations (firsthand or from media) to construct an evidence-based account for natural phenomena.	**LS3.A: Inheritance of Traits** • Young animals are very much, but not exactly like, their parents. Plants also are very much, but not exactly, like their parents. **LS3.B: Variation of Traits** • Individuals of the same kind of plant or animal are recognizable as similar but can also vary in many ways.	**Patterns** • Patterns in the natural and human designed world can be observed, used to describe phenomena, and used as evidence.

Figure 4.2 1-LS3-1. Caption.
Source: NGSS Lead States. (2013). *Next generation science standards: For states, by states.* Washington, DC: The National Academies Press.

Table 4.2 Daily Learning Intentions

Learning Intentions: What are we learning today? Why are we learning it? What will this help me do?
Content Learning Intention: I am learning about the similarities and differences between animals and their young (disciplinary core ideas).
Social-Emotional Learning Intention: I am learning that scientists work together to make observations (science and engineering practices).
Psychomotor Learning Intention: I am learning that scientists record observations as evidence so that they can go back and find patterns (writing or illustrating).
Behavioral Learning Intention: I am learning how active listening is a way to show respect for my peers (character education).

"For us, we look at the first big idea, 'young animals resemble their parents,' and look at other curricular documents that are a focus in our school division and school. For example, we have spent a lot of time on character education and social-emotional learning. It is important that we embed that into all aspects of our teaching and learning. These are things that cross all disciplines." Mr. Reinhart is referring to division-wide and school-wide initiatives that support their learners' growth and development beyond cognitive outcomes. This also includes those initiatives related to the division and school's strategic plan or school improvement plan. "We have a focus on literacy this year and have made it one of our school goals in our school improvement plan. So, we will be looking for ways to build the literacy skills of my learners through science." They develop their learning intentions and place them into the lesson plan template (see Appendix B; Table 4.2).

"We will make daily changes to the content learning intention, but likely focus on the other learning intentions during the entire progression. However, some days we really zero in on one learning intention over the other learning intentions."

Ms. Shay and Mr. Reinhart worked together with their colleagues to establish learning intentions by deconstructing the big ideas.

Deconstructing Big Ideas

To get to the point of writing learning intentions, we have to return to the metaphor of the umbrella and look under the umbrella.

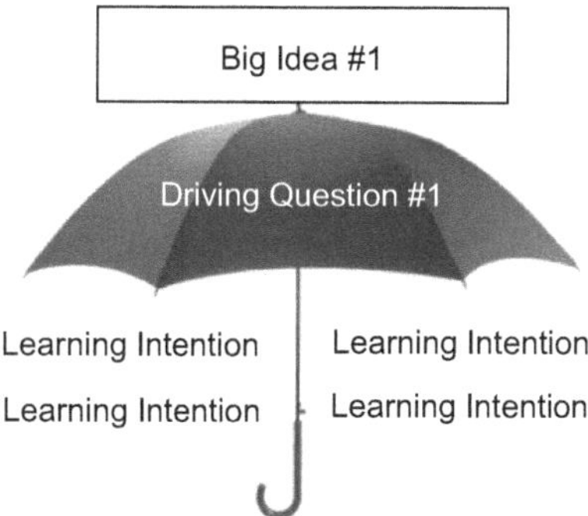

Figure 4.3 Deconstructing Big Ideas.
Source: Author created.

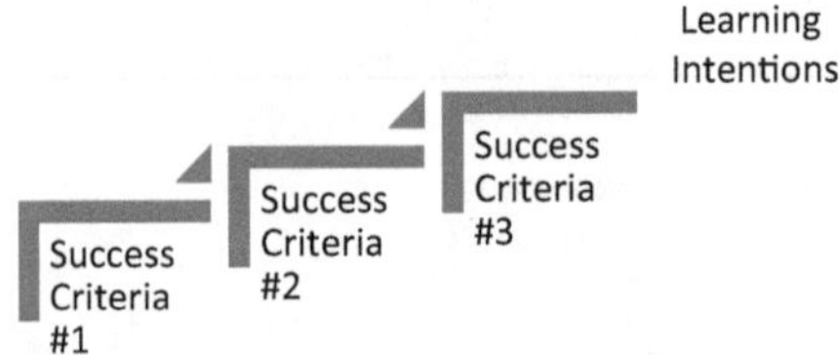

Figure 4.4 Success Criteria Leading to a Learning Intention.
Source: Author created.

Learning intentions are established from breaking down the big idea into smaller chunks. For example, if the big idea for Mr. Reinhart and his colleagues is "young animals resemble their parents", then the team must decide how to break that big idea down into smaller learning chunks that build upon each other and result in building capacity in our learners to answer the driving questions. This is where a pacing guide is helpful in deciding how long to devote to a single big idea and how many chunks to deconstruct that big idea into.

A pacing guide is a curriculum document that is generated at the district, division, or school level that provides the suggested amount of time to devote to specific content, skills, and understandings throughout the school year. This guide helps us to pace our instruction. We want to be clear here in that a pacing guide is the suggested pace of instruction and should provide general guidelines for pacing. Pacing guides that dictate the number of days, class periods, or even minutes to devote to specific learning are both inappropriate, ineffective, and in direct contradiction to what we know about how students learn. If extra time is needed to guide learners toward the understandings represented by the big ideas and to build capacity in our learners to answer the driving questions, then we should take that time. Furthermore, pacing guides that dictate time and are implemented in a way that does not allow any variance in that time de-professionalize us as teachers (Figure 4.4).

For Mr. Reinhart and his team, "our pacing guide suggests that we devote ten days to this standard and thus, should plan for three days on the big idea that young animals resemble their parents. However, our initial assessment data suggests are learners have considerable prior knowledge in this area and we may be able to bank some of this time for later units where their prior knowledge is not as strong." If Mr. Reinhart and his colleagues are going to plan for three days, they should then deconstruct the big idea into three content-learning intentions. Given that the science and engineering practices and crosscutting concepts are the same for the entire standard, the social-emotional, psychomotor, and behavioral learning intentions are likely to remain the same during the three days.

Research to Classroom Practice Tasks

Having seen multiple examples and two nonexamples of learning intentions, what do you believe the essential characteristics are of learning intentions?

Characteristics of Learning Intentions

As illustrated by Ms. Shay and Mr. Reinhart, the establishing of learning intentions is different from writing learning intentions that establish what the learning is for the day, why the learning is important, and what this learning will help learners do. From the previous examples, we can

Table 4.3 Open versus Closed Learning Intentions

Open Learning Intentions	*Closed Learning Intentions*
I am learning about the similarities and differences between animals and their young.	I am learning how deer fawns differ from their mothers.
I am learning that scientists work together to make observations.	I am learning to work with a partner to make observations.
I am learning that scientists record observations as evidence so that they can go back and find patterns.	I am learning to write five observations about animals in my science notebook.
I am learning how active listening is a way to show respect for my peers.	I am learning to listen to my peers.

identify essential characteristics of learning intentions that answer these questions in a way that maintains a focus on learning and not on a checklist or agenda item. First, learning intentions should be independent of a particular approach, strategy, or example. Take Ms. Shay's learning intentions about the parts of a plant. Her expectations are that learners gain an understanding of the generalizable big idea that plants have parts, and those parts help the plant to survive. This is very different than a contextualized learning intention, such as "we are learning about the parts of a geranium." Or, as another example, in Mr. Reinhart's classroom, "I am learning to write the characteristics of a white-tailed deer in my science interactive notebook" versus, "I am learning that scientists record observations as evidence." In these two examples, the removal of a specific context provides a generalizable understanding that will transfer beyond Ms. Shay or Mr. Reinhart's classroom.

Second, learning intentions should be open rather than closed. We want to establish a learning experience that allows for all learners to actively engage in the learning, leverage their strengths to be a contributing member of the community, and allow for a variety of options to support and scaffold their learning when necessary. Let's look at the open learning intentions of Mr. Reinhart and his colleagues and demonstrate what they would be if they were closed (Table 4.3).

From Table 4.3, we can see that closed learning intentions restrict our approach to teaching and our students' approach to learning. Take for example learning how deer fawns differ from their mothers. This level of specificity may appear to enhance the clarity of what learners are supposed to learn. However, this limits the thinking about how young animals resemble their parents. We want our learners to understand this big idea beyond deer fawns. Furthermore, learners who bring different prior experiences and background knowledge may not see this big idea with a deer but can relate to a camel, flamingo, or an animal that is something they have observed in their own lives. When we look at the intention focused on five observations in a science notebook, we run into a similar challenge in equity of access and opportunity. For learners who have a physical disability, do not yet have the fine motor skills for writing, or maybe speak a different language, this closed learning intention may appear out of reach for them. Opening up the intention to include recording observations allows us and our learners to engage with the learning intention using their strengths (e.g., drawing, using an electronic talker, or using pictures).

Lastly, learning intentions should be student centered. Learning intentions should use first-person, student-friendly language. There is a difference between "the student will understand the relationship between young animals and their adult parents" and "I am learning about the similarities and differences between animals and their young." First-person pronouns send the message of ownership and responsibility on the part of the learner. Again, if learners are going to know their current level of understanding, reading a learning intention that is from their perspective, in their language, sets the tone that they are the ones doing the learning and not some abstract individual from a sentence written in third person.

Opportunities for Reflective Practices

Take a few moments and review the essential characteristics of learning intentions. Have you observed this in your own learning experiences as a student?

Sharing Learning Intentions

Once we establish our learning intentions, we must share them with our learners. Again, if they are expected to know their current level of understanding and know where they are going next in their learning, we must share the learning intentions with them. If they are expected to know what they are learning, why the learning is important, and what this learning will help them do, we cannot keep the learning intentions a secret. What often happens in the planning and implementation of daily learning experiences is that we devote time to establishing learning intentions only to keep them between us and our colleagues. Then learners engage in these learning experiences without any awareness of the intention behind that learning. Yet the sharing of learning intentions is easier said than done. Not impossible but not as simple as writing them on the board or displaying them on the screen. When it comes to sharing learning intentions, the inclusive early childhood classroom presents challenges that are different from classrooms in higher grade levels. Mainly, the challenge comes from the reading level of the learners and the common use of stations in the early childhood classroom. This brings about two questions that must be addressed. First, how do I share learning intentions with learners who may not be able to read them yet? Second, how do I share learning intentions when using centers?

Opportunities for Reflective Practices

How do you think we support learners in knowing the learning intention when they may not be able to read the learning intention yet? How about centers?

The answer to both questions involves us deconstructing learning intentions with our learners and the use of pictures or visual representations of learning intentions linked to the words.

Deconstructing Learning Intentions

Returning to the classrooms of Ms. Shay and Mr. Reinhart, when observing their classrooms, we find that they open up their science blocks by deconstructing the learning intention.

Ms. Shay begins instruction by bringing her learners to the carpet. "We read, in unison, the learning intention as I point to each word. Then we brainstorm and predict what we are going to be learning today. The students get to ask questions, share their predictions, and then share their prior knowledge. I literally breakdown the learning intention."

Similarly, Mr. Reinhart asks his learners to read the learning intention with him and then "talk to a neighbor and generate questions they have about the day's learning. Sometimes I ask them to paste the learning intention in their science notebooks and circle the words they know, underline the ones they don't know, yet. Then we briefly talk about those terms."

In both classrooms, these teachers recognize that the terminology or academic vocabulary is challenging. However, they do not shy away from this challenge; instead, they use it as a teaching opportunity to build academic vocabulary within the context of science learning.

Visual Representations

A second option for sharing learning intentions is providing visual representations or gestures along with the words that are challenging for the students. This linking of an image, visual, or gestures to specific words in the learning intention allows all learners the access and opportunity to know the learning intention and, at the same time, provide a concrete link between the words and their meanings. Mr. Reinhart points out, "I provide images for science words that learners may struggle with. Plus, I have a consistent image of a brain, along with a gesture that cues my students into the learning intention. I start each class by pointing to my brain and announcing, 'Today we are learning.'" This is also a way to support learners who speak English as a second language. Building concepts of words at the same time learners are developing science content, skills, and understandings is an efficient and effective use of instructional time.

Learning Intentions and Centers

Finally, the use of centers can bring about challenges with sharing learning intentions. For example, do we put our learning intentions at the front of the room that are associated with each center? This approach would likely lead to double-digit learning intentions on the board, too many for young children to internalize in a single location. Instead, learning intentions should be located next to each center; presented in first-person, student-friendly language; and supported with images and visuals. For example, the learning intention for the kitchen center should be, as you might have guessed, next to the kitchen center. The learning intention for the literacy center should be next to the literacy center. The establishing and sharing of learning intentions for centers should make it very clear to learners what they are learning at that center, why that learning is important, and what this learning will help them do.

Research to Classroom Practice Tasks

How will you establish and share learning intentions with your students? Use the template in Appendix B to establish learning intentions, ensuring that they have the aforementioned essential characteristics.

Once we have established and prepared to share our learning intentions, our attention must turn to the success criteria. What does successful learning look like?

Establishing and Sharing Success Criteria

While learning intentions establish and share the focus, importance, and utility of our learning, success criteria establish and share what successful learning looks like in our classrooms. Much work has been done on the role of learning intentions and success criteria in effective teaching and learning (see Almarode & Vandas, 2019; Fisher, Frey, Amador, & Assof, 2019). These two concepts go hand in hand as we implement high-quality, high-impact daily learning experiences. Just as learning intentions help learners know their current level of understanding and where they are headed next in their learning, success criteria help them to monitor their own progress, decide when to seek and give feedback, and select the right tools for their learning. These, as you may recall, are all characteristics of an assessment-capable visible science learner (see Table 4.1).

Success criteria, then, present clear parameters that establish what success looks like in their learning. This is our way of explicitly showing learners the target for the day. We acknowledge that learning is a lifelong process and does not end with the conclusion of the school day, but learners must have visible milestones toward which they monitor and guide their learning. Success criteria articulate the evidence we are looking for and that learners must produce to demonstrate their progress toward the learning intention, big idea, and driving question (Ainsworth & Donovan, 2019). Let's take another look at the work of Mr. Reinhart and his colleagues.

"When we develop our success criteria, we look at them from several different angles. For example, what would a learner do if they had mastered the learning intention for the day? In other words, a learner who really knows how young animals are similar and different from their parents would say and do what? The answers to this question help us generate success criteria." Establishing the criteria for success requires Mr. Reinhart and his colleagues to engage in content analysis. Using the learning intention as the end point, what actions would lead a learner to demonstrate mastery of that learning intention? Success criteria can be viewed as steps along the way to meeting the learning intention. Again, what would a learner say or do if they had reached the learning intention?

Opportunities for Reflective Practices

Consider a learning intention that you have established for an upcoming daily learning experience. What would a learner say or do if they had successfully reached the learning intention?

Using Mr. Reinhart and his colleagues as an example, let's go through the process of establishing success criteria for each of the learning intentions in Table 4.2. To begin, we want to make sure we are clear on what makes good success criteria. Consider each of the following learning intentions.

I am learning about the similarities and differences between animals and their young.
I am learning that scientists work together to make observations.
I am learning that scientists record observations as evidence so that they can go back and find patterns.
I am learning how active listening is a way to show respect for my peers.

Table 4.4 Examples and Nonexamples of Success Criteria

Success Criteria Option #1	*Success Criteria Option #2*
1. I can fill in a Venn diagram about an animal and its baby. 2. I can tell my neighbor five things that are on my paper. 3. I can do this at a volume level 1.	1. I can identify how an adult animal is the same as and different from its young. 2. I can record my thinking. 3. I can explain my thinking using my science words. 4. I can ask questions to better understand what others are thinking.

As you recall, the last learning intention, the one directed toward behavioral learning, takes into consideration the character education initiative within Mr. Reinhart's school division and applies to all areas of the day. He and his colleagues are integrating this learning into science. Furthermore, Mr. Reinhart and his colleagues do not intend to develop separate lists of success criteria for each learning intention. Instead, they want to blend together the content, social-emotional, psychomotor, and behavioral learning outcomes to make it clear to their learners that these work in tandem and should not be seen as separate, siloed outcomes. This reflects the definition of science as more than just facts but also an integrated discipline composed of a body of knowledge, set of processes, and way of knowing (Bell, 2008). "My team and I recognize that expecting our first-graders to engage with 8, 9, or 10 success criteria is ridiculous and unrealistic. We try to think of two or three success criteria that learners can sink their teeth into and use to monitor their own learning."

Table 4.4 presents two sets of success criteria related to the learning intentions developed by Mr. Reinhart and his colleagues.

If you had an immediate reaction to the three success criteria in Option #1, you are justified in that reaction. Those success criteria resemble a set of instructions or an agenda. Not to mention, the third success criteria is not about learning but about classroom management. Yes, classroom management is important, but the students are not learning "level 1." These students are learning to explain their thinking and ask questions. Level 1 is simply the specific context. A second concern with the listed success criteria in Option #1 relates directly to our desire to provide an inclusive early childhood science learning environment. If our success criteria provide a specific context, approach, or strategy, we can inadvertently exclude learners. For example, by providing success criteria that name a Venn diagram and writing, as we also mentioned in our discussion of learning intentions, can unconsciously exclude learners who have a physical disability, do not yet have the fine motor skills for writing, or maybe speak a different language. This specific success criteria may appear out of reach for them, for now. By opening up the success criteria, we make other options available for demonstrating success using their strengths (e.g., drawing, using an electronic talker, or using pictures) and then focus on providing small group or one-on-one interventions to target these skills at a different time. We should not allow them to be barriers to demonstrating that they understand that there are similarities and differences between animals and their young, that scientists work together to make and record observations, and that we must engage in appropriate interactions when talking about science ideas. These understandings are independent of learners' ability to write or speak the primary language of the classroom and their disability status.

> **Research to Classroom Practice Tasks**
>
> Having seen examples and nonexamples of success criteria, what do you believe the essential characteristics are of success criteria?

The four success criteria in Option #2 focus on exactly what the student will do if he or she understands, at this point in his or her learning journey, that there are similarities and differences between animals and their young, that scientists work together to make and record observations, and that we must engage in appropriate interactions when talking about science ideas. Thus Mr. Reinhart and his team put these success criteria into their daily learning experience lesson plan (see Appendix B; Table 4.5).

Specifically for the last understanding, this is a long-term learning intention, and today, Mr. Reinhart and his colleagues choose the skill of asking probing questions or clarifying questions as one aspect of that understanding. In a subsequent learning experience, the focus may then be on providing feedback to their peers. Again, this returns us to the rather passionate discussion about professionalism and pacing guides. The decision about how to develop success criteria and where to focus our attention for broader ideas, such as the science and engineering practices or aspects of social-emotional and behavioral learning outcomes, are professional decisions we make based on our desired outcomes and, more importantly, who are learners are and where they are in their own learning journeys.

Deconstructing Learning Intentions

How we move from learning intentions to success criteria is very similar to how we move from big ideas to learning intentions. Only now, our focus is on what the learner will say and do to demonstrate that he or she has reached the specific learning intention. Success criteria are established by breaking down the learning into concrete, measurable actions. The verb in each

Table 4.5 Learning Intentions and Associated Success Criteria

<table>
<tr><td>Learning Intentions:
What are we learning today? Why are we learning it?
What will this help me do?</td><td rowspan="2">Success Criteria:
How will we know we are successful?
1. I can identify how an adult animal is the same as and different from its young (content).
2. I can record my thinking (psychomotor).
3. I can explain my thinking using my science words (behavioral).
4. I can ask questions to better understand what others are thinking (social-emotional).</td></tr>
<tr><td>Content Learning Intention:
I am learning about the similarities and differences between animals and their young (disciplinary core ideas).
Social-Emotional Learning Intention:
I am learning that scientists work together to make observations (science and engineering practices).
Psychomotor Learning Intention:
I am learning that scientists record observations as evidence so that they can go back and find patterns (writing or illustrating).
Behavioral Learning Intention:
I am learning how active listening is a way to show respect for my peers (character education).</td></tr>
</table>

success criteria communicates the specific action that we are looking for and that our students aim to demonstrate. Again, this must be concrete and measurable. The success criteria, "I understand that young animals are similar to their adult parents" is not measurable. What does it mean to understand? However, learners who can identify similarities and differences, record those observations, explain their thinking, and ask probing questions understand this idea. Identify, record, explain, and ask are the four verbs in the success criteria established by Mr. Reinhart and his colleagues. Therefore, we are looking for our learners to do just that, and they should be prepared to demonstrate each of those skills. The number of success criteria that come from this deconstruction will depend on what we believe is realistic for our learners. The pacing guide mentioned in our discussion plays a role here as well. Knowing that the suggested time for a particular standard or unit can also help us make decisions about when to introduce specific success criteria.

Mr. Reinhart and his team remind us that "again, our pacing guide helps us decide which success criteria to emphasize on what day. We have three days to space out learning and therefore three days to support their progression toward this particular learning intention. So, we can spend one day helping our learners ask questions and another day on the different types of questions like clarifying or probing questions."

Characteristics of Success Criteria

From the previous examples, we can identify essential characteristics of success criteria that will help our learners answer the question, how will I know I have learned? This also helps us to focus our attention on what we look for from our learners. And, as we will see in upcoming chapters, strong success criteria help us develop formative assessments, select our instructional approach, and identify evidence-based practices. Let's look more closely at these characteristics, many of which we identified in the previous reflection.

First, success criteria should be independent of a particular approach, strategy, or example. We pointed this out in reference to the success criteria, mentioning a Venn diagram. To demonstrate success, we want learners to compare and contrast, not simply use a Venn diagram. Venn diagrams are one way to organize a learner's thinking around similarities and differences, but there are other ways. The removal of a specific approach, strategy, or example moves the focus to the learning process and not the product.

Like learning intentions, success criteria should be open and include a range of ways for demonstrating success. Mr. Reinhart wants to articulate what success looks like in a way that allows for all learners to actively demonstrate their learning, leverage their strengths to be a contributing member of the community, and allows for a variety of options to support and scaffold their learning when necessary. We have mentioned this before, but it is worth mentioning again that closed success criteria restrict how learners can "show what they know."

Lastly, success criteria should be student centered. They should use first-person, student-friendly language. There is a difference between "the student will identify the similarities and differences between young animals and their adult parents" and "I can identify how an adult animal is the same as and different from its young." Like learning intentions, first-person pronouns send the message of ownership and responsibility on the part of the learner. Again, if learners are going to know what their successful learning looks like and where they are going next, reading success criteria that are from their perspective, in their language, sets the tone that they are the ones demonstrating their own learning and not some individual named "student."

At this point in our journey, we notice that there is a commonality between the establishing and sharing of learning intentions and success criteria. This is because they go hand in hand. However, there is a slight difference with success criteria in that how we share them is not restricted to an "I can" statement. Let's look closer at this difference, as well as the commonalities between learning intentions and success criteria.

Sharing Success Criteria

Once Mr. Reinhart establishes success criteria, he and his colleagues must share them with their learners. Again, they are expected to know their current level of understanding and know where they are going next in their learning. To monitor their learning, we must share what success looks like. This may seem intuitive, but how often do we, as teachers, have an idea about what success looks like and never tell our students? Then learners engage in these learning experiences without any awareness of what the target is for their work. When it comes to sharing success criteria, the inclusive early childhood classroom again presents challenges that are different from classrooms in higher grade levels. Once again, how do I first share success criteria with learners who may not be able to read them yet? Second, how do I share learning intentions when using centers?

Opportunities for Reflective Practices

How do you think we support learners in knowing the success criteria when they may not be able to read the learning intention yet? How about centers?

Demonstrating Success Criteria. Mr. Reinhart asks his learners to think about the success criteria. "I share the success criteria with them and have them ask me questions or give examples of things they might be doing today during our science learning. Furthermore, I use this time to model success." What Mr. Reinhart is talking about is the different ways we can share success criteria. In addition to "I can" statements, we can use exemplars and modeling to show our learners what success looks like. For example, Mr. Reinhart might use work from previous years that show how learners kept track of similarities and differences through Venn diagrams, t-charts, a double bubble graphic organizer, or simply written in their interactive science notebooks. If this is not possible, we can create a model and walk through what makes this a "good example." "I often ask my learners to look at my work and tell me what makes my work successful and where do I need to spend a little more time. This exercise helps them see both examples and non-examples."

Visual Representations

Another option for sharing success criteria is to provide visual representations or gestures, along with the words that are challenging for the students. This is the same approach we can use with learning intentions and links an image, visual, or gestures to specific words in the success criteria that allows all learners the access and opportunity to know what success looks like and the academic vocabulary for that success. Returning to Mr. Reinhart's classroom, he offers, "I often take pictures of learners being successful at social-emotional and behavioral success criteria. Then, I place those pictures next to success criteria so that learners see themselves as the models of what success looks like. Plus, many of these pictures can be used for different criteria, allowing me to reinforce previous criteria alongside new criteria."

Success Criteria and Centers

Finally, back to the use of centers and the challenges brought about by having learning occur at different locations in the room. We should approach this the same way we approach learning intentions. Success criteria should be located next to each center, presented in first-person, student-friendly language, and supported with examples, models, images, visuals, and/or pictures. That is, the success criteria for the contents and container center should be, as you might have guessed, next to the contents and containers center. Likewise, the success criteria for the literacy center should be next to the literacy center and truly support their decision making about how to engage in text as it relates to the learning intention. The establishing and sharing of success criteria for centers should make it very clear about what successful learning looks like at that center, above and beyond playtime.

Research to Classroom Practice Tasks

How will you establish and share success criteria with your students? Use the template in Appendix B to establish success criteria, ensuring that they have the aforementioned essential characteristics.

Quantity versus Quality

As we wrap up our work on learning intentions and success criteria, we now move into selecting the model of instruction that best aligns with the learning intention and success criteria, designing formative assessments and checks for understanding to monitor student learning, creating rigorous tasks within the particular model of instruction that allows learners to engage in authentic learning across all domains, and evaluating the progress learners have made toward the learning intention and success criteria. However, we need to reiterate the issue of quantity versus quality. How many learning intentions and how many success criteria should I have each day?

There is no one right answer to this question. There is, however, a wrong answer. The wrong answer is that there is an ideal number that should be established and shared each day. This is wrong. Depending on the nature of the content, skills, and understandings (the what); where our learners are in their journeys; and who they are in terms of background knowledge and prior experiences, we may have days that zero in on one or two success criteria. Other days may involve three success criteria. Again, the wrong answer to the question of how many is to provide a set number. A better way of thinking about this is to consider this reflective question: How many learning intentions and success criteria can my learners realistically work toward so that they all experience some level of success to celebrate at the end of the learning experience? The answer to that question will give us the best chance of identifying the ideal number of learning intentions and success criteria.

Professional Learning Tasks

1. Returning to the science standard of learning you are unpacking, develop learning intentions and success criteria for a daily learning experience. Complete the template in Appendix B.
2. Using those learning intentions and success criteria, develop different ways of sharing them with your current or future learners.
   - How will you deconstruct the learning intention with your current or future learners?
   - What images could you use? How about sharing them in different languages?
   - What examples or exemplars could you use to share with learners what success looks like?
3. Devote time to looking at examples of learning intentions and success criteria online. Practice providing constructive feedback as if you are the mentor to these teachers and collaborating with them to help them improve their learning intentions and success criteria. Refer to the essential characteristics presented in this chapter for support in analyzing these online examples. Of course, you are not going to actually contact these individuals. This is to enhance our understanding of what makes a good learning intention and success criteria.
4. Now that we have established learning intentions and success criteria, we must begin to think about how to design learning experiences. Although we will devote significant time to this in Chapters 5 and 7, we have to start looking for ways to creating rigorous and authentic learning experiences early. One of the ways is to identify resources in the community. This helps learners see who uses this content, practices, and understandings in their daily lives. Using the "Community Resource Task" in Appendix E, develop an interview protocol for engaging your learners in student conferences or one-on-one interviews.

Family and Community Engagement

1. **Make teaching and learning a collaborative effort:** The development of learning intentions and success criteria leads to a monstrous to-do list as we begin to design and implement learning experiences (i.e., Chapters 5 and 7). One way to engage the family and the community is to identify needs and tasks that can be supported by someone other than us. This is the time to capitalize on community resources available to you in your school. There is a task at the end of this chapter that will explore this effort a bit more on page ##.

   This is also a time to seize the opportunity to include families in your classroom. Using the information obtained from the family questionnaire generated in the previous chapter, offer specific tasks to families based on their strengths, interests, and availability. For this to be successful, we must set aside time to share information and impressions frequently, especially after conversations with parents, guardians, and other community members. Be sure to acknowledge everyone's unique contributions as members of a "team." Families and community members are part of the team!

2. **Document learning and share it:** Sharing examples of student learning keeps parents and guardians current about their children's progress and achievements. One way is to create a learning journal for your students that captures specific milestones, experiences, or learning accomplishments. This can be shared on a weekly basis or at any increment of time that you select for your classroom. If you return to the "Family and Community Engagement" sections in the previous chapters, you will see that we have looked at different digital tools for connecting with families and the community. These same tools can be helpful in documenting and sharing learning. For example, Seesaw and Dojo are two possible tools for doing this across a digital platform if creating physical portfolios. Set aside some time to explore other tools for documenting and sharing learning.

   Another option for this documenting and sharing of learning is to provide sentence stems, question starters, or additional resources that support parents and guardians engaging in discourse about their children's learning. The goal is to help family members take part in conversations about what their child is learning, why they are learning it, and what success looks like for this particular learning experience. We can provide specific examples of how to connect in-class learning to the home environment and what resources are available to family members. As we will see in upcoming "Family and Community Engagement" sections, these resources can be sent home with learners well before they start a particular unit. This pre-exposure can be very helpful to our students. In addition, family members may not be comfortable or certain talking about specific content, practices, and understandings or do not know how to best support their child in this learning. We can help!
3. **Create a daily communication system:** Let's be honest, we still must have a way to communicate with parents or guardians on a daily basis that is not feasible through digital and electronic pathways. Remember, in the interest of inclusion, we cannot assume families will have access to Seesaw, Dojo, or other tools. One of the easiest ways to establish daily communication is through learners' backpacks and with folders. For example, have a pocketed folder where "Things for Home" go in one pocket and "Things to Return to School" go in the other pocket. This daily communication might include notes or newsletters for parents/guardians ("Things for Home") or permission slips ("Things to Return to School"). However, if we set up this system for daily communication, we have to follow through and check folders each and every day. We must also encourage and remind families to do the same.

5 Implementing Daily Learning Experiences

Models of Instruction

With clear learning intentions and success criteria established and ready to share with our learners, we direct our attention to the specific characteristics of the daily learning experience. As we have identified several times over the past several chapters, each step in our journey to plan, design, and implement high-quality, high-impact inclusive learning experiences is interconnected with every other step. For example, we cannot effectively design learning intention and success criteria without understanding the big ideas that our young students should develop through the learning experiences. Without an analysis of the standards, we cannot identify those big ideas. To ensure that we devote the necessary time and attention to what learners "need" to know and not what is just "neat" to know, we have to take into account our learning progressions and the evidence generated from initial assessments to decide where we start within our progressions. Now, we use our work up to this point to design the learning experiences that will move our learners toward the learning intentions as evidenced by the success criteria.

Learning experiences are structured around models of instruction and use evidence-based practices to maximize science learning. Models of instruction, or approaches to teaching, are frameworks based on specific theories about how we learn and provide a guide for implementing instruction (see Estes & Mintz, 2015; Joyce, Weil, & Calhoun, 2003). One helpful way of thinking about these approaches is that they help us structure the thinking and doing of our learners as they engage in learning experiences. We will consider eight different models of instruction.

1. Direct Instruction
2. Concept Attainment
3. Cooperative Learning
4. The 5E Model
5. Inquiry-Based Learning
6. Project-Based Learning

Although there are additional models of instruction and a thorough treatment of these models would evolve into a book in and of itself (e.g., Estes & Mintz, 2015; Joyce, Weil, & Calhoun, 2003), our purpose here is to simply introduce each model and understand the relationship between my learning intentions, success criteria, and the specific model of instruction we choose to frame the day's learning experiences.

Research to Classroom Practice Tasks

Devote some time to exploring the models of instruction and identifying similarities and differences across each of the models. In addition, making some predictions about the types of learning intentions and success criteria might lead you to select one model over another.

Identifying a model of instruction into which we structure our learning experiences must result from our careful consideration of what we want our students to learn, why they are learning, what they can do with that learning, and how they know they will be successful. This is easier said than done. Oftentimes, our particular approach to teaching is selected because the model is our favorite or dictated to us through a curriculum. For example, science is often presumed to be best taught through inquiry. After all, children are like little scientists and should thus engage in science just as a scientist would engage in science. First, the belief that science is best taught through inquiry is not supported by the research (see Adams & Engelmann, 1996; Almarode et al., 2018; Forness et al., 1997; Hattie & Donoghue, 2016; Klahr and Nigam, 2004) And while young learners are curious, ask lots of questions, and are constant explorers, the child-as-scientist perspective is also not fully supported in the cognitive development of scientific reasoning (e.g., Amsel & Brock, 1996; Chen & Klahr, 1999; Sodian, Zaitchik, & Carey, 1991; Strand-Cary & Klahr, 2008; Zimmerman, 2000, 2007). Strand-Cary and Klahr (2008), for example, point out the necessity of science instruction in developing specific science skills captured in the science and engineering practices (NGSS Lead States, 2013). Therefore, we should identify our model of instruction based on our specific expectations and learning outcomes. There should be complete alignment between the learning intentions, success criteria, and our approach to teaching.

Let's venture back to Ms. Campbell's classroom from Chapter 1. She used a driving question to frame learning for her students in a series of centers. The phrasing of the driving question is very important. When we first met Ms. Campbell, the use of the pronoun "we" did not seem significant. Now, incorporating our discussion on models of instruction with the analysis of the standard, we can better understand why she decided to use cooperative learning to get at the day's learning (Figure 5.1).

She intentionally, deliberately, and purposefully modeled the skill of questioning and then provided a learning experience that immersed her learners into cooperative learning groups so that they could collaboratively produce evidence to answer a question. These science and engineering practices were embedded in the content of vibrating materials and the production of sound. The main point here is the intentional, deliberate, and purposeful nature by which she selected her model of instruction: inquiry-based instruction within cooperative learning groups. And this all started with the analysis of the standard.

Opportunities for Reflective Practices

Reflect on the level of intentionality in Ms. Campbell's teaching. How intentional are you in your thinking about each daily learning experience in your future or current classroom? What surprises you about Ms. Campbell or any of the teachers featured in this book?

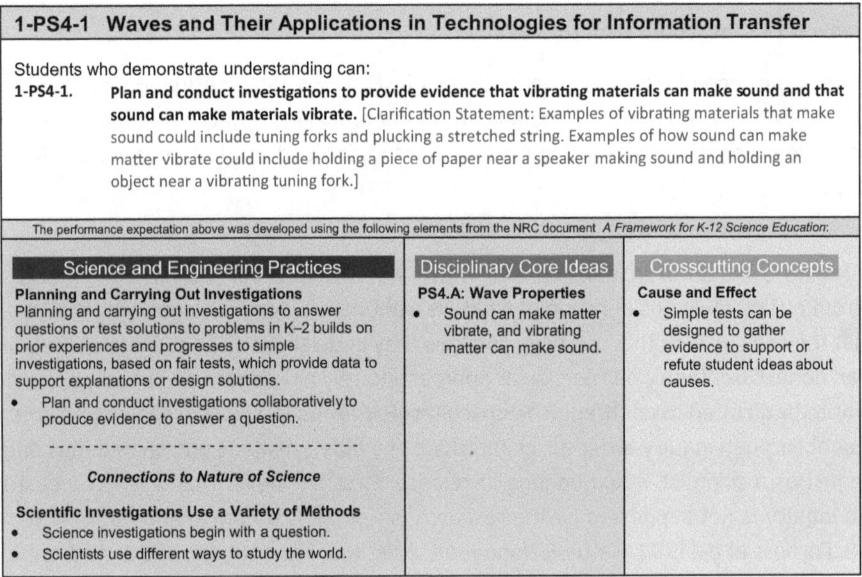

1-PS4-1 Waves and Their Applications in Technologies for Information Transfer

Students who demonstrate understanding can:

1-PS4-1. Plan and conduct investigations to provide evidence that vibrating materials can make sound and that sound can make materials vibrate. [Clarification Statement: Examples of vibrating materials that make sound could include tuning forks and plucking a stretched string. Examples of how sound can make matter vibrate could include holding a piece of paper near a speaker making sound and holding an object near a vibrating tuning fork.]

The performance expectation above was developed using the following elements from the NRC document *A Framework for K-12 Science Education*:

Science and Engineering Practices	Disciplinary Core Ideas	Crosscutting Concepts
Planning and Carrying Out Investigations Planning and carrying out investigations to answer questions or test solutions to problems in K–2 builds on prior experiences and progresses to simple investigations, based on fair tests, which provide data to support explanations or design solutions. • Plan and conduct investigations collaboratively to produce evidence to answer a question. - - - - - - - - - - - - - - - - ***Connections to Nature of Science*** **Scientific Investigations Use a Variety of Methods** • Science investigations begin with a question. • Scientists use different ways to study the world.	**PS4.A: Wave Properties** • Sound can make matter vibrate, and vibrating matter can make sound.	**Cause and Effect** • Simple tests can be designed to gather evidence to support or refute student ideas about causes.

Figure 5.1 NGSS Standard 1-PS4-1.
Source: NGSS Lead States. (2013). Next generation science standards: For states, by states. Washington, DC: The National Academies Press.

Different Models of Instruction

Ms. Campbell selected cooperative learning because that was the best approach for the day's learning. Had the learning intention and success criteria been different, her approach would have been different as well. There is no one right approach for teaching and learning science in the inclusive early childhood classroom. As Ms. Lamb planned out her learning experiences around the physical characteristics of insects, she would likely have been led to a direct instruction approach to move her students forward in naming the head, abdomen, and thorax. Then she may have decided to use an inquiry-based approach to support their comparing and contrasting of insects with other insects and spiders. Again, there is no one right approach for teaching and learning science in the inclusive early childhood classroom. Let's look more specifically at the eight previously mentioned approaches and take the same approach modeled by Ms. Campbell and Ms. Lamb - identifying the approach that aligns with our learning intentions and success criteria.

Direct Instruction

Direct instruction is an approach to teaching that is structured, sequenced, and facilitated by the teacher (Estes & Mintz, 2015). This approach requires that the teacher initiate the learning experience by hooking learners' attention and establishing relevancy. Why are we learning this, and what will we be able to do with this learning? This involves activating the background knowledge and prior experiences of students so that the new content, skills, and understandings can be assimilated into that knowledge of those experiences. This leads to the introduction of the new learning and relies heavily on teacher modeling, offering learners opportunities to engage in guided practice, giving and receiving feedback, and then closing out the learning experience with independent practice.

Ms. Lamb did indeed decide to use direct instruction to support her learners in naming and identifying the parts of an insect. "I started the lesson by having them join me on the rug and giving each of them plastic magnifiers. I wanted to hook them into learning by letting them see different insects. I asked them questions, they made observations, predictions, and got to hear from their peers about different bugs. That allowed me to introduce the three parts of an insect, now that they had experience with what an insect even looked like, and eventually return to the magnifiers for guided practice." What Ms. Lamb has shown us is that direct instruction has a place in the early childhood classroom. She then provides multiple opportunities for her young learners to engage in independent practice at various locations and centers around the room.

Direct Instruction in Ms. Lamb's Classroom

- Ms. Lamb introduced the topic to her learners through an instructional hook - looking at insects with plastic handheld magnifiers.
- She then introduced the learning intention and success criteria using words, images, and gestures.
- Using pictures and insect specimens, she presented the three parts of an insect to her learners. This also involved gestures and a song.
- Her young learners practiced using their own insect specimens, while Ms. Lamb monitored their learning and provided feedback.
- Throughout the day, her young learners had opportunities to engage in independent practice at the art center, the science and discovery center, and the literacy center.
- Ms. Lamb used artifacts from each center to evaluate her learners and make decisions about where to go next with this particular part of the learning.

Before we move to our second model of instruction, let's address some challenges with direct instruction.

Direct instruction is misunderstood. In many conversations, direct instruction is used synonymously with lecture, teacher-talk, sit-and-get, or passive learning. This is unfortunate given that the benefits of this model of instruction, when done correctly, speak more to the balance of control between the teacher and his or her students. Direct instruction is teacher driven and highly effective in the acquisition and consolidation of specific knowledge and skills (Almarode et al., 2018). However, this approach should require learners to actively engage with that content and those skills through questioning, academic discourse, and practice.

Opportunities for Reflective Practices

Compare and contrast your beliefs about direct instruction with what you now know about direct instruction.

To plan for direct instruction, we would devote considerable time to thinking about how we would hook our learners, activate prior experiences and background knowledge, present the

Activity Element & Time (in minutes)	**Procedures and management** *Step-by step procedures including questions and main points – visualize what you are going to say to the students.)*	**Students** *(Describe what the students will be doing as a result of your instructions.)*
Introduction		
Event 1		
Transition		
Event 2		
Transition		
Event 3		
Transition		
Conclusion:		

Figure 5.2 Planning Template.

content and skills; what type of guided practice is necessary; how to provide feedback, and how to structure opportunities for independent practice. Guided practice and independent practice opportunities should be very focused on supporting learners' acquisition and consolidation of the content and skills. A template for doing so is found in Figure 5.2 and Appendix B.

Notice the emphasis in the third column on what students will be doing as a result of our actions or instructions. This is vital if we are to monitor how we structure the thinking and doing of our learners as they engage in the learning experiences. As we will see shortly, there are other models that place the control of learning into the hands of the learner. Now that we have introduced one of the models of instruction, it may be helpful to plot this along a continuum of control. As we discuss each additional model (Figures 5.3–5.10), we will add that model to Figure 5.2.

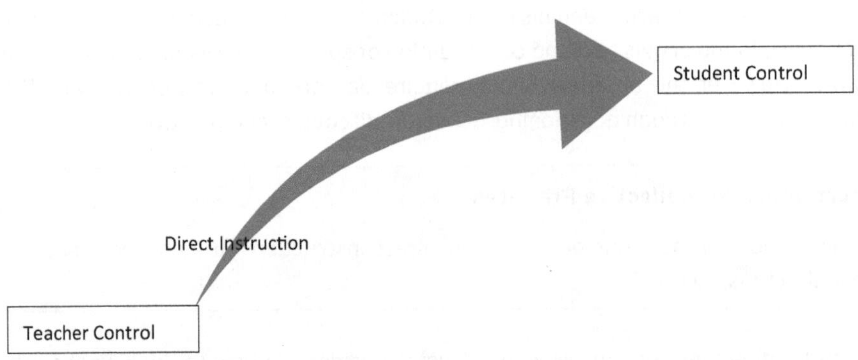

Figure 5.3 Models of Instruction and the Continuum of Control.

But remember, what makes a particular model of instruction effective in moving student learning forward is not the model itself but the alignment between the specific model and what we want our students to learn, why they are learning, what they can do with that learning, and how they know they will be successful. There is an exception. Scripted curricula would fall even farther to the left than direct instruction, but we are not including that approach in our discussion, as research indicates this is not an effective model, having very little influence on student learning (Loughran, 2013; Milner, 2013).

Now let's look at the concept-attainment model.

Concept-Attainment Model

We want to see how different models of instruction can be used within the same standard or unit and at the same time understand how we align student learning expectations with a particular model. So, we will look in on Ms. Lamb as her learners move through their learning progression and are ready to understand what makes an insect an insect and not a spider. "For this part of their learning, I want them to understand what makes an insect different from other living things. Really, they are engaging in developing the concept of an insect. So, for this, we have a completely different approach from when we are learning about the parts of an insect or how they impact our world."

Concept attainment is just that, a model for scaffolding and supporting learners' development of a particular concept. For example, matter, cycles, climate, change, part-whole relationships, and energy are examples of concepts that leaners must understand and be able to generalize in science learning. Thus learners must begin to cognitively define the boundaries of what the concept entails, as well as what that concept does not entail. This is done through structured inquiry (Joyce, Weil, & Calhoun, 2003). The goal of this structured inquiry is to support learners as they identify key characteristics of the concept. In early childhood science, this weaves academic vocabulary and academic discourse with observing, analyzing, comparing and contrasting, and drawing conclusions. This model of instruction relies on the construction of two sets of examples: those that possess the essential characteristics of the concept and those that do not.

"This is one of my favorite models of instruction because the thinking really falls on my learners. Once I have my concept, in this case insects, I carefully prepare my two sets of examples. But hear me when I say this, my yes examples cannot be ambiguous. For this to work with my learners, the yes examples have to allow them to clearly identify characteristics of insects." What Ms. Lamb is referring to is the importance of being intentional about the examples we select in this model of instruction. If we do not devote planning time to develop these two categories, there is a high likelihood that learners will not develop a clear understanding and might even form misconceptions.

Concept Attainment in Ms. Lamb's Classroom

- Ms. Lamb introduces the day's learning intention and success criteria. In most instances of concept attainment, she uses the driving question to frame the learning. In this case, the question is, What can I do, as an artist, to help citizens understand the difference between insects and spiders?

- She then presents the concept-attainment sheet on flipchart paper (see Figure 5.4).
- Ms. Lamb then presents "yes" and "no" examples and tapes them to the flipchart. Three examples in each column is a good place to start, but this can vary depending on the learners.
- She then asks her learners to observe, analyze, and compare and contrast. She uses intentional questioning to scaffold these processes and in some cases models them for her young learners. At this point in the model, the focus is on finding similar characteristics in the "yes" examples and how the "no" examples differ from each other.
- Ms. Lamb records their thinking and what they identify as characteristics on the flipchart paper.
- She continues by adding more examples in each column and repeating the processes of observing, analyzing, and comparing and contrasting.
- Ms. Lamb begins to bring this to a close when she observes that her learners are beginning to narrow in on the essential characteristics of the concept. In this case, it is an insect. She encourages them to come up with examples of their own to analyze with the group.
- She then uses the list of student-generated attributes to ensure that her learners come to a consensus about the essential characteristics. Her line of questioning and feedback helps to keep students headed in the correct direction and away from misconceptions. Once identified, she helps students define an insect using the list of identified attributes.
- To ensure that her learners have developed an understanding of what makes an insect an insect, she can verify this by using additional examples and have learners place the examples in the "yes" or "no" category.

One feature of this example worth noting is that the learners in Ms. Lamb's classroom knew the concept as insect. Another approach with this model is to not let learners know the concept and have them both identify and define the concepts. This may or may not be appropriate for your learners and is part of our professional decision making. Either way, we map this out and carefully plan for concept attainment using Appendix B, as shown in Figure 5.2.

One of the many benefits to concept attainment is that this can be done as a whole-group activity or implemented in a small-group setting. Ms. Lamb points out that "when working in small groups, learners now are engaged in concept-attainment and cooperative learning at the same time. However, I have to make sure they have the necessary social-emotional, behavioral, and language skills to successfully engage in this in a small-group setting. So, I usually start with and model this with the whole-group early in the year and then turn it over to them later in the year."

Research to Classroom Practice Tasks

Concept development is a model of instruction that has many similarities to concept attainment. Gather information about concept development and compare and contrast these two models. When might you use one over the other? What would concept development look like in your future or current classroom?

Ms. Lamb's Flipchart Concept Attainment Sheet.	
Yes, that's an INSECT	**No, that's not an INSECT**
•	•
•	•
•	•
•	•
ATTRIBUTES of INSECTS	
1.	
2.	
3.	
4.	
5.	
So, what is an insect?	

Figure 5.4 Ms. Lamb's Flipchart Concept-Attainment Sheet.
Source: Author created.

Cooperative Learning

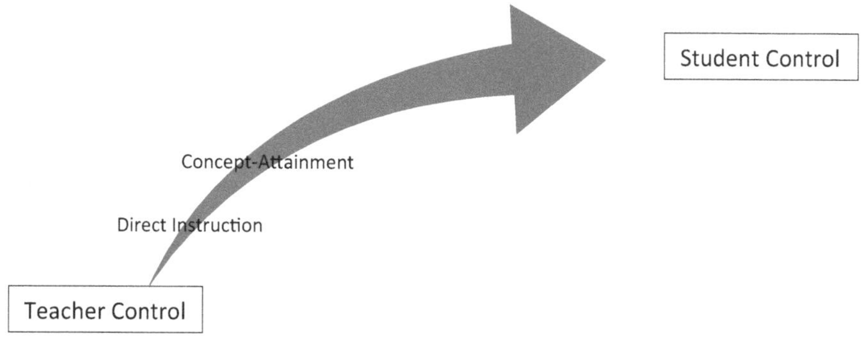

Figure 5.5 Models of Instruction and the Continuum of Control.

Ms. Campbell used cooperative learning in an inquiry-based instructional model. As you may recall, she wanted to support her learners in collaboratively producing evidence to answer a question about vibrations and sound. Cooperative learning is often treated as an independent model of instruction. However, recent work has suggested that collective learning is a valuable aspect of many other approaches to teaching and learning (see Fisher, Frey, & Almarode, 2020). Learning is a social activity. Opportunities to discuss learning, exchange ideas, challenge or question ideas, and reason through science concepts are essential to learning (Zembal-Saul, McNeill, & Hershberger, 2012). How Ms. Campbell structures the interaction between herself and her students, student to student, or even student to material is an essential component within the planning and implementation of daily learning experiences. Specifically, Ms. Campbell has structured these interactions around a question that requires them to generate evidence to answer.

Our point here is this: The models of instruction are not often distinguishable in planning, designing, and implementing high-quality, high-impact teaching and learning in the inclusive early childhood science classroom. Again, it matters more that the approach aligns with the learning expectations. However, we do want to look at what the research says about cooperative learning. For this, we turn to the seminal work in the field.

David Johnson and Roger Johnson (1999) identified five basic elements that allow successful small-group learning: positive interdependence, face-to-face interaction, individual and group accountability, group behaviors, and group processing. For the benefit of our young learners, this triggers a shift in the roles of teachers and students. There had long been evidence that cooperative learning can lead to significant gains in student learning (Hattie, 2012). However, when we look closer at the decisions Ms. Campbell made prior to implementing centers, she did not just throw learners into stations and tell them to work together on a task. This requires, at times, the direct instruction of social-emotional, behavioral, and language skills. She points out that "my learners need support and scaffolding in what it means to work together in a group. To do this, I begin with a very structured approach. I provide clear directions, provide fill-in notes at each center that help keep them focused on the learning within the center, and I even assign roles to each member of the group. Over time, I do not necessarily have to provide this level of support."

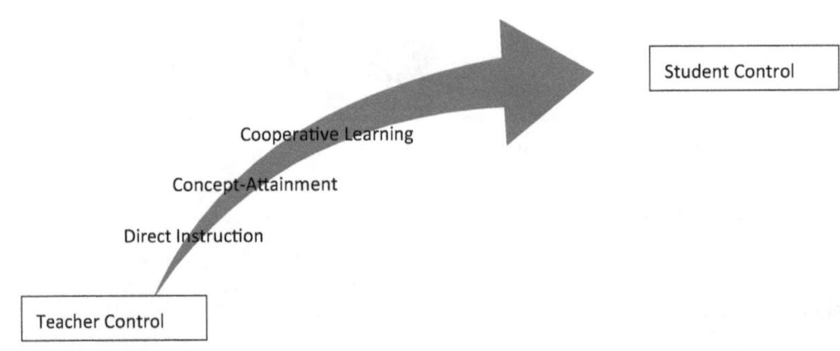

Figure 5.6 Models of Instruction and the Continuum of Control.

Cooperative Learning in Ms. Campbell's Classroom

- Ms. Campbell first decides what social-emotional and behavioral outcomes will benefit from learners engaging in cooperative learning. She also looks at the nature of the content, skills, and understandings to decide if these are best approached through collective effort or individual experiences.
- She then develops a plan for how to hold each learner individually accountable. This might include fill-in notes or some individual record keeping that each learner is responsible for during the work.
- Based on where her learners are in self-regulating their engagement, she may or may not assign roles to support equal participation. Either way, learners are given the expectation that they will leverage their strengths for the benefit of the group.
- Finally, Ms. Campbell ensures that the classroom climate is set up for positive team interaction.

As we think about cooperative learning, both as a model of instruction and as an approach that we can embed within other models, we must really focus on the other learning outcomes for our students. Cooperative learning requires a higher level of social-emotional and behavioral skills. At the same time, we want our learners to leverage their own strengths for the benefit of the group.

Research to Classroom Practice Tasks

Within cooperative learning, what are different strategies for ensuring

- individual accountability,
- equal participation,
- simultaneous interaction, and
- positive team interaction?

How might this be reflected in our learning intentions and success criteria?

The 5E Instructional Model

The 5E instructional model (Bybee, 1997, 2015; Bybee & Landes, 1990) is also a blended model of instruction that is structured into five learning stages: (1) engagement, (2) exploration, (3) explanation, (4) elaboration, and (5) evaluation. Learners move through problem solving that encourages them to approach science concepts in a way that challenges their beliefs and promotes self-reflection and elaboration of those concepts (Bybee & Landes, 1990). Let's look at each aspect of the 5E model and then apply this approach to the early childhood classroom.

Engagement. This is the initial step that encourages learners to activate background knowledge and prior experiences. This activation helps to focus learners on the specific learning intentions and success criteria for the day's learning. As with other approaches, this can take the form of an individual or group task or discussion. The main idea is to get learners thinking about the new learning but also placing the new learning within the context of background knowledge and prior experiences, even if they are misconceptions.

Explore. At this step in the model, learners incorporate the science and engineering practices into a hands-on, minds-on task. This task is purely for exploration, and, therefore, not linked to formal instruction about the concepts, skills, and understandings associated with the task. Unlike engagement, where learners can work together with their peers, explore comes with the expectation that learners will work in cooperative learning groups. This is one of the reasons we label this as a blended model.

Explain. In this step, the verb "explain" applies to both the teacher and the learners. Learners have the opportunity to explain their understanding from the exploration. This requires us to ask clarifying and probing questions before we then initiate direct instruction and introduce the content and skills that support the expected understanding. One area that should receive special attention is the development of misconceptions. In the end, this step in the process closes with learners being able to explain their thinking about the concepts, skills, and understandings.

Elaborate. Following explain, learners are encouraged to elaborate on their new learning through collaborative interactions with their peers. For example, learners might engage in academic discourse with their peers to better understand a particular concept. Learners may ask additional questions that allow them to engage in further inquiry and develop some type of presentation or model. Elaboration may also include the application of concepts, skills, and understandings to other disciplines.

Evaluate. Although we will turn our attention to this particular aspect of inclusive early childhood science, within the 5E model, this is where learners are evaluated on both their thinking and doing. Given that the 5E model values more than just facts (i.e., science as a body of knowledge), evaluation in the 5E model must include performance assessments in addition to traditional assessments (adapted from Duran & Duran, 2004).

Opportunities for Reflective Practices

We have referred to the 5E model as a blended model. What other models of instruction do you see embedded in the 5E model?

In the introduction of this book, we had the opportunity to observe Ms. Rogers introduce or, as we know now, engage her learners in sinking and floating. Her use of the S-T-W engaged learners by activating background knowledge and prior experiences. Then as you might recall, they were asked to experiment with a variety of objects to identify characteristics of objects that float and objects that sink. This is how Ms. Rogers brought the explore step to life. Then as she worked with her learners during circle time and morning meeting, she gave them many opportunities to explain their thinking, as well as receive direct instruction about sinking and floating. In the end, the elaboration and evaluation were embedded in other stations or around the room. A literacy-rich station offers learners the opportunity to read and write about sinking and floating. With a variety of picture books and print books, Ms. Rogers's young learners interact with a variety of images and words as they work on emergent literacy skills (i.e., letter recognition, phonological awareness, word recognition). There is a station that links mathematics

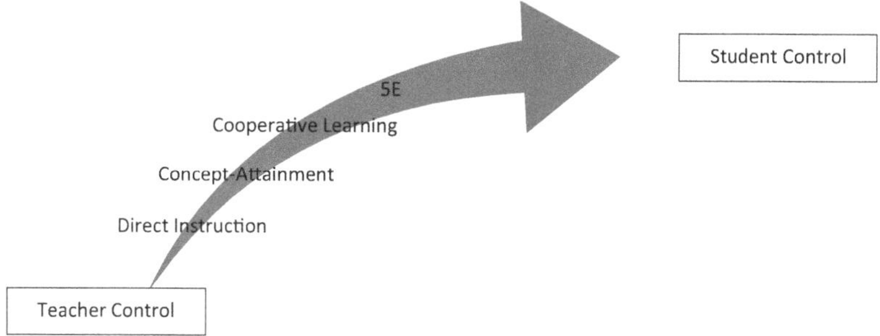

Figure 5.7 Models of Instruction and the Continuum of Control.

to sinking and floating that has learners graph data related to how many pennies a container can hold before it sinks - not to mention an art station as well. The final culminating task requires that learners design and construct their own object and test to see if the object sinks or floats. As you might suspect, learners will get to make revisions and adjustments to their design (e.g., repeated trials). Figure 5.7 shows the 5E model relative to the other models and where they fall on the continuum of control.

As we have mentioned with previous models, this can be planned out using the template in Appendix B and shown in Figure 5.2.

The last three models of instruction that we will look at in this chapter are two models that are frequently embedded in the previous models. For example, the exploration step of the 5E model often results in inquiry-based learning. Similarly, cooperative learning is implemented to solve an authentic problem in science. And, finally, early childhood science is often integrated across multiple disciplines and involves a project that ties it all together.

Inquiry-Based Learning

Ms. Cornish decided to engage her learners in an inquiry-based task around the big idea that living things have needs that are required for them to survive. In Chapter 3, we learned that her driving question for this big idea was how can I, as a scientist, discover what plants need to survive? "When we began this unit, I wanted them to immediately engage in inquiry because this was a topic that lends itself to concrete experiences we could produce in the classroom. This is different from learning about the planets. We can actually grow plants in our classroom or outside in a class garden." For this particular big idea and driving question, Ms. Cornish wanted to

1. develop the questioning skills of her kindergarteners;
2. enhance their communication about science content, skill, and understandings;
3. promote cooperative learning;
4. tackle an authentic question; and
5. introduce them to the analysis of data and drawing of conclusions.

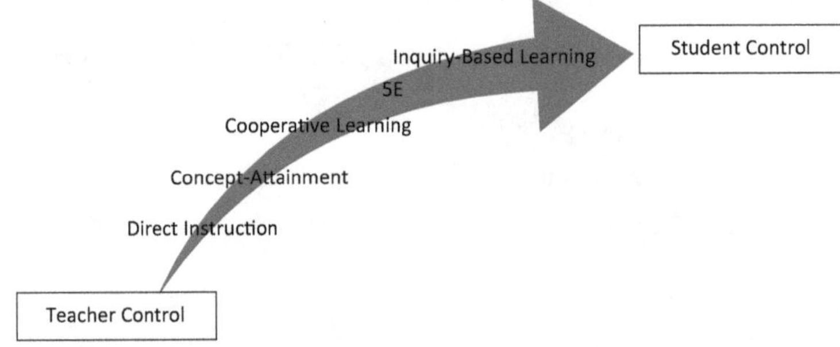

Figure 5.8 Models of Instruction and the Continuum of Control.

Inquiry-based learning provides learning experiences that yield each of these learning outcomes. However, there is one word of caution when using inquiry-based models. "I know that I have to monitor their thinking very closely during this experience. If I notice that a learner or group of learners is missing essential background knowledge or prior experiences that will hinder their ability to successfully navigate a line of inquiry, I have to provide that support." Ms. Cornish brings up a very important point. Without the necessary background knowledge and prior experiences, inquiry-based models can lead to misconceptions or down the path of imaginary solutions. The approach we want to take is to carefully monitor student progress and provide that foundational learning when needed. This can be done through one-on-one instruction, small-group, or whole-group direct instruction. Then learners can go right back into the inquiry task.

Inquiry-Based Learning in Ms. Cornish's Classroom

- After introducing the driving question for the day's learning experience, Ms. Cornish uses a brainstorming strategy to get her kindergartens to ask questions about the needs of plants.
- Most of the responses to this brainstorm are learners' answers to the driving question, which requires Ms. Cornish to model and coach them into turning their answers into a question that they will explore.
- She then scaffolds and supports her learners as they set up their inquiry task. Some place potted plants in the closet and near the window. Others put their plants in soil, while others use gravel.
- Over a period of two weeks, learners make observations, begin to analyze their data, and draw conclusions.
- Ms. Cornish supports her learners in communicating their findings and sharing them with the school community.
- As part of closure to this learning experience, Ms. Cornish devotes time at the end of this process to consolidate what her students learned from their inquiry task.

As we quickly notice, this went beyond a single day and required careful coordination within the classroom. Ms. Cornish makes sure that this approach incorporates characteristics common in all inquiry-based learning experiences. First, learners have significant control over the learning process but require very close monitoring by us to ensure they have the background knowledge, prior knowledge, and supplies to move forward in their learning. And, second, we continuously model and engage learners in questioning that guides their processing of what they observe in the inquiry experience.

Opportunities for Reflective Practices

Where might inquiry-based learning be an ideal approach for teaching and learning in the inclusive early childhood science classroom?

There is no magic time frame for an inquiry experience. When using the 5E model, the inquiry task may begin and end in one block of time. This particular experience took time for the plants to grow. What did Ms. Cornish and her learners do while they were also monitoring their plants? Continue to move through the learning progression. In fact, the inquiry task continued to serve as an anchor task when they needed examples of how plants change their environments (e.g., pushing through the soil, growing toward the sunlight) and the effect of humans (e.g., plants that were watered with unclear water). "In fact, my learners were so excited about this inquiry experience, they asked to build our own garden." Which, by the way, leads to project-based learning.

Project-Based Learning

Over the past several years, project-based learning has garnered significant support as a means for enhancing student learning through authentic learning experiences (see Buck Institute for Education, 2020). Just as Ms. Cornish's learners recognized the relevancy of what plants need to survive, project-based learning models seek to create that level of authenticity right from the start. For Ms. Cornish, the nature of the inquiry experience, along with the driving question, her learners found themselves engaged in a project-based learning experience as they applied the concepts and thinking from the needs of plants to a community garden. This is an important point we cannot overlook. When we use driving questions to engage our learners in the big ideas for a unit or standard, we also set the stage for project-based learning. Let's return to the examples of driving questions from Chapter 3.

The phrasing of each driving question in the last column follows the pattern of "how can I, as..." After the "as" is a role that the learners are to assume in responding to the question. This response is a project. For example, with the question, "What can I do as an artist to help citizens understand the difference between insects and spiders?" learners can develop a brochure, poster/pamphlet, or an infomercial that addresses the question. We certainly don't want to be redundant, but we hope by now that the connections across each of these chapters are obvious and clear. For both Ms. Lamb and Ms. Cornish, the development of project-based learning requires as much planning and preparation as any of the other models. This can be mapped out in the template in Appendix B, and it is shown in Figure 5.2. We have to consider the following elements of project-based learning.

LEARNING PROGRESSION FOR MS. LAMB'S LEARNERS	BIG IDEA	DRIVING QUESTION
IMPORTANCE AND IMPACT OF INSECTS	Everything in our environment has an important role.	How can I, as a scientist, inform my community about the importance of insects?
PHYSICAL CHARACTERISTICS AND ANATOMY	The parts of an organism work together to help it to survive.	How could I, as a teacher, create a model of an insect that helps others understand the parts of an insect?
HOUSEHOLD AND GARDEN INSECTS	Organisms thrive in an environment that meets their needs.	Could I, as a horticulturalist, create a guide to help citizens identify insects that might be in their home or garden?
COMPARING AND CONTRASTING INSECTS WITH OTHER INSECTS AND SPIDERS	Organisms are classified based on their characteristics.	What can I do, as an artist, to help citizens understand the difference between insects and spiders?
LEARNING PROGRESSION FOR MS. CORNISH'S LEARNERS	**BIG IDEA**	**DRIVING QUESTION**
NEEDS OF PLANTS AND ANIMALS	Living things have needs that are required for them to survive.	How can I, as a scientist, discover what plants need to survive?
IMPACT OF HUMANS ON THE ENVIRONMENT	The decisions we make have an impact on the world around us.	What can I, as an environmental advocate, create to show my community how they impact the environment?
PLANTS AND ANIMALS CHANGE THEIR ENVIRONMENT	Living things adjust their environments to meet their needs for survival.	How can I, as a student, document the different ways plants and animals change their environment?

Figure 5.9 Big Ideas and Driving Questions.

Content. Before we allow our learners to begin work on their projects, we have to work collaboratively with our learners to articulate the mission of the project. Again, our driving question does this, but we want to make sure everyone in our classroom is focused on that mission.

Project Goals. This element of the approach allows us to co-construct goals with our learners. What do we want to get out of this project? With regard to the school garden, Ms. Cornish and her learners decided that they wanted to produce healthy vegetables for lunch in the cafeteria.

Background Knowledge and Prior Experiences. As the teacher, we have to make sure we are aware of what learners must already know, understand, and be able to do if they are going to successfully navigate the project. When background knowledge and prior experiences are missing, we have to have a plan in place to ensure that we address this need and, as soon as possible, get the learners back into the project.

Cooperative Learning Groups. How will we group learners? As we have pointed out in our discussion of cooperative learning, how will we promote individual accountability, equal participation, simultaneous interaction, and positive team interaction?

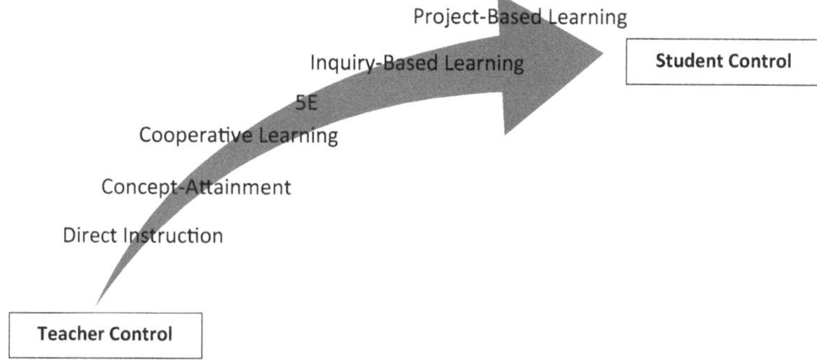

Figure 5.10 Models of Instruction and the Continuum of Control.

Agendas, Schedules, and Check-Ins. To promote self-monitoring and self-regulation, we must provide a time line with benchmark points for checking learners' progress. Plus, learners need to be aware of how much time they have available at certain points in the project.

Resources and Materials. We have to provide the necessary resources and materials that learners may need to work on the project. This may change as cooperative learning groups will think of something we did not think to provide.

Assessment. Finally, we have to develop our tools for assessing students' knowledge, skills, and understanding during and after the project. This can include both traditional and performance-based assessments. But keep in mind that we will need to have both individual assessments and group assessments.

Figure 5.10 shows all of the models we have discussed and where they fall on the continuum of control.

Opportunities for Reflective Practices

Looking at your driving questions, what do you need to think about in transforming those driving questions into project-based learning experiences?

Inclusion through Models of Instruction

We devoted a significant amount of time overviewing models of instruction that provide structure to our learning experiences and give careful consideration to what we want our students to learn, why they are learning, what they can do with that learning, and how they know they will be successful. Although we have not mentioned the word *inclusion*, the reason for selecting the models that we did revolves around their capacity to accomplish the following:

1. Ensure each member of our classroom community is an active participant in the learning.
2. Each member of the community is valued, and his or her contributions are recognized as vital for the success of the entire community.
3. Provide support and scaffolds so that each individual has the access and opportunity for successful learning.

We want to close this chapter by explicitly talking about the role of inclusion in each of these models. For each model, we must adjust the input, processing, and output expected by our learners to reflect the strengths of each learner. We can provide support to learners through translating materials into their primary languages, using pictures and images, tiering the guided and independent practice opportunities, using heterogeneous groups, offering different types of media (e.g., leveled readers, digital recordings, access to computers and the Internet), providing different manipulatives at different stations or centers, providing graphic organizers or thinking papers, and the list goes on. The models of instruction provide the structure, we have to adapt the content, processes, and products so that everyone, and we mean everyone, has equity in access and opportunity to learning and success.

Opportunities for Reflective Practices

Look back over each of the models discussed in this chapter. How do they not only provide a structure for learning experiences but also provide opportunities for inclusion?

Professional Learning Tasks

1. Returning to the science standard of learning that you are unpacking, based on your learning progression, learning intentions, and success criteria, what models of instruction might scaffold and support your students' learning? Using Appendix B, map out a learning experience using one of the models.
2. There are other models of instruction besides the ones we explored in this chapter. What are those models? Plot them on the teacher-student control continuum. Then develop resources that will help you decide when to use these other approaches.
3. As we mentioned in this chapter, there is no one right approach for teaching and learning science in the inclusive early childhood classroom. This opinion is not shared by everyone in our field. Take time and read up on the varying perspectives about the teaching and learning of science in the inclusive early childhood classroom. However, focus your search on the research. Rather than opinions, what does the research say?
4. You have seen examples of stations throughout each of the chapters in this book. Stations can be used with multiple models of instruction. From cooperative learning to project-based learning, stations or centers are simply a way to use small-group instruction. Let's walk through a process for developing stations around science content, practices, and understandings. For this particular task, we will focus on cooperative, collaborative learning infused with concept attainment, inquiry, and project-based learning. Using the "Science Express Task" in Appendix F, develop a series of cooperative, collaborative learning stations.

Family and Community Engagement

1. **Be present at drop-off and pickup.** Greeting learners at the door is an important strategy for supporting classroom cohesion and a positive classroom climate. When our students arrive at our classroom doors with their families, greeting them is key to engagement as well. For example, welcome both the student and their family to the classroom and share a detail or two about their child, comment on the child's

progress in a particular area of science, and point out an accomplishment related to their science learning. We all know that the morning can be busy with so many tasks (e.g., setting up the room, announcements, a possible faculty meeting). However, ensuring that we are at the door to greet our learners is paramount. We should plan for it. Greet them with enthusiasm and, when possible, acknowledge the student and their family's arrival in some special way. For example, introduce the other students by saying, "Xavier and his uncle have arrived at our classroom this morning. Someone come and say hello." This serves several purposes: it makes Xavier feel welcomed, makes his uncle feel more at ease about Xavier being there, and teaches (and models) the importance of greeting and acknowledging others.

2. **Vary the activities and ways to engage**. Again, let's refer back to the family questionnaire. An inclusive early childhood science classroom means that we are inclusive of families as well. How do we make every family active participants in their children's learning, ensure that every family member is valued and his or her contributions recognized as vital for the success of the entire community, and create ways for every family member to have the opportunity to engage? The answer is to vary the activities based on the strengths of our learners' moms, dads, uncles, aunts, cousins, etc. Try to plan activities such as informal breakfasts, picnics, class trips, and fairs featuring educational books and toys throughout the school year. Eliciting ideas for these events from families may encourage them to be more involved in developing and planning. Be sure to consider the schedules of family members to ensure that they all have opportunities to participate.
3. **You can never communicate too much.** Whether in person (parent-teacher conferences, calls home, or home visits), through printed materials (newsletters, portfolios or work samples, school bulletin boards) or digital (website/blog, Seesaw, Dojo), try to make frequent contact with families. Return to the daily communication with folders shared in the previous chapter. This is just one way to ensure that the lines of communication are open! To further engage families and the community, be sure to ask whether the information being shared is useful and how it can be improved, both in terms of content (e.g., what we are learning in class, why we are learning it, what success looks like, and ways to engage with their children in regard to the learning) and accessibility (e.g., timing, format, and clarity). This is an excellent opportunity to engage families in the decision making and planning for learning experiences and opportunities in the community to further support the learning experiences in the classroom.
4. **Develop a sense of community among families.** A good way to start building a sense of community inside and outside of the classroom is to create a family contact list. Along with that contact list, offer families a chance to share "what they do." For example, if one of your students' uncles is a carpenter, take the opportunity to share that with other families. You never know when other families in your classroom may need a carpenter. Maybe another family has a locally owned business. Again, this promotes both family and community engagement. Be sure to include teachers, aides, and other relevant school personnel. Highlighting the strengths of all members of the classroom community – students, families, and other community members – makes teaching and learning science a collaborative endeavor. They are *our* students.

6 Implementing Daily Learning Experiences

Developing Assessments

When we plan, design, and implement high-quality, high-impact teaching and learning, we must also think through how we will know if learners are progressing toward the learning intentions and success criteria and when they have met the learning expectations. We cannot simply start a direct instruction, concept-attainment, or project-based learning experience and see it through to the end without monitoring or gathering and collecting evidence of that learning. What we are talking about here is assessing student learning. Assessments allow us to check for understanding, monitor learners' progress, and, in the end, provide evidence that they have arrived at the learning outcomes. Through checks for understanding and progress monitoring, we keep a close eye on the learning progress of our learners during the learning experience so that we can make immediate and necessary adjustments to the daily learning experiences should they not make progress toward the day's learning outcomes. Through artifacts gathered and collected during the learning experience, we can identify when learners have demonstrated that they met the learning intentions and success criteria. Assessments not only provide valuable evidence and information but also contribute to the building of assessment-capable visible science learners. If we are to ensure that our learners develop into assessment-capable visible science learners, we must also ensure that they know how they are progressing toward the learning intentions and success criteria. Learners, as they develop into assessment-capable visible science learners, use the checks for understanding to seek and receive feedback, monitor their own learning, and make adjustments to their learning progression when needed to continue moving forward in that learning. In the end, they use assessments to recognize when they have met expectations and are ready to move on in their learning journey.

Formative versus Summative Assessment

The most commonly used terms related to assessment are "formative" and "summative," and they were first discussed at length in the late 1960s (Scriven, 1967).

> **Opportunities for Reflective Practices**
>
> We have all likely heard of formative and summative assessment. What do you understand these terms to be, and what role do they play in teaching and learning in the inclusive early childhood science classroom?

Formative assessment is typically defined as an assessment that is done during instruction and for purposes of making informed decisions about where to go next. On the other hand, summative assessment is defined as an assessment after instruction that captures the amount of learning. From the perspective of the inclusive early childhood science classroom, Ms. Campbell's fill-in notes for her learners to glue into their interactive science notebooks are formative assessments. For a summative assessment, Ms. Campbell might ask her learners to complete a "test" on what causes sound and/or the planning of investigations at the end of the week. We often recoil at the term "test" in early childhood, but that is not a necessary reaction. Both formative and summative assessments have their place in teaching and learning. For example, Ms. Campbell not only needs to monitor her learners' progress within the learning experience but also, at some point, she needs to assess whether her learners have met the expectations across the learning outcomes. Plus, her learners need to be able to monitor their own learning and recognize when they've "got it."

Yet this way of thinking about assessment might be contributing to the visceral response of testing, which is often associated with high-stakes testing and grades. What if we looked at assessment through the lens of (Earl, 2003) the following?

- Assessment of learning
- Assessment for learning
- Assessment as learning

These three perspectives focus less on the assessment and more on the purpose of the assessment. If we focus on the purpose of the assessment and make that purpose clear to our learners, we stand a better chance of avoiding the negative connotations associated with assessing (i.e., testing, grades, high stakes, developmental appropriateness) and redirect our attention back to learning.

Assessment of Learning. The purpose of this type of assessment is to truly determine if learners can demonstrate that they have arrived at the cognitive, social-emotional, behavioral, and psychomotor outcomes. Put differently, assessment of learning encourages both us and our learners to look at artifacts or products of a learning experience and, using the learning intentions and success criteria as the measuring stick, see if we have met expectations. An example of this in Ms. Lamb's classroom would be her formal assessment of learners identifying the parts of an insect or sequencing the life cycle of an insect. Although learners may practice this throughout daily learning experiences (assessments for and as learning), she uses this assessment to see if they have "got it."

Assessment for Learning. The purpose of this type of assessment is to use artifacts or products as evidence to inform where we are headed next in the learning progression. Together with our learners, we are using assessments for learning to make just-in-time decisions about the next learning experience (Novak et al., 1999). We will refer to these as checks for understanding in that they happen multiple times throughout the learning experience as we regularly "check" to see our learners' level of understanding or ascertain where they are in their progress toward understanding science content and skills at various points in the learning experience. An example of this is would be the "science discovery" center in Ms.

Lamb's classroom. As learners used the bug lab lightbox, she would check their understanding of the parts of an insect or the sequencing of the life cycle through observation and asking clarifying or probing questions.

Assessment as Learning. This final purpose for assessment is to allow learners to check and monitor their own learning. These are moments during the learning experience that offer opportunities for learners to see their own thinking and learning and then make their own decisions about their learning progression. Assessments as learning include a self-reflection, self-monitoring component that truly supports learners in their journeys toward assessment capability. For example, Ms. Lamb provides multiple anchor charts and supporting materials that allow learners to not only engage in a rigorous learning task but also collaborate with peers and other resources to see how well they are learning the content, skills, and understanding.

Opportunities for Reflective Practices

It is not about formative versus summative but the purpose for assessing. Take a moment to compare and contrast the three purposes for assessing. What are some examples from your own classroom or that you have observed in classrooms?

The key idea in this chapter is not the development of high-stakes assessments for young children so that we can assign them a grade. Instead, the point of developing assessments is to check for understanding, monitor progress, and collect and gather evidence that our learners are making progress toward the learning intentions and success criteria. If they are making progress or demonstrate that they have met expectations, keep going. If not, change something in the learning experience to enhance progress. What matters most is not that we assess but that we assess with a purpose (Table 6.1).

Specifically, in this chapter, we will look at the development of assessments of, for, and as learning. We will return to a more detailed look at the assessment of learning in Chapter 8 when we self-reflect and self-evaluate our teaching by evaluating our students' learning.

Table 6.1 Developing Assessments with a Purpose

	Purpose	*Examples*
Assessment of Learning	What have students learned, and how much have they learned?	Tests, performance-based assessments, standardized tests, or protocols
Assessment for Learning	How are my learners progressing toward the learning intentions and success criteria?	Checks for understanding and progress monitoring techniques (e.g., observations, interactive notebook entries, student conversations)
Assessments as Learning	How am I (the student) making progress in my (the student's) learning?	Anchor charts, collaborative learning, reflective questioning

Source: Author created.

Developing Assessments of, for, and as Learning

Developing assessments requires us to return to our learning intentions and success criteria yet again. We see a pattern emerging here in the value of having strong learning intentions and success criteria for identifying a model of instruction and, now, developing assessments. Looking back at Chapter 4, we recall that success criteria articulate what evidence learners must produce to demonstrate their progress toward learning intentions (Ainsworth & Donovan, 2019). Therefore, and this is very important, our assessments of, for, and as learning should generate that evidence, making the evidence visible both to us and our learners. Consider the following learning intentions and success criteria in Figure 6.1 from Ms. Campbell's classroom.

The verb in each of these statements makes it clear how Ms. Campbell's learners can show what they know. They also guide the evidence we should aim to gather and collect to check for understanding, monitor progress, and determine what and how much students have learned. Ms. Campbell's assessments need to provide students' opportunities to describe, record, explain, and use.

Opportunities for Reflective Practices

Brainstorm how many different ways a learner can describe, record, explain, and use.

When developing our assessments, the first place we look is the criteria for success that have been explicitly shared with our learners. When Ms. Campbell analyzed the standard and

Learning Intentions and Success Criteria for Ms. Campbell's Learners.

<u>Learning Intentions:</u> What are we learning today? Why are we learning it? What will this help me to do?	<u>Success Criteria:</u> How will we know we are successful?
<u>Content Learning Intention:</u> I am learning about the causes of sound (Disciplinary Core Ideas). <u>Social-Emotional Learning Intention:</u> I am learning how scientists work together to plan and conduct investigations(Science and Engineering Practices). <u>Psychomotor Learning Intention:</u> I am learning that scientist record observations as evidence so they can go back and find patterns (writing or illustrating). <u>Behavioral Learning Intention:</u> I am learning about collaborating in answering scientific questions (Character Education).	1. I can describe how objects produce sound (Content). 2. I can record my thinking (Psychomotor). 3. I can explain my thinking using evidence from my experiments(Behavioral). 4. I can use my peers ideas to better explain my thinking (Social-Emotional).

Figure 6.1 The Day's Learning Intentions and Success Criteria for Ms. Campbell's Class.

mapped out her students' learning progressions, she built her learning intentions and success criteria so that she could easily identify ways to gather and collect the evidence of, for, and as learning. This is why we emphasize the measurability of these success criteria.

Assessments of, for, and as Learning Should Be Opportunities to Respond

If recognizing that the verb is key in developing our assessments, are there characteristics that these assessments should have to ensure that we generate that evidence, making the evidence visible both to us and our learners? The answer is yes. In other words, how did Ms. Campbell arrive at her assessments? She took two ideas into consideration:

1. Assessments of, for, and as learning should come from multiple contexts (e.g., individual, small group, written, out loud, informal).
2. These assessments should make student thinking visible.

Each of these characteristics is possible if we offer our learners multiple opportunities to respond. These opportunities to respond offer learners' multiple pathways for actively progressing toward that destination. Only when learners are actively progressing toward the destination do we, as teachers, have the necessary information about their progress to make decisions about where to go next.

Opportunities to respond include any strategies, activities, or tasks within the learning experience that make student thinking visible and allow both us and our learners to see where they are in the learning progression. If you recall from our previous discussion on the SOLO Taxonomy, the only way to know if learners are at the prestructural, unistructural, multistructural, relational, or extend abstract level is to observe learning and thinking, as shown in Figure 6.2.

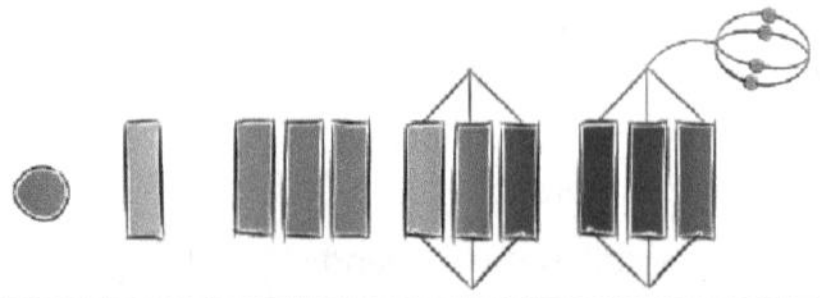	General Characteristics
Prestructural Thinking	learners focus on irrelevant ideas or avoid engaging in the content,requiresusto support the learner in acquiring and building background knowledge
Unistructural Thinking	learners have a single idea or component related to the concept; learners at this level identify, name, and follow simple procedures
Multistructural Thinking	learners then begin to acquire multiple ideas that are combined into a coherent description
Relational Thinking	learners are identifying relationships between concepts or ideas
Extended Abstract Thinking	learners formulate big ideas and generalize their learning to a new domain

Figure 6.2 The SOLO Taxonomy and Characteristics of the Thinking.

Opportunities for Reflective Practices

How does making our learners' thinking visible relate to the SOLO Taxonomy? What is the benefit of creating opportunities to respond that incorporate multiple contexts?

When Ms. Campbell plans her assessments, she shares, "I think about all of the different ways I can give my learners opportunities to describe, record, explain, and use. But the opportunity to respond has to show me their thinking. It has to take what they are thinking and bring it out into the classroom. Only then can I make decisions from those assessments." What Ms. Campbell is talking about is the difference between opportunities to respond that make thinking visible versus those that keep the thinking of learners hidden. Let's look at several examples of where learners are not provided opportunities to respond, and thus their thinking is hidden from the teacher and themselves.

In the introduction of this book, Ms. Rogers engaged her learners in a learning experience about sinking and floating. If she wanted to assess her learners to see if they could describe characteristics of things that float or sink, she would need to do more than ask her learners to circle images on a handout that they believe would float. We do not want to discredit the use of a sorting task. However, sorting objects into two groups, one that sinks and one that floats, is not the same level of complexity as the verb describes. If the verb of the assessment does match the verb of the success criteria, we don't truly know what our learners know, understand, and are able to do. Returning to Ms. Campbell's classroom, if she simply had them make sounds at each of the centers, as enjoyable as that be, she does not gain insight into whether her learners can describe, record, explain, or use ideas. Thus she arrives at the following plan, shown in Figure 6.3.

We will return to the third column in Figure 6.2 toward the end of this chapter. For now, let's focus on where Ms. Campbell planned out the ideas in the second column.

Success Criteria	Assessments of, for, and as Learning	Evidence
I can describe how objects produce sound (Content).	Interactive notebook sheets, exit ticket	
I can record my thinking (Psychomotor).	Interactive notebook sheets	
I can explain my thinking using evidence from my experiments (Behavioral).	Questioning, think-pair-share, student conversations at the centers	
I can use my peers ideas to better explain my thinking (Social-Emotional).	Questioning, think-pair-share, student conversations at the centers	

Figure 6.3 Ms. Campbell's Success Criteria Assessment Development Template.

Assessments of, for, and as Learning Should Come from Multiple Contexts

Thinking about our assessments as opportunities to respond opens up the options or contexts for generating evidence. Yes, entrance tickets, exit slips, quizzes, and unit assessments are examples of opportunities to respond. However, think-pair-shares, classroom discussions, questioning, laptop dry erase boards, and journal prompts are also examples of opportunities to

CONTEXT OF OPPORTUNITY TO RESPOND	DESCRIPTION	EXAMPLES
Individual	Each individual student has an opportunity to respond.	An individual student answering a question; completing an exit ticket; one-on-one conversation, listening to a student explain his or her thinking
Small group	A small group of students generates a response; three, four, or five students contribute to a single response.	A group of students complete a science task, answer questions, meld individual summaries into one that represents the thinking of the group, or complete a science experiment
Whole group	All students in the class respond to the same question or prompt.	Choral response; using clickers or respose devices, where responses are representative of the class as a whole; Kahoot or Poll Everywhere questions; responses on dry erase boards
Silent	The response does not involve social interaction.	Exit ticket, short constructed response, writing a summary, journal reflection
Out loud	The response involves social interaction or dialogue between learners and teacher.	Think -pair-share, turn and talk, read aloud, cooperative learning task, discussion circles
Formal	The response is formally recorded.	Summaries in an interactive notebook, exit slip, data from plickers, students rate their progress against the success criteria paired with evidence of their work
Informal	The response is not formally recorded.	Conversations with/between peers or the teacher, response to impromptu questions, quick verbal checks

Figure 6.4 Multiple Contexts for Opportunities to Respond.

Source: Adapted from Almarode, J., & Vandas, K. (2019). *Clarity for learning: Five essential practices for empowering students and teachers*. Thousand Oaks, CA: Corwin Press.

respond. As shown in Figure 6.4, whether they are done individually, in small groups or as a whole group, formally or informally, silent or out loud, opportunities to respond are purposeful and intentional moments that make student thinking visible and allow both the teacher and learner to observe learning progress.

Opportunities for Reflective Practices

What are other examples in each of the contexts in Table 6.3?

Notice that certain opportunities to respond fit into multiple categories. For example, an exit ticket is a formal opportunity to respond that is silent and individual. Furthermore, these opportunities do not require a number recorded in the grade book. Informal opportunities to respond are often impromptu checks for understanding that inform the next steps in teaching and learning. While informal, to get the most out of providing students an opportunity to respond, they should be planned for and thoughtfully aligned with instruction. Opportunities to respond come in many varieties, opening the door for us to use them on a regular basis to monitor learners' progression toward the learning intentions and success criteria. Providing opportunities to respond should be a routine, not an occasional, occurrence. The role of opportunities to respond in student learning is well documented in the literature as formative assessments (Black & Wiliam, 1998; Hattie, 2009, 2012). The more time that is devoted to providing learners with opportunities to respond, the higher student achievement climbs (Black & Wiliam, 1998; Hattie, 2012; Marzano, 2007).

Assessments Should Make Student Thinking Visible

As our content becomes more rigorous, opportunities to respond become increasingly more important so that teachers have a firm awareness of whether students are progressing in the learning content, skills, and understandings. This can only happen if both our learners and us spend the necessary time to make thinking visible. For Ms. Cornish, she emphasizes that "when it comes to living versus non-living things, I cannot take anything for granted. Just because they identify which thing is living does not mean they are clear in their understanding. I have to get them to share their thinking."

Mr. Reinhart focuses on planning, developing, and implementing opportunities to respond so that he can see students' thinking about the similarities between adult animals and their young. "I want them to actively process these concepts and take an active role in their learning by developing an enhanced awareness of their own progress." Each of the teachers featured in this book strives to make thinking visible in their assessments of, for, and as learning. There are several ways to make learners' thinking visible (Ritchhart, Church, & Morrison, 2011):

1. Ask learners to provide descriptions of terms, concepts, ideas, procedures, or processes.
2. Encourage learners to develop explanations and interpretations of concepts, ideas, procedures, or processes.
3. Check that learners' reasons, explanations, and interpretations are accompanied by evidence.
4. Ask learners to take different viewpoints and perspectives on concepts, ideas, procedures, or processes.

5. Ask learners to make connections between what they are learning and what they have already learned.
6. Ask the right question – this will get students to reveal their thinking.Let us look at each of these six characteristics individually and with examples.

Tasks that make thinking visible should ask learners to *provide descriptions of terms, concepts, ideas, procedures, or processes*. This is different from asking learners to give a definition or simply repeat a specific process or procedure. For example, Mr. Reinhart could have his learners describe the young of an adult animal rather than simply identify which young animal goes with which adult animal. Ms. Rogers could have her learners describe the specific characteristics of objects that float, listening for the essential characteristics in their descriptions. Ms. Shay might ask her learners to describe the plant rather than simply list off the parts. The main purpose of this assessment is to engage learners in academic discourse to better see their thinking. This can be done verbally, in writing, or using assistive technology.

Tasks that make learning visible should also encourage learners to *develop explanations and interpretations of concepts, ideas, procedures, or processes*. Instead of simply answering a question or responding to a prompt, information about learners' progress is clearer if they have to provide an explanation for a specific answer. As part of learners' explanations, we should encourage them to *incorporate evidence to justify their explanations and interpretations*. Because of this evidence, we can better determine where the learner is in the learning progression. In Ms. Cornish's classroom, learners should be expected to not only answer a question about animals and plants changing their environments but also provide an explanation for their interpretation or response. This can be done using different pathways as well (e.g., verbally, written, or with technology). Explanations, interpretations, and justifications can be incorporated into any opportunity to respond by simply asking students, "What makes you say that?"

If we ask learners to *take different viewpoints and perspectives on concepts, ideas, procedures, or processes*, we are better able to unpack the level of depth in their understanding. For learners to look at an idea from a viewpoint other than their preferred perspective requires that they analyze the idea, extract the essential characteristics, and then compare and contrast those characteristics with the characteristics as they would be seen from the students' preferred perspective. Take for example the human effect on the environment. If Ms. Cornish were to ask her learners about their effect on the environment, the final aspect of the learning progression, they may find this question to be a bit of a challenge. However, by asking them to think of this question in terms of an animal in a polluted pond or in a habitat cluttered with trash, learners may be able to make the connections she is looking for in her students' thinking. The added element of this task will provide reliable and valid evidence for learners' ability to generalize the skills and concepts to different contexts. Which skills did the learners generalize to the different scenarios, and which ones were not generalized to this new scenario?

One technique for encouraging different viewpoints is to ask a provoking question that makes learners consider that viewpoint.

- What would happen if all objects could float in water?
- What would happen if plants could walk like animals?
- What would happen if sound could only travel through a solid?

Developing a strong understanding of individual concepts, ideas, procedures, or processes is important. However, finding connections across different content areas and generalizing understanding is the goal of teaching and learning in the early childhood science classroom. Can our learners use knowledge and understanding from one area and apply that learning to another area? This requires practice. This requires us to support learners in making connections between writing, mathematics, and authentic experiences outside of the classroom. *The connections that students make between what they are learning and what they have already learned* must be visible so that teachers and learners can see the interconnectedness of concepts, ideas, procedures, or processes.

Other Examples:

> An elementary science teacher can help learners make connections by using thinking maps or concept maps that relate two concepts in science. For example, how are the needs of living things related to how they change their environment? How do the parts of the plant help it to survive? What is the relationship between the force with which I strike an instrument and the nature of the sound it creates?

If we want to make student thinking visible, we have to ask the right questions. *Asking the right questions gets students to reveal their thinking.* There are two broad categories of questions: open and closed (Allen, 2001; Boaler, 1998; Dohrenwend, 1965). The most salient difference between these two broad categories of questions is the type of thinking involved in responding to an open versus a closed question. Consider the following three examples in Figure 6.5.

Semantically, the difference in these questions is subtle. In terms of thinking, one provides an opportunity to make thinking visible, while the other leads to simply getting an answer. *Getting students to reveal their thinking requires us to ask the right question.* In all three examples, the first question is a closed question, while the second is an example of an open question. The words *best* and *most important* close the responses down to one acceptable answer. The exchange of these words in the second question for phrases like *your ideas* and *some differences* opens the question up for multiple acceptable answers that open the door to teachers asking, "What makes you say that?"

	Question 1		Question 2
Example 1	What are three characteristics of living things that make them different from non-living things?	Or	Let's list a few characteristics of living things? What about non-living things?
Example 2	What is the most important difference between an insect and a spider?	Or	What are some of the differences you can think of between an insect and a spider?
Example 3	What is the reason things sink?	Or	What are your ideas about sinking and floating? Can you give me some examples?

Figure 6.5 Examples of Open and Closed Questions.

Returning to Figure 6.3, we were left wondering where Ms. Campbell came up with her assessments of, for, and as learning. Just as we have seen in all of the classroom examples, there is a high level of intentionality behind everything these teachers say and do. There is an equal amount of intentionality in what they ask their learners to say and do. To ensure that we see this connection, Ms. Campbell and her colleagues focus on the verbs in the success criteria to guide the development of assessments that should provide evidence that learners can, indeed, demonstrate those verbs. Then, Ms. Campbell and her team develop assessments of, for, and as learning that draws from multiple contexts and makes thinking visible.

However, we must remember, our assessments are only as good as the evidence they provide. And that evidence is only as good as the decisions we make based on that evidence. Let's turn our attention to that last column in Figure 6.3. How do we plan for the gathering and collecting of evidence?

Opportunities for Reflective Practices

Before reading on, summarize what is meant by making thinking visible? What are some ways we can ensure that learners' thinking does not remain hidden in our classrooms?

Evidence from Assessments

The last column in Figure 6.2 directs our attention to the evidence that we will be gathering and collecting from these assessments. Every assessment of, for, and as provides opportunities for both us and our learners to generate evidence about learning. However, we have to plan for this gathering and collecting of evidence. Ms. Lamb has developed a comprehensive list of assessments of, for, and as learning for her students' learning around insects. These assessments involve multiple contexts and make thinking visible. "Now I have to think through what I am looking for in these assessments. Before I walk in the door, I need to know what to listen for, look for, and watch for from my learners." For us to leverage assessments to know where to go next with student learning, we have to target our noticing of what evidence learners generate in those assessments. Ms. Lamb emphasizes, "Without thinking through what I am looking for, I run the risk of inadvertently missing something that is important in moving a learner forward in the progression."

The source for us to generate this evidence comes from the content knowledge associated with a particular topic. This is where our own professional learning comes into play. For Ms. Lamb, she has to make sure that she has the necessary content knowledge to know what evidence will indicate that a learner is making progress toward the learning intention and success criteria. "I will spend time reading and researching topics to make sure I have a strong foundation in what my students are learning. It is my responsibility to ensure that they are getting accurate knowledge, the necessary skills, and the precise understandings within science."

Opportunities for Reflective Practices

To ensure that you have the necessary content knowledge to recognize and articulate evidence of learning, where would you go to build your own content knowledge?

Table 6.2 Ms. Campbell's Evidence-Gathering Plan

Success Criteria	*Assessments of, for, and as Learning*	*Evidence*
I can describe how objects produce sound (content).	Interactive notebook sheets, exit ticket	Look for explicit statements relating to vibrations, sound
I can record my thinking (psychomotor).	Interactive notebook sheets	Correct use of terminology (e.g., vibrate, investigation, evidence, sound)
I can explain my thinking using evidence from my experiments (behavioral).	Questioning, think-pair-share, student conversations at the centers	Clear and coherent links between variables in the experiment and observations - do not have to use the term "variables"
I can use my peers' ideas to better explain my thinking (social-emotional).	Questioning, think-pair-share, student conversations at the centers	Active listening cues, please, thank you, learners summarize or paraphrase

Returning to Ms. Campbell's classroom, she and her colleagues have developed a plan to gather evidence (Table 6.2) that is aligned with the "I can" statements. As she states, "We really spent time thinking about how we wanted to evaluate our learners' understanding during the lesson. We made this a central part of our planning conversation."

Ms. Campbell and her colleagues have multiple methods of gathering evidence about students' learning. Furthermore, these assessments allow her to imbed evaluation into the very model of instruction selected for the day's learning: cooperative learning and inquiry-based learning. "I want to monitor their learning progress along the way so that I can make decisions now rather than waiting until the opportunity has passed and we have to recreate the context. Plus, a lot of my assessments require students to engage with each other. I am always monitoring how they approach the learning and then make meaning of that learning. Oh, and how they get along." This last statement reflects her use of assessment for and as learning rather than solely focused on the assessment of learning - after the learning experience has ended.

Planning to Collect Evidence. In addition to planning the evidence to be gathered, we have to develop ways of collecting or organizing the evidence. Collecting an entrance ticket, exit ticket, or other student-generated artifacts is one way of obtaining the evidence. In addition, there needs to be a way of organizing evidence so that we can make meaning of that evidence and decide what to do with it. In addition, there are rich conversations, interactions, and actions that occur outside of tangible artifacts collected that can also be used to determine impact. Ms. Campbell describes the importance of having a way to keep track of what is going on in the classroom. "When learners are working at their centers, engaged in the task, or whaling away on an instrument, I need to make sure I jot down what I am seeing and hearing so that I can reference this evidence at a later time. I use a record-keeping sheet that I keep close by during class." When we look at this record-keeping sheet, we see that Ms. Campbell maintains her focus on the criteria for success but broadens her view of evaluation to capture student learning beyond how they respond to a single handout or activity. "When I observe them engaging in academic discourse and working collaboratively with their peers, I get a feel for their buy-in and whether or not they see the value in what we are doing in class."

Table 6.3 Ms. Campbell's Success Criteria Assessment Development Template

SC	*Observed Doing*	*Heard Saying*	*Saw Writing*
I can describe how objects produce sound (content).			
I can record my thinking (psychomotor).			
I can explain my thinking using evidence from my experiments (behavioral).			
I can use my peers' ideas to better explain my thinking (social-emotional).			

Source: Adapted from Sweeney, D., & Harris, L. S. (2017). *Student-centered coaching. The moves.* Thousand Oaks, CA: Corwin Press.

When we gather evidence through seeing and listening, we gain insight into learners' understanding, dispositions, and motivations. If our assessments of, for, and as learning are from multiple contexts, we have to be prepared to collect evidence from multiple contexts as well.

Anticipating Misconceptions. Simply by experiencing the world around them, learners process and organize information from many sources (Rutherford & Ahlgren, 1990). As a result, they come to our science classes with already formed ideas about the world. These prior ideas are often composed of fragmented, incomplete, or naïve beliefs about scientific phenomena. The ideas are not typically consistent with accepted scientific views (Bass, Contant, & Carin, 2009). For example, learners can have misconceptions about living and nonliving things, liquids, light rays, sound, and geoscience processes. Some of the most common misconceptions are the following:

- Animals are living because they move, but plants are nonliving.
- Anything that pours is a liquid.
- When liquids evaporate, they just disappear.
- Electric current is used up in bulbs, and there is less current going back to a battery than coming out of it.
- Light rays move out from the eye in order to illuminate objects.
- Loudness and pitch are the same thing.
- Suction causes liquids to be pulled upward in a soda straw.
- Earth is flat.
- The phases of the Moon are caused by shadows from Earth falling on the Moon.
- Seasons are caused by the changing distance of Earth from the Sun (see Driver et al., 1994).

The final aspect of developing assessments involves reflecting on our own content knowledge and pedagogical content knowledge. Ms. Campbell has the experience and has developed the expertise associated with early childhood science. This means that she is aware of misconceptions that surface in the classroom. "Having taught this before, I am aware that many things that learners know about sound are either incomplete or misconceptions about how sound really works. Even now, I still spend time anticipating where my learners might need additional support or misinterpret the phenomenon through the lens of a

Table 6.4 Multiple Contexts for Opportunities to Respond

Misconception	*Ways to Address Misconception*

Source: Author created.

misconception." What are some possible misconceptions? What did the initial assessments tell me about my learners? We must carefully monitor learners as they engage in content, skills, and understandings, especially as they begin to monitor their own learning and apply their prior experiences and background knowledge to avoid the development of misconceptions or the self-verification of previously held misconceptions. When we develop assessments that draw from multiple contexts and make thinking visible, we have a greater chance to recognize errors in scientific reasoning and support conceptual change (Driver et al., 1994; Wandersee, Mintzes, & Novak, 1994).

The template in Appendix B (see Table 6.4) provides space for us to anticipate misconceptions.

Once we have identified a misconception or error in scientific reasoning, our learners must be appropriately challenged to recognize that their personal theories and scientific explanations are in conflict with scientific views. This can be done by circling back and providing direct instruction of the scientific principle or scaffolding and supporting their new learning through additional learning experiences that focus on reshaping their knowledge, skills, and understanding. But again, this is something we plan for in developing assessments of, for, and as learning.

Opportunities for Reflective Practices

Thinking about the misconceptions in science, what are some ways you would address misconceptions in your current or future learners?

Developing Assessments in the Inclusive Early Childhood Science Classroom

Assessments are opportunities for learners to show what they know. Whether this is at the end of a unit or series of daily experiences (assessment of learning) or during the learning process, the value of assessments lies in the information those assessments provide us and our learners. This is reflected in the second column of Table 6.1. The assessments must provide the essential information needed to answer those questions of purpose. To gather and collect this essential information from all of our learners, we have to expand our view of how to do it. Having learners show what they know is possible beyond writing it out, for example. To ensure that our learners are active members of the classroom community, even in our assessments, we have to provide multiple pathways for them to show what they know. Ms. Shay shares, "I try and find as many ways as possible for learners to share their thinking. Sometimes it is with words, sometimes, with pictures. Then, there are times they act it out and times they write it out."

The pathway through which learners demonstrate their knowledge, skills, and understandings should represent the same level of complexity as the learning intention and success criteria. However, the package, so to speak, of the knowledge, skills, and understandings must ensure that there are not barriers simply because we are focused on having them complete a worksheet or handout. Plus, welcoming learners to show what they know through a pathway of their choice ensures they are seen as valuable members of the community and have the opportunity to share their success with their peers. In the end, the assessments we develop should reflect three questions related to our teaching and learning in the inclusive early childhood science classroom (Hattie, 2012):

1. Where are we going? - This is to ensure that we anchor the development of assessments in the learning intentions and success criteria.
2. How are we going? - This is to ensure that the assessments provide the evidence that they are moving toward the learning outcomes.
3. Where do we go next? - This ensures that we do something with the evidence that is gathered and collected.

We will devote Chapter 8 to the response to question #3. For now, we have developed our assessments of, for, and as learning. Let's move to rigorous task design within our models of instruction from Chapter 5.

Professional Learning Tasks

1. Returning to the science standard of learning you have been working with for the past several chapters. Develop assessments for an upcoming daily learning experience. Once you have aligned those assessments with the level of complexity articulated in the learning intentions and success criteria, verify the balance of your assessments. Are your assessments developed of, for, and as learning? Use the template in Appendix B.
2. Using the assessments developed in the previous professional learning task, what modifications must be made to those assessments to ensure that all learners have equity of access and opportunity to "show what they know"?
3. To better anticipate your learners' responses, devote time to research the most common misconceptions for a topic you are going to teach in the future. Return to the "Misconceptions Interview Task" in Appendix D. What does the research say about addressing these misconceptions?
4. Through checks for understanding and progress monitoring, we keep a close eye on the learning progress of our learners during the learning experience so that we can make immediate and necessary adjustments to the daily learning experiences should they not make progress toward the day's learning outcomes. Through artifacts gathered and collected during the learning experience, we can identify when learners have demonstrated that they met the learning intentions and success criteria. Appendix G provides a process for generating checks for understanding. Using the guiding questions, develop a series of checks for understanding that provide evidence of learning, evidence for learning, and evidence as learning.

Family and Community Engagement

As we conclude our discussion about developing checks for understanding and progress monitoring, we want to tie in family and community engagement. These assessments, although designed to inform our instruction, require that we communicate information about a child's progress in science learning. This can and will get difficult from time to time. However, if we have truly created an inclusive learning environment for both learners and their families, we are better positioned to have these very important conversations with families. Let's look at a few tips to ensure that the engagement of families remains high even when sharing concerns about a child's progress in science learning.

1. **Listen first - seek to understand:** When working with young children, there is a high probability that we will have blind spots in understanding our young learners. Listening to what parents or guardians have to say is very important. Their perspective will help shine a light on blind spots and help us make decisions about how to meet the cognitive, social-emotional, behavioral, and psychomotor needs of their children. Conversations with family members where we listen and seek to understanding provide much more information than was asked of them and offer cues about whether they need more information about a particular issue and whether they are prepared to hear what we have to say.
2. **Begin with the positives:** Do not hit parents or guardians with negative information right from the start. When talking with family members, start by identifying strengths in their science learning. Setting a positive tone will ensure that parents or guardians do not walk away feeling as though the entire experience was negative - that is never the case. Plus, this will set a positive tone and help even defensive parents or guardians feel as though you see the strengths of their children. In more cases than not, you will likely share the same impressions about strengths and opportunities for growth. The challenge is often how to initiate a conversation without pointing fingers at anyone about being overly sensitive or unnecessarily concerned. Remember, this is someone's child - their pride and joy. They see them as special - we should do the same.
3. **Come at it from different angles:** Conversations about school can be stressful, regardless of whether the discussion is about "good news" or concerns about learning. For some family members, their past experiences in school have left them uncertain and even skeptical about communicating with us. You should make sure that any information you have to share with parents or guardians is supported by evidence. This is not a "gotcha" and should not be presented as evidence in a trial. Instead, offering examples whenever possible will allow the parents or guardians to share examples from home. Yes, you guessed it, these examples from home may help us better understand how to meet the cognitive, social-emotional, behavioral, and psychomotor needs of their children. Be sure to ask the parents or guardians to confirm what they have heard and if they can work with us to move the students' learning forward.
4. **We are not doctors - do not diagnose:** During the school day, we get to see our learners in different settings (e.g., small group, whole group, cafeteria, playground).

This gives us a chance to observe learners in settings with other learners and settings that may not be replicated at home. When communicating with parents or guardians, do not jump to conclusions or diagnose the student. Instead, do everything you can to gather detailed information that could be helpful in working with the parents or guardians to meet the cognitive, social-emotional, behavioral, and psychomotor needs of their children. Remember, the point of this communication or form of engagement is to help the learner be successful.

5. **Wait time is important:** We live in the world of teaching and learning. This world is full of jargon, acronyms, and terminology that is not common in everyday language. Yep, Tier 3 vocabulary (see Chapter 1). Communications with parents or guardians about their children's progress may stir up feelings associated with their experiences in school or feelings of guilt and helplessness. Be sure to provide opportunities for parents and guardians to understand your concerns. Let them ask questions. Provide a means for them to communicate with you after they have had time to process the information. Again, the point of this communication or form of engagement is to help the learner be successful, *not* to simply say, "Well, I let their family know, now it is up to them."
6. **Finally, let parents or guardians have a turn.** Get parents' or guardians' feedback about their children's learning experiences in your classroom. There just may be something you are doing or not doing that will make a world of difference. Your efforts and willingness to be a flexible, well-informed, and enthusiastic collaborator in the teaching and learning of their children will create healthy relationships with families.

7 Implementing Daily Learning Experiences

Task Design

Task design is an essential component of inclusive early childhood science teaching and learning. Tasks represent the pieces of work to be done or undertaken within the learning experience or model of instruction. For example, within a model of instruction, there are specific things learners will do that, in the end, result in them moving forward in the learning progression. While concept attainment might be the particular model of instruction, the tasks within that model are the specific elements of the model that are designed to actively engage learners in the content and skills (e.g., sorting, writing, describing, analyzing, documenting, drawing conclusions, designing experiments). The tasks that we design provide our young students with opportunities to actively engage with the content and skills, ultimately building and supporting their enduring understanding of ideas about how the world works. Task design should foster, nurture, and sustain all learners' engagement in the highest level of complexity possible so that they can acquire and consolidate their learning. This, of course, includes learning across all domains: cognitive, social-emotional, behavioral, and psychomotor.

However, task design is not as simple as downloading an activity or exercise from Pinterest, Teachers Pay Teachers, or pulling a premade activity out of a teacher's resource guide that accompanies our curriculum. Designing tasks that maximize the time learners are engaged with and successful in the learning of content, skills, and understandings is paramount in high-quality, high-impact inclusive early childhood science learning. These pieces of work or undertakings should scaffold and support learners as they make meaning of the science phenomenon, apply science and engineering practices, and develop an enduring understanding of how the world works.

The amount of time allotted to science teaching and learning is far less than other subject areas and aspects of the school day (Pianta, Belsky, Houts, & Morrison, 2007). And although we do not want to be alarmist, one of the implications of these findings is that we must maximize the time we do have for science teaching and learning. Maybe we don't have as much time as we would like, but we can make intentional, deliberate, and purposeful decisions about the tasks we design so that we provide high-quality, high-impact learning experiences that maximize student learning in the time that we do have for science. That is the key focus of this chapter. What makes a task high-quality and result in high-impact learning? Are there ways to design a task that will effectively support our learners in making meaning of the science phenomenon, applying science and engineering practices, and developing an enduring understanding about how the world works? The answer is yes.

We will once again visit the classrooms of Ms. Rogers, Ms. Campbell, Ms. Shay, Ms. Cornish, and Mr. Reinhart and analyze the specific tasks they designed and provided for their learners. This will lead us to three key ideas:

1. In an inclusive early childhood science classroom, tasks must be rigorous.
2. We can make adjustments to any task so that all learners have equity of access to the highest level of complex thinking possible and the potential to be successful.
3. There are essential characteristics of a rigorous task that should inform our design and implementation of those tasks.

Let's start with rigor - and that is quite a loaded term and should be fun to explore.

Opportunities for Reflective Practices

Describe rigor. What do you mean when you say rigor? Providing some specific details, what makes learning rigorous learning?

Rigor in Inclusive Early Childhood Science Teaching and Learning

High-quality, high-impact teaching in the inclusive early childhood science classroom maximizes the time that learners are engaged with and successful in the learning of important outcomes (Berliner 1987, 1990). The "engaged with" part of that statement is where we want to direct our attention. The desire to increase the rigor of learning in our classrooms is evident in our most recent revisions of learning standards (e.g., Common Core, NGSS, and C3 Framework in Social Studies) and our renewed focus on 21st-century skills or college and career readiness initiatives. One word that keeps popping up is rigor. Rigorous standards, rigorous learning, rigorous tasks. However, this term is too ambiguous to be helpful for our work with young learners. If we were to ask every one of our colleagues what rigor was and what it looked like in their future or current classrooms, we would likely get as many different responses as the number of colleagues we asked.

When the topic of rigor comes up among Mr. Reinhart and his colleagues,

> the focus immediate jumps to making it hard. I struggle with this because making something hard does not necessarily make it rigorous or lead to better learning. For example, it can be hard for a six-year old to sit still for 30 minutes. But does that mean sitting still is rigorous. I have an even harder time thinking about this in terms of science content.

Ms. Cornish agrees.

> The word hard comes to mind when rigor is discussed in our planning block. I could have them make daily observations in a science journal each night at home, but to what end? I could also ask them to use vocabulary or perform tasks in science that are clearly out of their zone of proximal development.

Ms. Shay jumps in with

> not to mention that we often are more comfortable pushing certain learners. Even if we do it inadvertently, there are some learners we challenge because we believe they can do it.

There are others we don't push when it comes to specific learning. But I believe they are both engaged in rigorous learning, right?

This internal struggle shared through a conversation with these teachers reflects the ambiguity around rigor. Barbara Blackburn (2018) defines rigor as "creating an environment in which each student is expected to learn at high levels, each student is supported so he or she can learn at high levels, and each student demonstrates learning at high levels (p. 13)." What this definition points out is that we play a vital role in ensuring our learning environment is rigorous. And that is the point we are trying to make here. We must engage in the intentional, deliberate, and purposeful planning for rigorous learning experiences. In addition, this definition does not speak to any quantity, a specific population of learners, or test scores or grades. So, as we try to reduce the ambiguity in the term "rigor," we must also look at misconceptions associated with the term. Table 7.1 contains several misconceptions related to rigor.

Table 7.1 Misconceptions about Rigor

Misconception	*Explanation*
Lots of work at home is a sign of rigor in early childhood science teaching and learning.	Oftentimes, we falsely believe that providing an abundance of "things" for learners to do at home with their parents, guardians, or caregivers is promoting rigor. This promotes inequity for learners who do not have access to the necessary resources outside of school.
More science content is better and should be pushed into early childhood classrooms sooner.	The coverage of more topics, tasks, and/or activities does not represent rigor. This misconception sometimes leads to expecting learners to engage with content, skills, and knowledge that are not developmentally appropriate. Learning takes time and has a strong developmental component. This may create gaps in learners' knowledge, skills, and understandings that cause problems later in their learning trajectory.
Not all of our learners can handle rigor.	Rigorous learning experiences are often set aside for certain learners whom we perceive are capable of handling that rigor. Statements like, "My babies can't do that," exemplify this misconception. This reflects deficit thinking and denies some learners the access to and opportunity for the highest level of complexity possible.
Scaffolding and support lessen the rigor.	The task does not have to be completed independently and without any help to be rigorous. This misconception perpetuates the internal belief of learners that "I should not ask for help." Scaffolding and support are essential components of all learning, for all learners.
Curricula and programs provide the rigor.	We often assume that the resources we are provided take rigor into account. Although this is not an unfair expectation, this is a misconception. We must analyze the expectations and tasks within our resources to make the necessary adaptations for the local context of our classroom. Those curriculum writers and program developers don't know our students as well as we do.
Standards of learning to create rigor.	Remember, standards tell us what to teach, not how. Rigor is about the "how" and should be informed by the "who." The "who" in this case are our learners. Simply put, standards do not create rigor; they create expectations for learning. Rigor comes in how we analyze, map, and implement daily learning experiences from those standards.
Rigor is an education fad.	Providing learners with daily experiences that maximize their growth and development is not a fad. This is what we do as teachers. This is the ethical and moral hinge point for inclusive early childhood science teaching and learning. Do we want to have an impact or not? If not, find something else to do.

Source: Adapted from Blackburn, B. R. (2018). *Rigor is not a four-letter word.* New York, NY: Routledge.

Opportunities for Reflective Practices

Take a moment and process these misconceptions. Are there some we have missed? Do you see yourself in any of these statements? How do each of these misconceptions directly contradict our goal of providing an inclusive learning environment in science? What efforts can be taken to address these misconceptions in us and our colleagues?

Let's return to our definition of inclusive early childhood science teaching and learning, first mentioned in Chapter 1, page 19.

> An inclusive environment for all learners - an environment that actively engages all learners, welcomes and embraces every learner as an important member of the community, and provides the necessary support to each learner so that they have an equal opportunity for success (see Jimenez, Browder, Spooner, & DiBiase, 2012; Spooner, Knight, Browder, Jimenez, & DiBiase, 2011).

These misconceptions about rigor in Table 7.1 directly contradict this definition. Yet if we see this definition as more than a definition, more than an expectation, but as a belief that drives our teaching of science, we quickly move away from misconceptions. Consider the following statements from the perspective of rigor as a necessary and sufficient condition for inclusion.

1. If we believe that all learners should and will be actively engaged in our learning environment, then all learners should and will be actively engaged in rigorous tasks.
2. If we believe all learners should be embraced as an important member of the community, then we will offer access and opportunity to all learners to engage in rigorous tasks.
3. If we believe learners should be provided the necessary support to have an equal opportunity for success, then we will make the necessary adaptations to tasks so that all learners can engage in the highest level of rigor possible.

As Blackburn (2018) points out, rigor is about quality, not quantity. Rigor is for everyone, not just a selected few. And, finally, rigor is about moving learning forward. This means we must intentionally, deliberately, and purposefully design our tasks to include elements that enhance the quality for all learners based on what they need to move their learning forward. This includes

- access to complex text;
- a focus on extracting and leveraging evidence from text to explain thinking;
- the opportunity to build background knowledge through informational text;
- a balance between conceptual understanding, procedural fluency, and the application of thinking and concepts; and
- integrating the above elements into the disciplinary core ideas, science and engineering practices, and crosscutting concepts.

For Ms. Campbell and Ms. Lamb, they successfully integrate the aforementioned elements into the tasks they design for their learners. Ms. Campbell shares, "One of the reasons I use a read aloud to anchor the lesson is to give my learners access to complex text and conceptual understanding. Oftentimes, the text I use provides both authenticity and a conceptual example of what we are learning. Then, I make fiction and non-fiction texts available at the reading center."

Main Book List:

- Bugs for Lunch by Margery Facklam
- Caterpillar to Butterfly-National Geographic
- Bugs, Bugs, Bugs by Bob Barner
- What is an Insect? by Susan Canizares
- Wonderful Worms by Linda Glaser and Loretta Krupinski
- Bees-National Geographic by Melissa Stewart
- Grasshopper-National Georgraphic by Melissa Stewart
- Insect Picture Encyclopedia by George C. McGavin
- Ants-National Geographic by Melissa Stewart
- The Very Busy Spider by Eric Carle
- The Very Hungry Caterpillar by Eric Carle
- The Very Grouchy Ladybug by Eric Carle
- The Very Quiet Cricket by Eric Carle

Figure 7.1 Texts Available for Ms. Lamb's Unit on Insects.

Ms. Lamb uses a similar approach. "I make sure I have a text-rich environment for my learners. For the insect unit alone, I have a vast collection of books (Figure 7.1)."

But, keep in mind, a rich-text environment is not the only way. Both of these teachers, as well as Ms. Rogers, ensure that learners have a balance between conceptual understanding, procedural fluency, and the application of thinking and concepts. For Ms. Rogers,

> I aim for them to experience the phenomenon or concept that we are learning about that week. Rather than focusing on just procedures like the water cycle dance or gestures for the parts of a flower, I want them to conceptually understand the science and then link that concept to skills or procedures.

Rigor is a necessary and sufficient condition for inclusive early childhood science. However, there is one aspect of rigor that is not addressed in the definition proposed by Blackburn (2018) or others in our field. How do we do it? In other words, how do we create an environment in which each student is expected to learn at high levels, each student is supported so that he or she can learn at high levels, and each student demonstrates learning at high levels? Without that valuable information, we may find ourselves slipping into misconceptions, not because we intended to but because no one helped us with the "how."

Difficulty versus Complexity

Doug Fisher, Nancy Frey, and John Hattie (2016) proposed a different way of thinking about rigor. Rigor is the intersection between difficulty and complexity within a given experience or task. For example, look at Ms. Campbell's station description for xylophones in Figure 7.2.

Center 1: Xylophones

5 different length metal tubes on a piece of ridged foam and a small wooden mallet form the xylophone for this rotation. Students use the mallet to explore how the length of the tube relates to the pitch. A longer tube has a lower pitch compared to a shorter tube. Journal questions for this rotation are: How are the bars different? How did the bars sound different?

Figure 7.2 Center #1 for Ms. Campbell's Lesson on Vibrating Objects and Sound.

Center 4: Cans

Students can make sounds whatever ways they want using a popsicle stick and metal can. For example, they can bang the stick on the bottom or sides of the can, run the stick up and down the ridges of the can, or rattle it around the inside of the can. The journal page for this rotation had a space for students to draw or write how they made sounds with the can.

Figure 7.3 Center #4 for Ms. Campbell's Lesson on Vibrating Objects and Sound.

The level of rigor for this particular center depends on the complexity and difficulty as represented by the expected actions and thinking that go into the completion of this center. The difficulty speaks to the amount of effort learners must put into using the mallet to explore and physically write their responses in their journals. The complexity speaks to the level of thinking required in this center. For example, Ms. Campbell's learners will have to think about the relationship between potentially two independent variables and one dependent variable (i.e., the length of the tube, the force of the mallet strike, and the dependent variable of pitch). While Ms. Campbell may not expect her learners to understand the concepts of independent and dependent variables, an added layer of complexity, they still must think about these relationships. Let's compare this with another center from the same lesson (Figure 7.3).

Opportunities for Reflective Practices

What do you notice about the differences in complexity and difficulty between Center #1 and Center #4? Why do you think that?

This particular center has a different degree of difficulty in that learners are not asked to just write in their journal; they are given the option to draw or write. For some learners, the act of writing is incredibly difficult, while drawing may require less effort. What if a learner has a clear understanding of the relationship between characteristics of the popsicle stick, the metal can, the force of the "mallet" strike or vibrations, and the nature of the sound but struggles to write or does not have the necessary vocabulary, yet, to formulate a written response? Ms. Campbell adjusts this level of difficulty by allowing learners to either write or draw in their science journals. More to this point, her decision to adjust the level of difficulty for this station is related to the increase in the level of complexity. Learners have a more open-ended task that introduces additional variables. For example, striking the can with the popsicle sticks is different than putting the popsicle sticks into the can and shaking the can. More variables lead to more relationships and greater complexity.

The interaction between difficulty and complexity produces the rigor in a given learning experience or task. What we have witnessed through Ms. Campbell's centers is that this is a balance that we must strike with our learners. What makes this particularly challenging is that the rigor or any experience or task must be considered from the perspective of the learner – not us. In other words, whether we consider something to be difficult and/or challenging is irrelevant. The learners determine the level of rigor. Let's unpack this a bit more. What we are not saying is that we, as teachers, do not have any control over the rigor. The exact opposite is true. We, through our planning, developing, and implementing of high-quality, high-impact learning experiences, must ensure that the tasks we design are difficult and challenging. What is difficult and challenging depends on our learners. Through our initial assessments, assessments of, for, and as learning, we must develop a clear picture of what is the right level of difficulty and complexity for the learners - finding the right level of rigor is how we move learning forward.

Opportunities for Reflective Practices

Summarize your own understanding of rigor. How would you integrate the concepts of difficulty and complexity into that summary?

Adjusting the Level of Difficulty, Not Complexity

Finding the right level of rigor that moves learning forward requires that we plan for different levels of rigor and prepare to make adjustments to the rigor as learners engage in learning tasks. Therefore, one of the key ideas is that we make adjustments to any task so that all learners have equity of access to the highest level of complex thinking possible and the potential to be successful. For Ms. Campbell, she planned for different levels of difficulty and complexity in the design of the tasks at each center. However, if we pay careful attention to exactly what Ms. Campbell adjusted, we see that she upped the complexity and lowered the difficulty.

> I identify the level of complexity expected of my students in the standard and share that through my learning intentions and success criteria. Then, I ensure everyone can engage at that level by adjusting the difficulty of the tasks. In some cases, I lower the difficulty and ramp-up the complexity. I don't ever lower the complexity. That is how I ensure I have high expectations and then scaffold and support my learners in meeting those expectations.

What Ms. Campbell is referring is a different way of thinking about inclusion through differentiated instruction. How do we not just design tasks but also implement them in such a way that the tasks actively engage all learners, welcome and embrace every learner as an important member of the community, and provide the necessary support to each learner so that they have an equal opportunity for success? And at the same time, how do we offer equity of access and opportunity to the highest level of rigor for all learners?

When designing and implementing tasks, adjust the level of difficulty, maintain the level of complexity. Let's look at a specific example of this as it relates to a separate performance-based task in Ms. Campbell's classroom (Figure 7.4).

Our Museum of Music

Challenging Task

Cooperative Learning Task: You and your team will create two different drums using different materials for each drum. Please be sure that the drums make different sounds. When finished, all groups will play their drums for the class and explain what materials were used.

Individual Writing Prompt: Tell me what you have learned about what causes sound.

Figure 7.4 Performance-Based Learning Task for Ms. Campbell's Learners.

> I wanted to give my learners a performance-based task that would allow me to assess their thinking and to see if they were able to pull all of the content, skills, and understandings together related to vibrations and sound. I also wanted to incorporate social studies and literacy into this task. This was a cooperative learning task but also had an individual component. I needed to see how they worked together and also hold them personally accountable for their learning.

The level of complexity of this task comes from the expectation that learners must create, compare, and contrast their two creations; explain their work; and then articulate their understanding of relationships through an individual writing prompt. On other hand, the difficulty comes from the effort they will need to construct the two drums from the given material. There is also one other source of difficulty that comes into play with a task like this one. If learners are not clear about what a drum truly is, they will likely experience enhanced difficulty in constructing one of their own. What makes the background knowledge and prior knowledge of this task influence the level of difficulty? The learning intentions and success criteria. The learning intentions and success criteria are related to understanding the relationships between materials, vibrations, and sound, not understanding what a drum is or is not. Therefore, this background knowledge and prior knowledge influence the difficulty of the task, just like the writing prompt. The point here is that we are far better at sorting out difficulty and complexity if we have established and shared our learning intentions and success criteria.

Another quick example of this comes from Ms. Shay's classroom. If her learning intention and success criteria focus on her learners' understanding of how the parts of the plant help it to survive, then she must consider what aspects of any task would make it difficult for a learner to engage in this complex content.

> If I have learners whose first language is not English, I can easily provide translations next to the parts of the plant. I can also let them share thinking in their native language. This removes the difficulty caused by a language barrier.

Opportunities for Reflective Practices

How do we sort out what influence's difficulty and what influences complexity? What are examples from your future or current classroom?

Ms. Campbell draws from her initial assessments, assessments of, for, and as learning to make decisions about how to adjust the difficulty of this particular task so that learners can truly engage a level of complexity that reflects where they are in their learning progression.

> What I do not want is for one of my students to truly understand the concept, but not be able to show me what they know or engage in the task because he or she struggles with reading, speaks a different language, or has a learning disability. None of those situations should stand in the way of my students learning about materials, vibrations, and sound.

So, Ms. Campbell provides the following scaffolds and supports aimed at reducing the difficulty but maintaining the highest level of complexity (i.e., create, compare, and contrast their two creations; explain their work; and then articulate their understanding of relationships) (Figure 7.5).

For the group task that requires researching and creating drums:

- Some groups will be provided with images of drums.
- Some groups will be provided audio or video resources about drums.
- Some groups will be provided with leveled readers where drums are include in the story or text.
- Some groups will be provided with a variety of text.
- Some groups will be allowed to select their own resources.

For the individual task/writing prompt:

- Some learners will be provided graphic organizers to summarize information.
- Some learners will be provided sentence frames for the independent writing.
- Some learners will be provided guiding research questions for the individual writing prompt.
- Some learners will be provided with no support for responding to the writing prompt.

Figure 7.5 Adjustments to the Difficulty of the Task.

As we read down the list of adjustments, we should have noticed an increase in the level of difficulty but no change in the complexity. During this task, each group and each learner will still create, compare, and contrast their two creations; explain their work; and then articulate their understanding of relationships. However, they are provided the necessary support to have an equal opportunity for success and access to the highest level of complexity. Plus, from the planning, designing, and implementation perspectives, we are developing one task and adjusting that task to meet all learners. In other words, inclusion does not require us to have 26 lesson plans, one for each learner. Inclusion does not require us to have 26 different versions of each center in our classroom.

There is one final aspect of difficulty and complexity that we need to address. If we do feel compelled to adjust the level of complexity, as Ms. Campbell did between Centers #1 and #4, move complexity up, never down. Complexity can be adjusted when learners have demonstrated a high level of proficiency with a topic instead of giving them more of the same or moving them into a different topic that is different from other learners in the classroom. This increase in complexity should move learners toward extended abstract thinking or the application of concepts and thinking. For example, Ms. Campbell upped the level of complexity in Center #4 by allowing her learners to freely explore the development of a musical instrument with a given set of supplies. Asking a learner to keep answering questions, doing experiments, or answering questions about a topic they have mastered is not helpful. Moving them on to the next topic is realistically manageable for us as teachers. In this case, up the complexity.

The template in Appendix B allows us to plan for this just as Ms. Campbell has here (Figure 7.6).

Template for Adjusting Difficulty.

F. ADJUSTING DIFFICULTY AND COMPLEXITY
Describe how you have planned to meet the needs of all students in your classroom with varied interest and learning readiness, English language proficiency, health, physical ability, etc. How will you extend and enrich the learning of students who finish early? How will you support the learning of students struggling with your learning intentions and success criteria?

Difficulty			
Complexity			

Figure 7.6 Template for Adjusting Difficulty.

Essential Characteristics of an Engaging Task

The last key idea for this chapter has to do with the nature or characteristics of the task. Yes, the tasks should be rigorous. And, yes, the tasks should adjust to offer all learners access to the highest level of complexity. However, these two previous ideas assume a motivated learner. In other words, how do we ensure that the task we design is one that learners will engage in during the learning experience?

What separates an engaging and rigorous task from one that learners are simply not motivated or interested in tackling is the nature of the engagement required to complete the task. Tasks that learners fail to see the value in often ask learners to simply repeat terms, concepts, ideas, procedures, or processes. In other words, finding the right level of difficulty and challenge must be followed up by finding the right level of engagement - not boredom. In 2015, Antonetti and Garver reported on data from more than 17,000 classroom walk-throughs and identified eight features of classroom tasks that differentiated those tasks that fostered, nurtured, and sustained student engagement from those that did not capture learners' attention. Let's look at these eight characteristics and use them as checks and balances for our own tasks.

Clear and Modeled Expectations. Do learners have a clear understanding of what they are supposed to know, understand, and be able to do? This characteristic refers us back to clear learning intentions, success criteria, learning progressions, exemplars, models, and examples. Do your learners know what success looks like, or are they blindly hoping to hit the end target that you have in mind for them?

Emotional Safety. Do learners feel safe in asking questions, making mistakes, or trying things out in the task? To be blunt, if learners feel threatened in our classrooms, they will not engage in any task. Preservation of self takes precedence over the completion of a task. This often shows up as disruptive behavior or apathy. If we truly have an inclusive learning environment, this particular feature of our tasks is present every time.

Personal Response. Do learners have the opportunity to bring their own personal experiences to the learning experience? Examples include any strategy or learning experience that invites learners to bring their own backgrounds, interests, or expertise to the conversation. This might be an activity that provides learners with the option to create their own analogies or metaphors, allowing learners to select how they will share their responses to a question (e.g., writing, drawing, speaking), or letting learners select the context in which a concept is explored (e.g., allowing learners to select a specific book or create their own problem). These examples have one thing in common: They allow learners to personalize their responses to meet their backgrounds, interests, or expertise.

Sense of Audience. Do learners have a sense that this work matters to someone other than the teacher and the grade book? This is much easier to accomplish in early childhood but is still something to be aware of when designing tasks. Tasks that give learners a sense of audience are those tasks that mean something to individuals beyond the teacher, and these tasks provide authenticity. A sense of audience can be established by cooperative learning or group work where individual members have specific roles, as in a jigsaw activity. Other examples include community-based projects or service projects that contribute to the local, school, or classroom community (e.g., conservation projects). As we recall our driving questions from Chapter 3, they naturally incorporate a sense of audience.

Social Interaction. Do learners have opportunities to socially interact with their peers? How about us? Providing learners with opportunities to talk about their learning and interact with their peers supports their meaning making and development of conceptual understanding. In addition, teachers and learners get to hear other students' ideas. Learning is social, and a quiet classroom stifles the social aspect of teaching and learning. Our tasks should provide multiple opportunities for learners to talk out ideas and exchange those ideas with peers. Academic discourse improves language and communication skills, along with understanding.

Choice. Do learners have choices in how they access the learning? As learners engage with content, skills, and understandings, we should offer choices around who they work with, what materials and manipulatives are available, and what approaches to learning they can use to move their learning forward. In addition, we should offer them multiple ways to show us their knowledge, skills, and understandings.

Novelty. Do learners experience the learning from a new or unique perspective? How can we present content in a way that captures their attention? Returning to our driving questions, how do we use a similar approach to provide learners with different perspectives that are different from their own? Having learners assume roles is one way to approach this particular characteristic of an engaging task. Getting the chance to be a scientist, doctor, botanist, veterinarian, environmental engineer, ice-cream maker, etc., can go a long way in fostering, nurturing, and sustaining engagement.

Authenticity. Do learners experience an authentic learning experience, or is the experience sterile and unrealistic (e.g., a worksheet versus a problem-solving scenario)? Authenticity simply means that the task reflects something that could or does happen in the world outside of the classroom. For example, growing a class garden (needs of living things), raising baby chickens (similarities and differences between adult animals and their young), creating a butterfly garden (insects), and building a boat to hold the greatest number of pennies (sinking and floating).

Opportunities for Reflective Practices

Take a moment and develop examples for each of the eight characteristics. How can we ensure that our rigorous tasks are ones that learners will engage in during the learning experience?

Ms. Lamb recognizes that engagement in rigorous tasks is essential if those tasks are to result in moving learning forward. "When I plan my tasks, I use the eight characteristics to ensure that the tasks are both rigorous and engaging. You can see I have almost all eight of these characteristics in my small and large group activities (Figure 7.7)."

Small group activities (planned)

- Bug Memory Match
- Building Bug Traps(daily thoughout entire unit)
- Drawing past experiences with insects/bugs
- Dissecting investigation
- Observations of live grasshoppers and crickets
- Creating 3D bugs with clay and collected items
- Investigating insects with microscope
- Drawing and labeling parts of an insect
- Compare and contrasting activity-chart/venn diagram/graph
- Picture match/identify
- Life cycle paper plate sequencing project
- Insect homes and habitats small group book reading
- Sort and classify bugs and insects

*Additional small group activities may be added depending on child interest and prior knowledge

Large group activities (planned)

- KWL Chart
- Read alouds daily with question and answer time (Vocabulary enrichment)
- What's missing? Insect identification and memory recall
- Moving and Learning-moving like insects
- Bug hunt outside (groups of 3 then whole group review)
- Which insect am I? clue game
- Draw a bug rhyme
- Insect sounds on cd- listen and identify
- Life cycle retelling/acting out

*Additional Large group activities may be added depending on child interest and prior knowledge

Figure 7.7 Small-Group and Large-Group Tasks.

Table 7.2 Planning for Task Materials

Materials Needed *List all materials that will be needed to teach this lesson.* *Who will be responsible for securing each item?*	
Materials	*Who is responsible for securing these materials?*

"There are times when I find learners drifting or not necessarily thrilled about a particular task. Almost every time I am missing one or more of these characteristics. Now, don't get me wrong. I don't include all 8 in every task."

Ms. Lamb is pointing out one of the most fascinating findings from Antonetti and Garver's (2015) research. To feel compelled to include all eight in every task is just as daunting as feeling compelled to design 26 different tasks for 26 different learners to truly be inclusive. Both of these are unrealistic. Antonetti and Garver (2015) found that when a task contained at least three of these characteristics, there was approximately 87% sustained engagement. When there were only two characteristics, there was approximately 17% sustained engagement. If only one was present, there was 0% (Antonetti & Garver, 2015). The rule is three or more.

As Ms. Lamb and the others plan out their tasks, they, of course, use the template in Appendix B to ensure they have what they need to implement these tasks (Table 7.2).

Task Design in Inclusive Early Childhood Science Teaching and Learning

The theme across the last several chapters is that our decisions about teaching and learning lay the foundation for including all learners in high-quality, high-impact science learning in the early childhood classroom. Task design is no different. Ensuring that our tasks evoke learners to actively engage in the experience, challenge them to operate at the highest level of complexity, and sustain that engagement depends on how we design our tasks. The task is where the rubber meets the road, per se. We can have amazing learning intentions and success criteria. We can have initial assessments that tell us where our learners are in the learning progression. We can even have a model of instruction that aligns with our expectations. However, if we fail to plan, design, and implement learning tasks that are rigorous and engaging, learning will not move forward.

Now, we also have to acknowledge that not everything will run as planned (Table 7.3). So, we have to think ahead about where we may need to make immediate and just-in-time adjustments.

And even then, we can expect the unexpected. The good news is that preparation lessens the disruption.

Table 7.3 What Could Go Wrong During the Learning Experience?

What Could Go Wrong with This Lesson and What Will You Do About It? *Think about this! It may help you avoid an embarrassing situation. This cannot include fire drills, interruptions due to announcements, weather, or other emergencies.*

As we close out our work on task design, we want to look ahead at what comes next. During the learning experience, while learners are deeply engaged in the learning tasks, we have to notice what they are saying and doing. Because, at the end of the task, the closing of the learning experience, the evidence collected from learners' artifacts and assessments of, for, and as learning allows us to evaluate our teaching by assessing their learning. Then we engage in this whole process again. Learning is a process.

Professional Learning Tasks

1. Returning to the science standard of learning you are unpacking based on your learning progression, learning intentions, and success criteria. Design rigorous and engaging tasks that embed three or more of the characteristics from Antonetti and Garver (2015).
2. Select one of your learning tasks and adjust the level of difficulty so that all learners in your current classroom can engage at the highest level of complexity. If you do not have your own classroom yet, consider scenarios where you would be compelled to adjust the level of difficulty.
3. Adjusting complexity and difficulty are approaches to differentiating instruction. Research other perspectives on differentiation. Then describe how you will approach inclusion through differentiation in your future or current classroom.
4. Appendix H contains a tool that allows you to analyze a task you have designed for your learners. The elements of this tool promote a thorough analysis of the characteristics of the task to ensure that the task is aligned, rigorous, and inclusive. Setting aside time for this thorough analysis will help you make adjustments to tasks when they are not aligned, not the appropriate level of rigor, or do not engage all of your learners. Select an upcoming task or one that you have already implemented and complete the "Assignment Analysis Task."

Family and Community Engagement

Parents, guardians, and family members have very different levels of availability to engage with their children's schools and classrooms. This absolutely should not be used for or against any individual. Parents or guardians may have work schedules that prevent them from devoting more than an hour of their time to volunteering in our classrooms. Other parents and guardians may find that they have several hours per week to lend a hand. Again, this absolutely should not be judged or have any influence on our perceptions of their children and home life. Instead, ensure that there is an open invitation for families and the community to engage in the teaching and learning of science in the inclusive early childhood classroom.

In this chapter, we will look at opportunities for parents and guardians who have more time during the week to engage with us. In the next chapter, we will look at opportunities for parents and guardians who have less time available during the traditional workday or workweek.

1. **Regular classroom support:** In the early childhood classroom, we can often use an extra set of hands for science demonstrations, experiments, and other tasks that might get a bit messy. In addition, the extra set of hands can often give us opportunities to support learners in small-group or one-on-one instruction. Now, remember, you are the highly trained professional. You are the one who must provide the specialized instructional support to learners. This extra set of hands should be used to help facilitate learning, not distribute teaching responsibilities. Take advantage of digital platforms for recruiting and securing class parents or guardians. For example, there are several online scheduling apps that allow family members to simply sign up for as much time as they are willing to share with you and your learners.
2. **Organize and support after-school opportunities:** The school day goes beyond dismissal for many of our students. Parents and guardians who have several hours per week to volunteer at school may want to engage in science learning by supporting and organizing after-school opportunities. There are so many ways to engage learners in science experiences outside of the traditional school day. Refer back to your family questionnaire generated in an early chapter. Using the strengths and interests of the adults who have ties to your classroom may allow you to form a science club, offer after-school science experiences, or support literacy in the content areas by creating a science reading club.

   Our role as teachers is to ensure that the after-school opportunities are aligned with the content, practices, and understandings that learners have experienced in the classroom or will experience in an upcoming unit. In the next chapter, we will generate ideas for finding the funding necessary to purchase the resources needed to support after-school opportunities. For now, take advantage of Facebook, Twitter, Instagram, your website, and newsletters to seek and secure volunteers to take on these after-school opportunities.
3. **Help produce school newsletters and other community outreach materials:** Over the past several chapters, we have looked at ways to engage families and communities through social media, newsletters, daily folders, and other resources. You may have felt a twinge of anxiety about the time needed to pull this off. That is both a fair and real concern. For parents and guardians who have time to engage in our classrooms on a regular basis, they can help here. When parents and guardians have regular contact with our students and become regulars in our classroom, they are able to see the "big picture" of our inclusive early childhood science classroom. They can then help post on social media, construct newsletters, check daily folders and stuff daily folders to go home with students, and compile resources that support science learning. For example, if you are providing non-fiction science texts for learners to read, have a volunteer compile those resources and place them in learners' backpacks to go home.

Again, this still calls for us to oversee the process and ensure that the materials are developmentally appropriate and align with the science content, practices, and understandings we are learning in the classroom.

8 Implementing Daily Learning Experiences

Assessment of Learning

Over the past several chapters, we have designed a daily learning experience through the selection of a well-aligned model of instruction, monitored through multiple checks for understanding, and supported by rigorous and engaging tasks. This combination of evidence-based practices has provided equity in access and opportunity for all students to make learning gains in our inclusive early childhood classroom. Although we used checks for understanding as a means for monitoring student progress toward the learning intention and success criteria, we must also devote time after the teaching and learning experience to further explore student learning. After the teaching and learning experience, we have to evaluate the learning to make decisions about where to go next or how we might need a different approach to the content, skills, and understandings. This is the assessment of learning introduced in Chapter 6, alongside assessment as and for learning. To do this, we will work through a reflective practice, based on evidence gathered during the learning experience and analyzed through a process of self-reflection and self-evaluation. This reflective practice will support us in noticing where our learners are now and what is the next step in their learning journey. Another way to think about this is with two driving questions (adapted from Fisher, Frey, Almarode, Flores, & Nagel, 2020):

1. What did we learn today?
2. Who benefited and who did not benefit from today's learning experience?

Before we move into the assessment of learning, we want to first turn our attention to the purpose of this approach and the why behind reflective practice. After all, if our learners seemed to do well during the day, why can't we just move on? All of the tasks went well and without a problem, what else is there to consider? The answer to this last question is learning. We have to consider student learning.

The entire premise of this book, introduced in the very opening pages, is that "our role is to work alongside these young learners to activate, guide, and support the actualization of this potential (p. 1)." This potential and actualization is represented by the learning outcomes across each of the learning domains in inclusive early childhood teaching and learning (i.e., cognitive, social-emotional, psychomotor, and behavioral). Therefore, the assessment of learning through reflective practice provides us with valuable information about the decisions we made in planning, designing, and implementing daily learning experiences. Did we make decisions that resulted in all students learning? If not, what are we going to do differently the next time? Did our decisions result in student learning for some learners but not all? If not, what are we going to do differently for those learners the next time? High-quality, high-impact teaching results in student learning. The assessment of learning helps us see this effect and make changes to ensure that we continuously activate, guide, and support the actualization of our learners' potential.

Quality Teaching in Inclusive Early Childhood Science

There are many different answers to the question, what is quality teaching? Although there is a large body of work on teacher evaluation (e.g., Darling-Hammond & Youngs, 2002; Lin et al., 2020), we want to look at how we engage in reflective practice rather than move beyond the scope of this book and look at teacher evaluation as a broader area with teaching and learning in the inclusive early childhood classroom. So what is quality teaching?

> **Opportunities for Reflective Practices**
>
> What is quality teaching? Summarize your own definition or conditions for quality teaching.

Research Viviane Robinson (2011) looked at how this exact question challenges our current view of how we should assess the quality of teaching. For example, quality is often assessed based on our teaching style. If our classrooms look and sound like we want them to, we are engaged in high-impact, high-quality inclusive early childhood science teaching. But what happens if our students don't meet achievement benchmarks? Well, in that case, we should use achievement data or benchmark data to determine the quality of the teaching. Thus if our learners meet the predetermined academic achievement or benchmark levels, then we engaged in high-impact, high-quality inclusive early childhood science teaching. Yet this still leaves unanswered questions, especially with regard to inclusive settings. If we are to ensure that all learners are active participants in the learning, are valued, and their contributions recognized as vital for the success of the entire community, then we have to also acknowledge that each learner is not starting from the same location in the learning. This should be obvious from the evidence generated by the initial assessments discussed in Chapter 3 and the discussion of the SOLO Taxonomy in Chapter 2. If we use academic achievement or benchmark levels as the standard for quality teaching, we ignore the unique identities of all students and their learning growth in our classrooms.

> **Research to Classroom Practice Tasks**
>
> What does the research say is "quality teaching"? Perform a miniature literature search and summarize what you find about the knowledge and skills of high-quality, high-impact teachers.

Quality teaching should be defined by the growth in our learners as a result of the access and opportunities we provide for their learning to occur. The access and opportunities for learning were explored in the previous chapter on task development. Here we are evaluating the growth in student learning as a result of that access and those opportunities. Did we provide the support and scaffolds so that each individual has the access and opportunity for successful learning growth? This brings us to the key focus of this chapter. We will take the evidence gathered from our initial assessments, checks for understanding, and artifacts generated from the daily learning experience to engage in reflective practice to make sense of our learners' growth, or lack of growth, and plan our next steps in planning, designing, and implementing daily learning experiences.

Using Data as Evidence of Learners' Growth

Each question, conversation, check for understanding, or artifact from any learning experience is data about learners' knowledge, skills, and understandings. This means we could easily get overwhelmed by the amount of data in any given learning experience. Furthermore, having a lot of data provides zero benefit if we do not know what to do with that data. Therefore, to initiate our reflective practice, we are best served by going back to the learning intentions and success criteria for the particular learning experience (Figure 8.1).

The learning intentions and success criteria, just as they guided our learners to know where to direct their energies in the learning experience, help us know where to direct our focus within the data.

> **Opportunities for Reflective Practices**
>
> How do you use data as evidence of student learning? What processes do you use in your school or classroom, or what processes have you observed in schools and classrooms?

Figure 8.1 Reflective Practice and the Assessment of Learning.

Mr. Reinhart devotes significant time to looking at his students' work.

> Before I do though, I pull up my big ideas, driving question, learning intentions, and success criteria to ensure I stay focused on exactly what it is I wanted my students to learn and what success looked like for this particular day or lesson. This keeps me focused and avoids me noticing things that may need to be a focus in the future but were not the focus for today.

What Mr. Reinhart is doing is ensuring that he keeps his focus on the target. If learners are supposed to learn that there are similarities and differences between animals and their young, he does not want to get sidetracked or distracted by learners' handwriting or spelling. Although handwriting is important, "If I get distracted and begin analyzing their handwriting and spelling, I will not use my planning time to see if learners have met the learning intention."

Mr. Reinhart then pulls the evidence he has gathered from the learning experience and aligns this evidence with specific learning intentions and success criteria. We likely notice that this aligning of evidence with specific learning intentions and success criteria takes us back to Chapter 6. As you recall from Chapter 6, we spent time planning the evidence we were going to collect to inform us about students' progress toward each learning intention and success criteria. This part of the process for evaluating learning simply looks back at this planning as a reminder of where we will look to find evidence of learners' growth. "For me, it is easier for me to simply list beside each of my learning intentions and success criteria the evidence I have available to me. What I find out, often unexpectedly, is that I do not have the evidence I thought I had for some of my learning intentions and success criteria." In this situation, Mr. Reinhart may have planned to gather evidence about a specific success criterion only to find that once in the learning experience, this may not have occurred the way he had planned for it to occur.

Using the template in Appendix C, we can record our self-reflection and self-evaluation so that the information is available as we move forward with the next steps. Specifically, questions VI and VII. Mr. Reinhart

> makes a note that I need to double-check and ensure that I have the evidence I need tomorrow. I simply make a note that tells me to verify LI, SC, and evidence alignment. Without this data, I cannot make the best decisions about tomorrow and beyond. I am missing evidence for one of my success criteria because I underestimated the time for one of my tasks and we did not get to everything today. So, I will have to gather that evidence tomorrow.

Reflective Questions

VI. As a result of planning and teaching this lesson, what have I learned or had reinforced about teaching?

VII. As a result of planning and teaching this lesson, what have I learned or had reinforced about myself?

As one final preparation before Mr. Reinhart looks closely at student work, he looks to see if he made any just-in-time adjustments to the lesson that were not necessarily included in the original plan (i.e., the aforementioned time situation). "This simply reminds me that I made an immediate change to the lesson progression because of something that happened in the moment. Oftentimes this is because learners say or do something that indicates I need to rethink how we are engaging in the learning experience. In any event, pulling that information out during my reflection reminds me to check and see if just-in-time adjustments affected my students' learning.

Reflective Questions

I. How did my actual teaching of the lesson differ from my plans? Why, specifically, did I make those changes?

The next part of the process is making sense of what the evidence tells us about our learners' knowledge, skills, and understandings.

Student Work Analysis

Artifacts are generated from our tasks and checks for understanding, and they provide evidence of learners' growth. Ms. Rogers uses both artifacts and checks for understanding to gain insight into her learners' thinking about sinking and floating.

> I really want to know where they are in their thinking. So, I listen to their conversations, ask questions, take pictures, and collect and gather items they produce at each center. These are invaluable to me as I take notice of how they are developing understanding about concepts and the use of specific skills.

Collecting and gathering artifacts and evidence is only part of student work analysis. We have to use them to gain understanding about student learning. By analyzing what learners say and do in these artifacts, we can gain insight into their thinking and where they are on the learning progression. In the end, this allows us to make decisions about where to go next in our teaching and their learning. These decisions are directly derived from the structure of observed learning outcomes or the SOLO Taxonomy. As Ms. Rogers has pointed out, this requires us to notice. Notice, in this situation, is more than just an observation.

Noticing. Teacher noticing is a specific skill in teaching and learning that has received a lot of attention over the past several years (see Sherin, Jacobs, & Philipp, 2011) as we have continued to try and understand what separates an expert teacher from his or her colleagues. Let's look at comments made by learners in Ms. Roger's classroom during the exploration of sinking and floating.

Big or heavy things sink.
Small or light things float.
Hollow things float.
Things with air float.
Things with holes sink.
Flat things float.
The sharp edge of an object makes it sink.
Vertical things sink.
Horizontal things float.
Source: Yin, Tomita, & Shavelson, 2008

These are all misconceptions about sinking and floating. In fact, you likely read through this list and immediately recognized that these statements were not accurate. In addition to these statements made by her learners, Ms. Rogers has drawings and sorting tasks to accompany the conversations, comments, and observations made by her learners. To truly evaluate the learning in her classroom, she has to move beyond collecting and gathering and actively seek to understand what the evidence says about her learners' content, skills, and understandings of sinking and floating. In other words, looking at artifacts and checks for understanding is not enough. What do we do about misconceptions? What do we do if learners have not progressed toward the learning intention and success criteria yet? Enter teacher noticing.

Research to Classroom Practice Tasks

Before engaging in the analysis of student work, research the possible misconceptions that young learners may have about the content, skills, and understandings associated with the topic. Ensure these are readily available as you move forward in evaluating learning.

Teacher noticing (Figure 8.2) is made up of three specific components: (1) attending to what is happening in our classrooms and with our learners, (2) analyzing what we see, and (3) deciding how to respond (Jacobs, Lamb, Philipp, & Schappelle, 2011). Ms. Rogers must not only attend to what her learners are saying and doing, but she must also analyze this evidence to make meaning or make sense of her learners' knowledge, skills, and understandings of sinking and floating. Then, use this assessment of learning to decide what to do next.

Like Mr. Reinhart, Ms. Rogers has already revisited her big ideas, driving questions, learning intentions, and success criteria. She quickly aligned her artifacts and checks for understanding

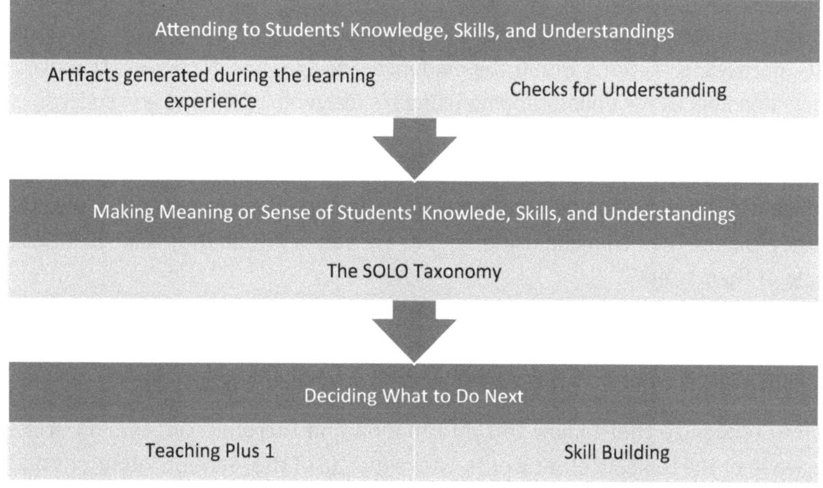

Figure 8.2 Teacher Noticing in the Inclusive Early Childhood Science Classroom.

to gauge whether she has the evidence she needs to figure out where her learners are in the learning progression. Now, she must engage in the process of teacher noticing.

An important point to note here is that teacher noticing is not an isolated task that is set aside for a discrete block of time. Ms. Rogers did not announce to her colleagues that they would be engaging in teacher noticing at 3:15 p.m. today. Instead, teacher noticing is an organic and continuous process that happens naturally for some of us and requires more deliberate focus for others. For example, Frederick Erickson (2011) notes that experienced teachers who have engaged in teacher noticing by continuously scanning student thinking and doing were able to triage what needed the most immediate response, were less distracted by learners who were simply compliant and well behaved but not demonstrating understanding, and were able to place what they noticed within the context of each individual learners' story. In other words, experienced teachers are always noticing. For those of us with less experience, we can build our teacher noticing skills through reflective practice and the assessment of learning (Santagata, 2011). That is exactly what we are doing right now and why we are using self-reflection and self-evaluating questions and structures in our assessment of learning. Overtime, and with practice, we will begin to engage in teacher noticing through a more organic and continuous process that happens naturally in our classrooms, collaborative planning meetings, grade-level meetings, and professional learning communities (PLCs). Let's look at each of the three aspects of teaching noticing and how this skill is both enhances and moves us through reflective practice and the assessment of learning.

Opportunities for Reflective Practices

Summarize the concept of teacher noticing. How would you self-evaluate your own ability to engage in teacher noticing? What challenges do you see with teacher noticing in your own classroom or future classroom?

Attending to Students' Knowledge, Skills, and Understandings. When attending to what our students have demonstrated that they know, understand, and are able to do, we must extract this evidence from the artifacts and checks for understanding. This requires us to look for specific words, phrases, or actions within the evidence. For example, Mr. Reinhart moves through the artifacts and checks for understanding using his learning intentions and success criteria as a reference point (Figure 8.3).

What do the artifacts and checks for understanding tell him? Can his learners identify how an adult animal is the same as and different from its young? Can his learners record their thinking? Can they explain their thinking using science vocabulary? Can they ask questions to clarify the thinking of their peers?

To use the evidence generated by the artifacts and checks for understanding, Mr. Reinhart has to combine his own expertise in this topic with his ability to see learning through the eyes of his students. This is what makes teacher noticing so challenging.

> I have to recognize that I know this information and therefore am coming at it from the expert side of the topic. In other words, I have met all of the learning intentions and success criteria, right? Otherwise, I should not be teaching it. What I have to do now is put myself in their shoes and interpret their responses as if I were just learning this for the first time.

Learning Intentions: What are we learning today? Why are we learning it? What will this help me to do?	Success Criteria: How will we know we are successful?
Content Learning Intention: I am learning about the similarities and differences between animals and their young (Disciplinary Core Ideas). Social-Emotional Learning Intention: I am learning that scientists work together to make observations (Science and Engineering Practices). Psychomotor Learning Intention: I am learning that scientist record observations as evidence so they can go back and find patterns (writing or illustrating). Behavioral Learning Intention: I am learning how active listening is a way to show respect for my peers (Character Education).	1. I can identify how an adult animal is the same as and different from its young (Content). 2. I can record my thinking (Psychomotor). 3. I can explain my thinking using my science words (Behavioral). 4. I can ask questions to better understand what others are thinking (Social-Emotional).

Figure 8.3 Mr. Reinhart's Learning Intentions and Success Criteria.

One learner in Mr. Reinhart's class decided to look at "baby frogs" and "adult frogs" as their example of adult and young animals. In this learner's interactive notebook, he kept mentioning the "little fish" and the "big frog." To an expert biologist, this would immediately be flagged as wrong and, quite likely, be classified as not making progress toward the learning intention and success criteria.

> Although Jacob's terminology is a not as precise as we would like it to be, he has demonstrated an awareness of a significant change in amphibians that is not there with mammals. For this learner, he gets the concept but needs additional support with his science terminology.

The need to see learning from the student's perspective was observed a second time in Mr. Reinhart's exploration of the artifacts and checks for understanding.

> "I had a learner that wrote in their interactive notebook that birds and reptiles were the same. This baffled me. There was no additional explanation, just that sentence. I could not figure out what this student was trying to say."

Rather than jumping to conclusions, Mr. Reinhart recognized that there was not enough evidence, and he needed to clarify this learner's thinking. "I know that this is new learning for them and I make every attempt to see this content through their eyes. In this case, I need more information." The next day, Mr. Reinhart engaged this learner in a one-on-one conference to get her to explain her thinking. What he discovered was that this learning had identified that both birds and reptiles lay eggs that hatch their young. This, of course, is an accurate conclusion. "I then asked Sherri to draw her thinking and then helped her form a sentence to explain her drawing. As it turns out, she had a clear understanding of the content. She needed additional support in explaining her thinking."

Opportunities for Reflective Practices

What additional professional learning might you need to ensure that you have the necessary content knowledge to successfully attend to students' knowledge, skills, and understandings? How difficult do you or will you find it to look at learning through the eyes of your students?

Mr. Reinhart documents his attending to students' knowledge, skills, and understandings in the organizer shown in Figure 8.4. This template is available in Appendix C.

Student Work Analysis.

I. Student Work Sample Analysis: Based on the artifacts and checks for understanding, what can you conclude about your students' learning? Did they learn? Who learned? What did they learn? What evidence can you offer that your conclusions are valid?

Look at the assessment data and identify who appears to fall into these 3 categories: (1) Gets it; (2) Has some good ideas, but there's still room for learning and (3) Does not get it, yet. Organize your responses to the following questions in a chart/table form similar to the one below.

	Gets It.	Has some good ideas, but…	Does not get it, yet.
a. What do they understand? How do you know?			
b. Where do they still need support? How do you know?			
c. What questions do I need to ask to clarify what is known and/understood?			

Figure 8.4 Student Work Analysis.

Making Meaning or Sense of Students' Knowledge, Skills, or Understandings. To make meaning of what students know, understand, and are able to do, we must revisit the SOLO Taxonomy. Looking back to Chapter 2, we need to revisit the original study by Biggs and Collis (1982).

> **Opportunities for Reflective Practices**
>
> Pause in your reading and return to Chapter 2. Take a few moments and review the SOLO Taxonomy. This will be helpful as we move forward here.

These two researchers looked at work samples and across several disciplines, such as mathematics, English, and geography (Biggs & Collis, 1982; Kirby & Biggs, 1981). Looking at student work generated during learning experiences, they identified five distinct patterns that later became known as the five components of the SOLO Taxonomy. As Ms. Shay points out,

> There are some of my learners that were unable to focus on the relevant knowledge, skills, and understandings about habitats. Several of them focused on irrelevant facts, concepts, or ideas such as colors and whether or not they would live there.

Some of Ms. Shay's learners focused on a single idea or one relevant aspect of the content, omitting key details in their responses.

> These learners were able to identify one thing really well. For example, they focused on one aspect of the habitat like shelter and did not recognize the other needs of living things. While a group of my learners included several pieces of information but have not yet arrived at the broader understanding of habitats expected in the learning intentions.

Some of her students were able to identify relationships between the facts, concepts, or ideas, moving beyond simply listing discrete pieces of information. "I do have a group of learners that applied the concepts and thinking to other content. For example, how zoos must replicate habitats in order for animals to survive outside of their natural habitat."

> **Opportunities for Reflective Practices**
>
> Using the current topic or content you are teaching or will be teaching in the very near future, determine a set of look-fors at each level of the SOLO Taxonomy. For example, what would a learner know, understand, and be able to do at the prestructural, unistructural, multistructural, relational, and extended abstract levels?

Ms. Shay arrived at this point in her assessment of learning by organizing student responses into the same five categories discovered by Biggs and Collis (1982). "I make sure that I devote time to making sense of my learners progress by organizing their thinking into the SOLO categories so that I can be intentional about where go next with the learning." Ms. Shay uses the template in Figure 8.5 to organize her sense making of student thinking. This is also available in Appendix C.

Deciding What to Do Next. After we have attended to and made meaning of learners' knowledge, skills, and understandings, we have to decide where to go next. This is the third

- Where is each student's learning within the framework of the SOLO Taxonomy? What evidence do you have to support your answer? Please provide student work samples.
- What ideas does each student need to work on next?

	Evidence from Artifacts or Checks for Understanding
Prestructural Thinking	
Unistructural Thinking	
Multistructural Thinking	
Relational Thinking	
Extended Abstract Thinking	

Figure 8.5 Student Work Analysis Reflection.

component of teacher noticing. In other words, in the assessment of learning, the evidence is only as useful if we let that evidence inform our decision making about the next learning experiences for our students. Again, making sense of learners where they are in their progression toward the learning intention and success criteria should also compel us to use this information to establish a level of challenge that will then move them forward. That is the essence of where to next. From the perspective of the SOLO Taxonomy, Biggs and Collis (1982) uncovered an effective and efficient way of thinking about "the next." Developmentally appropriate next steps for learners is teaching one step beyond the learner's current level on the SOLO, also known as the "plus one rule" (Biggs and Collis, 1982; Figure 8.6).

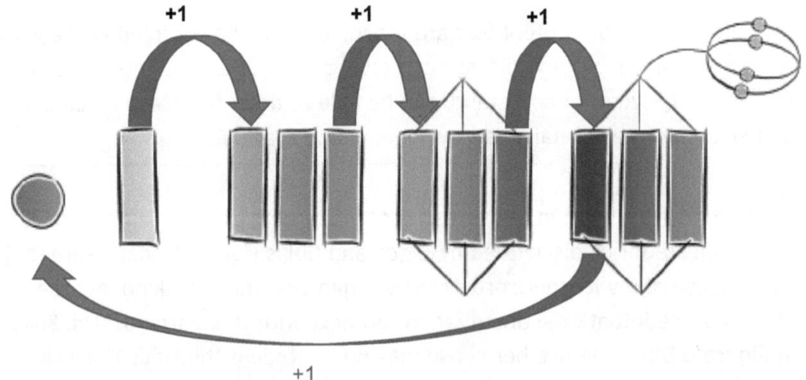

Figure 8.6 The Plus One Rule of the Structure of Observed Learning Outcomes.
Source: https://pamhook.com/2012/01/20/creating-solo-taxonomy-symbols-in-many-colours/

Where to next should include an appropriate level of challenge, which Biggs and Collis (1982) found to be plus 1 from their current level thinking. Ms. Cornish points out that

> this is so helpful in making sure I am focused on 'what to do next' really means. Oftentimes, what to do next means to move to the next topic in the pacing guide or the next page in the planner. With the SOLO, I now might be supporting learners as they identify and understand relationships in our learning about living things. Other learners are working on applying their thinking to new contexts or situations. Then, for others, I might need to engage in small-group instruction for learners that are still working on the foundation of the needs of living things. This keeps me from moving too fast or too far for my learners, but creating the right level of challenge.

The real reward comes when our learners are successful in putting forth the effort to meet the challenge.

> If the activity or task is overwhelmingly difficult (i.e., greater than plus 1), learners most likely will not put forth the effort to complete the task because they recognize they do not have the necessary knowledge, skills, and understandings, yet.

Opportunities for Reflective Practices

What is the plus 1 rule? What would this look like in your current classroom or future classroom for a specific topic?

Ms. Cornish is pointing out the value of using SOLO Taxonomy in moving learning forward. Oftentimes, in our classrooms, we believe moving forward involves going on to the next thing. In some situations, we recognize learners "don't quite get it" but are not clear on what to do about them not "getting it." By using the plus 1 rule, we can resist the belief that moving on to the next topic is the only option for what to do next.

If learners are working at the prestructural level, we should direct our focus toward moving them to the unistructural level. If they are working at the unistructural level, we should aim for the multistructural level, multistructural to relational, relational to extended abstract. We may find that we have to engage our learners in skill building around psychomotor learning outcomes, provide supports for behavioral learning outcomes, implement enrichment tasks for cognitive learning outcomes, and/or further instruction for social-emotional outcomes.

The SOLO Taxonomy provides scaffolding for us as inclusive early childhood science teachers, guiding our assessment of learning in a meaningful way. The possibilities of teaching and learning based on the nature of learners' thinking rather than on the "ability levels" of learners provide us with a way to think about how to facilitate the next steps in our learners' progression toward learning intentions and success criteria across all domains. Learners experience natural ways to extend their understanding through intentional opportunities to connect new information with prior understanding. This allows for a truly inclusive learning environment – focused on thinking, not demographics. Shifting the lens from what a learner can or cannot do to the place on the SOLO Taxonomy where that learner's prior experiences and opportunities provide the groundwork for moving forward – deciding what to do next

- demands that we see each learner as an active participant, valued by the community, and with the potential for successful learning.

Ms. Cornish uses the following template to organize her thinking around what to do next. This is also available in Appendix C.

Reflecting on What to Do Next

II. Describe how you will incorporate developmentally appropriate practice in a better or more thorough way if you were to teach this lesson again.
III. Based on the assessment data you collected, what would you do/teach next if you were the classroom teacher?

The Value of Evidence

There are challenges we often encounter in our self-reflection and self-evaluation. Those challenges have to do with the following:

- Why am I spending time on this process?
- What data is relevant to the conversation?
- Where do I get data?
- When do dig into my data?
- How do I interpret my data?

Moving through the process depicted in Figure 8.1 provides several benefits in the assessment of learning by highlighting the value of the evidence. Let's look at each of these five challenges and how the process for using data as evidence of growth addresses each of these challenges.

Along with many of our colleagues, we may not see the relevance of this aspect of teaching and learning. Ms. Campbell identified this challenge early in her career.

> I was not sure why my team and I had to devote so much time to this process. After all, they either did or did not do well at the centers and that is clear from their interactive notebooks. I was not sure what to analyze.

This is not a unique stance and represents a disconnect between data and how that data can and should inform our next instructional decision. This process begins with big ideas, driving question, learning intentions, and success criteria so that the connection between what we want our students to learn and the information in front of us is explicit. What exactly are we looking for in this evidence? This is similar to Mr. Reinhart and his concern over what to focus on in this process. The difference is that Mr. Reinhart knew the relevance of this process before Ms. Campbell did.

> However, I discovered that there were things I did not know about my learners simply because my checks for understanding weren't enough. Early on, I walked away from this process with my own next steps for what type of data I needed to gather and analyze so that I felt more confident in my decisions about where to go next with my learners.

Another benefit to carefully engaging in self-reflection and self-evaluation has to do with evidence overload. By starting with the big ideas, driving question, learning intentions, and success criteria, we know what evidence is not relevant to the conversation and avoid evidence overload. We often arrive at collaborative planning or grade-level meetings with endless amounts of data. In the era of accountability, schools and classrooms collect a lot of data. Knowing what data to focus on as evidence of learning and what data to leave alone for this conversation really depends on those initial elements of our planning (Robinson, Phillips, & Timperley, 2002). Ms. Cornish points out

> Our school is in school improvement. As a result of this status, we had so much data that we were often overwhelmed by the quantity. In fact, there were times my colleagues and I were not sure what data to look through during a meeting. I am sorry to admit that many times we simply didn't use any data and drew from our past experiences.

To be clear, experience matters. However, evidence of learning allows us to be more precise, accurate, efficient, and effective in making decisions. The process in Figure 8.1 allows us to discern between data and evidence.

Ms. Shay notices

> I often struggled getting access to the evidence. There were many conversations where I found myself acknowledging that learners were not making progress. Then, when my colleagues and I looked for evidence to back support or refute my assessment, I didn't have access to the evidence.

By devoting time to aligning the evidence and then looking at what the evidence says about student learning, we are more likely to change our approach in planning for, collecting, and organizing evidence for learning. Knowing that we will always follow a learning experience with the self-reflection and self evaluation of evidence holds us personally accountable for ensuring that this important information is available (Park & Datnow, 2009).

> It did not take long for our team to change our conversations about evidence of learning. Once we saw the relevancy of this process and how the assessment of learning improved the growth of our students, we carved out time during our plan to think ahead and ensure we had a plan for collecting and organizing evidence. We are much more efficient and effective at incorporating this information into our decisions about where to go next.

The fourth challenge has to do with time. Although we may think that time refers to "when am I ever going to have time to do this?" That is not what we are talking about here. Yet let's address the previous question. The process of using data as evidence of growth has a powerful effect on student learning (Lee, Chung, Zhang, Abedi, & Warschauer, 2020). This impact alone should justify any amount of time devoted to this process. We also believe that when relevancy and accessibility are addressed, along with the capacity to make meaning of the data, the benefits will eliminate any concern over time.

However, this is not the time we are referring to in this fourth challenge. Time in this context refers to when we use the evidence. Many of our collaborative planning meetings, grade-level meetings, and/or PLCs focus so much on getting through a planning template or document provided by the school that we simply move through a series of steps to ensure all aspects of the template are complete. In fact, as Ms. Lamb points out, "We used to just look at the pacing guide and then plan the next day's learning experience. We did not work data into the conversation at all." This is what we mean by time, not knowing when to bring evidence of learners' growth into the conversation (Robinson, 2011). The answer to this question is simple, on the surface. Any time the conversation comes up about where we are going next, evidence from prior learning experiences must be in the conversation. Again, on the surface, that answer appears simple. However, keep in mind that where we are going next involves establishing and sharing learning intentions and success criteria, selecting the model of instruction, designing formative assessments, and creating tasks. To be clear, evidence should inform all aspects of our teaching and learning. When evidence indicates learners are growing, keep going. When evidence indicates learners are not growing, we should change what we are doing.

Finally, the last challenge has to do with our capacity to make meaning or make sense of the evidence (Robinson, 2011). To make meaning or make sense of the evidence requires us, as professionals, to have a clear understanding of the content, skills, and understandings. Each of the teachers we have highlighted in this book knew their subject matter just as well as they knew how to teach the content, skills, and understandings. For Ms. Rogers, she had to have a clear understanding of what factors influenced whether something would float. For Ms. Campbell, to make sense of students' responses from their centers, had to have a strong command of vibrations and sound. This content knowledge also requires us to know the possible misconceptions (see Chapter 6) that come into play, along with the developmental trajectory of learners' as they engage with this content, skills, and understandings. Ms. Rogers points out

> "Before I start a new unit, I do my own exploration of the topic. I read and experiment with things before I ever introduce the concepts to students. I make sure I find all of the possible misconceptions learners may have so that I can spot them in the evidence. I also try and break down the concept and skills so that I can identify what is missing that I can help them to fill in.

Opportunities for Reflective Practices

Take a moment and review these five challenges to self-reflection and self-evaluation. Do you see yourself in any of these scenarios? How has this information changed your thinking? What role will evidence play in your assessment of learning? Did we leave any challenges out?

Self-reflection and self-evaluation are not easy. This process requires that we open ourselves up to feedback and change. However, being aware of the challenges that come with this process allows us to engage in the process with a more critical eye. An eye that recognizes that we have come upon the challenge and, maybe this time, overcome it. Then and only then can we engage in the type of self-reflection and self-evaluation that truly focuses on evidence gathered during the learning experience and analyzed by noticing where our learners are now and what the next steps are in their learning journeys.

The template in Appendix C will help scaffold our journey through questions like the ones that follow.

Reflective Questions

Reflection

I. Describe at least one way you could incorporate developmentally appropriate practice in a better or more thorough way if you were to teach this lesson again.
II. Based on the assessment data you collected, what would you do/teach next if you were the classroom teacher?
III. As a result of planning and teaching this lesson, what have you learned or had reinforced about young children as learners?
IV. As a result of planning and teaching this lesson, what have you learned or had reinforced about teaching?
V. As a result of planning and teaching this lesson, what have you learned or had reinforced about yourself?

Professional Learning Tasks

1. Locate student work samples from your own classroom or samples from your own classes at your college or university. Complete the reflective practice and assessment of the learning process in Figure 8.1. Use the template in Appendix C to guide your thinking.
2. Using the student work analysis chart in Figure 8.3, where would you place the students or, if you are using your own work samples, where would you place your students? How would you respond to the student work analysis reflection questions in Figure 8.4?
3. What is the difference between data and evidence? Using the discussion from this chapter, what role does evidence play in high quality, high-impact teaching and learning in the inclusive early childhood science classroom?
4. Refer back to the start of this chapter and the question, who benefited and who did not benefit from my instruction? As you engage in the "Student Work Sample Analysis" in Appendix C, sort your learners into two groups: those who made progress toward the learning intentions and success criteria and those who did not make progress toward the learning intentions and success criteria. Looking closely at those who did not make progress, reflect on who these learners are. Do they share a common background or demographic characteristic? If so, this is an equity issue? For example, if all of these learners are classified as having a low socioeconomic background, what professional learning do you need to better meet their needs? What changes might you make in your teaching and learning to ensure that all learners make progress?

Family and Community Engagement

As we begin to close out our time together, although this does not signify the end of the work in providing an inclusive early childhood science learning environment, let's look at a few more strategies to promote family and community engagement. In Chapter 7, we looked at the ways that parents, guardians, and community members could engage during the day or week. This chapter looks at ways to engage across a longer time span - a month or over the course of the school year. Again, these are suggestions that can be offered to families and the community through social media, newsletters, and personal visits to homes and locally owned and operated businesses.

1. **Join the parent-teacher organization or association (PTO or PTA):** The PTA or PTO is a great way for families and the community to stay informed about school events and provide a support system to the school and teachers. If parents or guardians, due to work schedules or other obligations, cannot commit to time in the classroom during the day, the PTA/PTO is a more reasonable option. These meetings typically occur outside of the typical workday or school-day hours. During these meetings, families and community members can hear about the many ways to provide school and teacher support.

   As a teacher, attending these meetings allows you to have contact with parents, guardians, and community members. These points of contact provide opportunities to use many of the strategies from the previous chapters (e.g., talking to parents or guardians, sharing information about your classroom, highlighting the work of your students, identifying specific resources or needs in your classroom).

2. **School board or board of education meetings:** This one gets a bit interesting. Every school division or school district has an elected school board or board of education. This board includes local citizens who provide oversight and guidance to the school or schools. Meetings for the school board or board of education are held in the evenings and offer great insight into what is going on in the school division/district. The board's agenda will provide a specific time for public comment so that the ideas and opinions of families, communities, and school personnel can be heard. Parents and guardians can run for office and be on the school board.

   As mentioned before, as a teacher, attending these meetings allows you to have contact with parents, guardians, and community members.

3. **Serve as a chaperone for school events:** Remember the "Community Resource Task" in Appendix E? If any of those community resources call for a field trip, you will need "all hands on deck" for the trip. Speaking of school boards, policies developed and implemented by boards of education require a specific ratio of chaperones-to-children. A way to promote family and community engagement is to invite parents or guardians to go along! Of course, you ensure that the group of learners the chaperone is responsible for includes their own child. What a great way for parents and guardians to spend time "learning" with their children?

   This same idea applies to school events, such as field day, STEM Day, and the science fair. Use all available platforms (e.g., Facebook, Twitter, Instagram, daily folders, drop-off and pickup times) to seek and secure these important volunteers.

4. **Participate in a fundraising event:** School budgets are tight and show no sign of getting better. Fundraisers are quite common in schools. When there is a need for resources and supplies that the school budget does not cover or cannot afford, there are other ways to secure those funds. Bake sales, car washes, and silent auctions are regular events at most schools. What these fundraisers all have in common is that they need individuals and families to either help "sell" items or volunteer to help coordinate these events. When families and the communities participate in these events, these are just more opportunities to engage with them and let them experience the value you and your school add to the lives of their children.

Conclusion

Over the past eight chapters, we have engaged in the intentional, purposeful, and deliberate process for planning, developing, and implementing high-quality, high-impact inclusive early childhood science teaching and learning. Our decisions focused on three guiding beliefs:

1. Science is more than just facts. Instead, science is a set of processes and a specific way of thinking.
2. The teaching and learning of science are important and valuable in the learning trajectory of all young children. And this value includes cognitive, social-emotional, psychomotor, and behavioral outcomes.
3. Science teaching and learning in early childhood should be inclusive and strive to build and support assessment-capable visible science learners.

These beliefs provided the motivation to answer the why, what, how, who, and when of teaching and learning science in the early childhood classroom. These question words represent the five major areas in our task - to work alongside these young learners to activate, guide, and support the actualization of this potential.

To truly actualize the potential of every young learner in our classroom, we have to ensure that they are in an environment that actively engages all learners, welcomes and embraces every learner as an important member of the community, and provides the necessary support to all learners so that they have an equal opportunity for success. This means providing the necessary compensatory and adaptive approaches to ensure equity of access and opportunity to the highest level of complexity in science content, skills, and understandings.

As you read the final words in this book, recall the work we have done over the past eight chapters:

- Analyzing what to teach
- Mapping out the progression of what to teach
- Establishing and sharing daily learning intentions and success criteria
- Aligning an approach to teaching that maximizes learning
- Developing assessments of, for, and as learning
- Designing rigorous and engaging tasks
- Evaluating the learning to make decisions about where to go next or how we might need a different approach to the content, skills, and understandings.

Whether you are currently in a classroom and the work in this book is for your continued professional learning or you are preparing for your first classroom and the work in this book is part of your preparation, keep the main thing the main thing: student learning.

At the end of the day, there is a young child on the other side of every decision we make in our classrooms. That means, the decisions matter because they matter. That also means we matter as their teachers. If all learners in your current classroom or in your future classroom are better off at the end of the day than they were at the start of the day just because they spent time with you, congratulations. You have done your job. And so I close with this. I have two children of my own, Tessa and Jackson. And my hope for them is that they experience high-quality, high-impact teaching and learning in science. I believe the contents of this book give us the greatest probability for that to happen with all learners. Because of Tessa and Jackson, what you have experienced over these past eight chapters is not just an academic exercise. It's personal. They help me keep the main thing the main thing. My hope is that teaching and learning in the early childhood science classroom are personal for you as well.

Now, go teach!

Appendices

Appendix A
Unwrapping the Science Standards

Topic________________________

<table>
<tr><td>Grade Level:</td><td rowspan="2">Date:</td></tr>
<tr><td>Standard(s):</td></tr>
<tr><td colspan="2">Disciplinary Core Ideas:

Science and Engineering Practices:

Crosscutting Concepts:</td></tr>
<tr><td>CONCEPTS: (nouns)
•</td><td>SKILLS: (verbs)
•</td></tr>
<tr><td colspan="2">LEARNING PROGRESSION:</td></tr>
<tr><td colspan="2">BIG IDEAS:</td></tr>
<tr><td colspan="2">DRIVING QUESTIONS:</td></tr>
</table>

Appendix B

A. Learning Intentions and Success Criteria

Learning Intentions:	*Success Criteria:*
What are we learning today? Why are we learning it? What will this help me to do?	How will we know we are successful?
Content Learning Intention: Social-Emotional Learning Intention: Psychomotor Learning Intention: Behavioral Learning Intention:	

B. Monitoring Learning

Success Criteria	*Assessments of, for, and as Learning*	*Evidence*

C. Procedure

Activity Element and Time (in minutes)	**Procedures and Management** *Include step-by-step procedures, including questions and main points. Visualize what you are going to say to the students. It might be helpful to script out what you are going to say, although, during the lesson, you do not need to use this language verbatim.*	**Students** *Describe what the students will be doing as a result of your instructions.*
Engage – Introduction		
Event 1		
Transition		
Event 2		
Transition		
Event 3		
Transition		
Conclusion:		

D. Materials Needed

List all materials that will be needed to teach this lesson.
Who will be responsible for securing each item?

Materials	*Who Is Responsible For Securing These Materials?*

E. Misconceptions or Alternative Conceptions

Anticipate how your students will respond to the tasks and activities of the lesson. Identify the possible misconceptions or alternative conceptions about the lesson content. Where do you think students will have difficulty? What questions will you pose or what changes will you make to help nurture students' thinking and understanding of the content?

Misconception	*Ways to Address Misconception*

F. Adjusting Difficulty and Complexity

Describe how you have planned to meet the needs of *all students in your classroom* with varied interests and learning readiness, English-language proficiency, health, physical ability, etc. How will you extend and enrich the learning of students who finish early? How will you support the learning of students struggling with your learning intentions and success criteria?

Difficulty			
Complexity			

G. What Could Go Wrong with This Lesson *and* What Will You Do About It?

Think about this! It may help you avoid an embarrassing situation. This *cannot* include fire drills, interruptions due to announcements, weather, or other emergencies.

Appendix C

Evaluation of Learning

I. How did your actual teaching of the lesson differ from your plans? Describe the changes and explain why you made them.

II. Student Work Sample Analysis: Based on the artifacts and checks for understanding, what can you conclude about your students' learning? Did they learn? Who learned? What did they learn? What evidence can you offer that your conclusions are valid?

Look at the assessment data and identify who appears to fall into these three categories: (1) gets it; (2) has some good ideas, but there's still room for learning; and (3) does not get it yet. Organize your responses to the following questions in a chart/table form similar to the one that follows.

	Gets it.	*Has some good ideas, but...*	*Does not get it yet.*
a. What do they understand? How do you know?			
b. Where do they still need support? How do you know?			
c. What questions do I need to ask to clarify what is known and/ understood?			

a. Where is each student's learning within the framework of the SOLO Taxonomy? What evidence do you have to support your answer? Please provide student work samples.

	Evidence from Artifacts or Checks for Understanding
Prestructural Thinking	
Unistructural Thinking	
Multistructural Thinking	
Relational Thinking	
Extended Abstract Thinking	

b. What ideas does each student need to work on next?

III. Describe how you will incorporate developmentally appropriate practice in a better or more thorough way if you were to teach this lesson again.

IV. Based on the assessment data you collected, what would you do/teach next if you were the classroom teacher?

V. As a result of planning and teaching this lesson, what have you learned or had reinforced about young children as learners?

VI. As a result of planning and teaching this lesson, what have you learned or had reinforced about teaching?

VII. As a result of planning and teaching this lesson, what have you learned or had reinforced about yourself?

Appendix D
Misconceptions Interview Task

Interviewing and talking to our learners is an effective way to understand the student's beliefs and understandings about a science topic or concept. Unfortunately, many of these strongly held beliefs about science topics or concepts are inaccurate. These misconceptions create barriers to future learning because learning science is a process of construction and reconstruction of previously held personal theories. That is, one of the most important influences on future learning is the prior knowledge or background knowledge of the learner. This task is designed to provide you with the experience of uncovering a student's beliefs and understandings about a science topic or concept, evaluating the validity or his or her understanding, and using this initial assessment to determine where to begin in the learning progression.

Task Description

- Using available resources, build your own background knowledge about the topic or concept. Then identify noted misconceptions about the topic or concept. For example, typing "misconceptions about the seasons" into an Internet search engine will provide a lot of information.
- Develop a series of open-ended questions that explore students' understandings of the topic or concept and uncovers their beliefs. Double-check to ensure that your protocol has questions that require students to contextualize the topic or concept, probe their understandings, and elicit their thinking about the topic or concept.
- Identify a random sample of learners in your classroom to interview.
- Conduct the interview, taking careful notes about student responses. Offer them the option of drawing their explanations if that is helpful.
- Once you have completed several interviews, use your notes and drawings from a student responses to uncover his or her beliefs and understandings about a science topic or concept, evaluate the validity of his or her understanding, and use this initial assessment to determine where to begin in the learning progression. Questions to guide your thinking include the following:
    - o What is the valid explanation of the topic or concept?
    - o What are the student's beliefs about or understandings of the topic or concept?
    - o Does the student have misconceptions about the topic or concept?

- o Are the student's beliefs and understandings of the scientific topic or concept accurate?
- o Where is this student developmentally (i.e., SOLO Taxonomy)? How does this relate to his or her explanation of the topic or concept?
- o How does this help you determine the starting point in your learning progression for this standard or chunk of the standard?

Helpful Hints for Questions

Do not just ask questions. Engage the student in a conversation. Respond to his or her answers with points of your own.

- The student you interview may be eager to hear about your own explanations. Avoid this by following up on student responses with probing questions.
- Students should share stories about their experiences with the topic or concept. This is valuable information.

Becoming more aware of strongly held misconceptions or alternative conceptions about science phenomena will help you anticipate, identify, and address these strongly held ideas in your inclusive early childhood science classroom.

Appendix E
Community Resource Task

Out-of-School Time Science and Informal Science Learning Environments

The overall goal of this task is to help you to become familiar with resources that exist outside the parameters of the classroom that can be used to facilitate science instruction in the classroom and to increase students' knowledge and understanding of the world. In addition, this task provides an opportunity to engage in the decision-making process associated with the selection and planning of appropriate out-of-school time science or informal science learning environments.

Locate community resources that can be used as an out-of-school-time science or informal science learning environments. The resource can be located *in* or *outside* of our specific town, city, or state. Remember, "virtual field trips" are an option. You must visit, physically or remotely, each community resource. Visit the sites that you have chosen and consider how you can use those sites as out-of-school time science or informal science learning environments. Use the following questions and guidelines to reflect on how this will support learners in meeting the learning intention and demonstrating the associated success criteria:

1. What and where is the site? Is this a walking visit, an official field trip, or a virtual field trip?
2. How is the site connected to the inclusive early childhood science curriculum (i.e., what you and your students are doing in the classroom)?
3. How is this site connected to the standards (state and national standards)?
4. How could this site be used to integrate other content areas into inclusive early childhood science? Or the other way around?
5. How does this site support physical, social, emotional, and cognitive development?
6. How does this site provide opportunities for promoting language development in inclusive early childhood learning?
7. How does this site provide opportunities to interlace *everyday concepts* and *scientific concepts*?
8. What opportunities to integrate *play pedagogy* are offered by this site?

9. How does this site promote an inclusive early childhood science environment?
10. How does this site fuse the boundaries between the learning that occurs in the home and in the inclusive early childhood classroom?
11. What would you do to prepare the class to visit this site? How would you follow up in your inclusive early childhood classroom after visiting this site?
12. What communication would you need to create to inform parents/guardians of your students in your class by describing the trip and obtaining permission for their son/daughter to attend the trip?

Build a database of community resources that not only support the learning intentions and success criteria but also create pathways for greater family and community engagement.

Appendix F
Science Express Task

This microteaching experience provides an opportunity to plan, implement, and evaluate science learning during cooperative, collaborative learning stations.

Reflective Questioning or Guidelines for Developing the Science Express

1. **Rationale**

   Why are you choosing these activities?

   A. Theory of learning: Use relevant theorists, such as Piaget, Bruner, or Vygotsky, as well as current research to justify your instructional approach. Discuss some of the basic tenets of the theory that influence how children learn science. For example, if you are planning activities for a third-grade class, what do we know about how eight-year-olds learn science?

   B. Developmental level: Discuss how ten-year-olds process information and interact with each other socially. Specifically, consider the appropriateness of this project for the age and stage of the children in the class. How will you design the activity to reflect the developmental level of eight-year-olds? Do any of the children have special learning challenges?

   C. Connection: Why choose these activities? How does it fit in terms of the learning intentions and success criteria?

   D. Purpose: The stations may coincide with the day's learning intention but can provide additional information that extends the learning or provides opportunities for review. Why are stations important to students' learning at this time? Is this an interdisciplinary group lesson? Why or why not?

2. **Content**

   A. What content, practices, and understandings are to be learned during each station?

   B. What standards, specifically disciplinary core ideas, crosscutting concepts, and science and engineering practices will be addressed in the stations?

   C. What additional standards are addressed (e.g., art, English language arts, mathematics, social studies)?

3. **Mapping It Out**
   A. Map out the arrangement of the stations and how learners will move from station to station. What will be the cue to wrap up working at one station, and what will be the cue for moving to the next station?
   B. How will you communicate the main ideas evident in the stations?
4. **Stations**
   A. The stations should provide opportunities for students to engage in inquiry learning. In addition, they should offer an opportunity for children to explore and experience the practices of science.
   B. Set up the activity. What can you do to facilitate cleanup? Should you put plastic on the floor? Are the required materials available? Are the materials safe? *Be creative to minimize the cost of your stations.*
   C. What trade books, websites, and other materials will be useful?
   D. What questions might be used to guide students as they explore the stations? What are the alternative explanations that might be offered?
5. **Evaluation**
   A. How will you evaluate the effectiveness of the station? How will you know the students gained additional information during this experience? Did they engage in inquiry? Did they gain additional information about how the world works? How will you know?

Will you develop a scoring guide that you can use for evaluating students? Will the scoring guide evaluate how well the students met the learning intentions and success criteria?

Appendix G
Checks for Understanding Task

Educational researcher John Hattie has devoted the last several decades to accumulating meta-analyses that look at influences on student achievement. This collection of meta-analyses includes tens of thousands of studies and more than 300 million students (Hattie, 2012). From this expansive collection of research on student achievement, six key findings have emerged:

1. Student achievement is strongly associated with teachers' belief that their primary role is to assess their effect on student learning.
2. Similarly, student learning is enhanced when teachers work together as they assess and understand their effect on that learning.
3. Teachers must base their classroom teaching on the prior knowledge and experiences of their students.
4. Students benefit from clear and explicit success criteria so that they know exactly what success looks like by the end of the learning experience.
5. Student achievement is strongly correlated when teachers use developmentally appropriate proportions of surface- and deep-level learning.
6. Student learning benefits when the expectation is not to just "do your best" but meet developmentally appropriate challenges (Hattie, 2012).

Specifically, the *check for understanding task* requires you to accomplish the following:

1. Design checks for understanding that are based on learning intentions and success criteria developed throughout this book.
    a. Your check for understanding should last between three and five minutes.
    b. The check for understanding should generate data on your students' understandings of the content and practices associated with a particular learning experience.

Checks for Understanding Reflection

Guiding Questions

The following questions will support your reflection about the checks for understanding.

I. Strategic Planning and Deliberate Use of Strategies

a. What was the nature of the thinking when designing your check for understanding?
b. How did you arrive at the final product, approach, or strategy?
c. How did you decide the topics, concepts, or ideas from the reading upon which to focus?

II. The Use of Student Voice and How Students are Understanding Content
a. What do you expect the students' responses to tell you about their learning?
b. What trends or patterns are you looking for in the students' responses?
c. What inferences will you be able to make about the students' levels of understanding?
d. What is the evidence you have to support these inferences?

III. Nature of the Feedback
a. What feedback will be provided by these checks for understanding? Feedback to you? Feedback to your students?
b. How will you use this feedback in your future teaching experiences?

IV. Gathering and Analyzing Data (after administering the checks for understanding)
a. Based on the previous analysis, what would be your next step instructionally?
b. What feedback would you give the students?
c. What is the evidence you have to support these next steps?
d. How would you adjust the learning for these students?
e. What led you to change the trajectory of the learning?

V. Overall Reflection
a. How has this experience changed your thinking about teaching and learning?
b. What, from this experience, will you apply to your future teaching experiences?

Appendix H
Assignment Analysis Task

Step 1: Determine the Key Features of the Assignment

Text Type (literary, informational, visual, multiple texts) **Text Length** (sentences, paragraphs, pages, etc.) **Text Complexity** (quantitative and qualitative values that suggest the grade range of the selected text, academic vocabulary)	
Output (verbal, no writing, note taking, one or two sentences, multiple short responses, one paragraph, multiple paragraphs)	
Length of Assignment (15 minutes or less, one or two class periods, multiple weeks, linked to an ongoing project quarter/semester/year)	
Student Thinking *SOLO Taxonomy* Unistructural Multistructural Relational Extended abstract	

Step 2: Assignment Analysis

1. Alignment with Standards
A standards-aligned assignment has essential features. First and most important, it must be grade-level appropriate and aligned to the learning intentions and success criteria. The assignment must embrace instructional shifts, including regular practice with complex texts; academic language; reading, writing, and speaking using evidence; and building knowledge through disciplinary core ideas, crosscutting concepts, and the use of science and engineering practices. The assignment has clear instructions so that students can fully understand what is expected of them. This may be through visuals, exemplars, or teacher modeling.

Assignment Analysis for Alignment with Standards:
2. Centrality of Text *The centrality of the text allows students to grapple with Tier 2 and Tier 3 vocabulary. Students have the opportunity to display increasing expertise in science and engineering practices through academic discourse. Specifically, an assignment fully reflects the role of literacy and academic vocabulary when engaged in disciplinary core ideas, crosscutting concepts, and the use of science and engineering practices.*
Assignment Analysis for Centrality of Text:
3. Cognitive Challenge *The cognitive work required ranges from simple to complex. Use The SOLO Taxonomy in your analysis.*
Assignment Analysis for Cognitive Challenge:
4. Motivation and Engagement *For learners to thrive and achieve at high levels, educators must embrace both the content of the curriculum and the design of instruction. Each of these elements affects student attention, interest, motivation, and cognitive effort and must be considered in the design of assignments. Specifically, we prioritize expectations, emotional safety, social interaction, authenticity, choice, novelty, sense of audience, and personal response. Students must be given some level of autonomy and independence in their tasks - with rigor (complexity and difficulty) maintained across all options. And the tasks must be relevant, as they focus on authentic experiences and give students the opportunity to make connections with the big ideas and driving questions.*
Assignment Analysis for Motivation and Engagement:
5. Adjusting the Level of Difficulty *Finding the right level of rigor that moves learning forward requires that we plan for different levels of rigor and prepare to make adjustments to the rigor as learners engage in learning tasks. Therefore, one of the key ideas is that we make adjustments to any task so that all learners have equity of access to the highest level of complex thinking possible and the potential to be successful. When designing and implementing tasks, adjust the level of difficulty, and maintain the level of complexity.*
Assignment Analysis for Adjusting the Level of Difficulty:

Source: Adapted from Santelises, S. & Dabrowski, J. (2015). *Checking in: Do classroom assignments reflect today's higher standards?* The Education Trust.

References

Adams, G. L., & Engelmann, S. (1996). *Research on direct instruction: 25 years beyond Distar*. Seattle, WA: Educational Achievement Systems.

Ainsworth, L., & Donovan, K. (2019). *Rigorous curriculum design: How to create curricular units of study that align standards, instruction, and assessment* (2nd ed.). Rexford, NY: International Center for Leadership in Education, Inc.

Allen, R. H. (2001). *Impact teaching: Ideas and strategies for teachers to maximize student learning*. Boston, MA: Allyn & Bacon.

Almarode, J., Fisher, D., Frey, N., & Hattie, J. A. C. (2018). *Visible learning for science. What works best to optimize student learning grades K-12*. Thousand Oaks, CA: Corwin Press.

Almarode, J., & Vandas, K. (2019). *Clarity for learning: Five essential practices for empowering students and teachers*. Thousand Oaks, CA: Corwin Press.

Amsel, E., & Brock, S. (1996). The development of evidence evaluation skills. *Cognitive Development*, 11, 523–550.

Antonetti, J., & Garver, J. (2015). *17,000 classroom visits can't be wrong*. Alexandria, VA: ASCD.

Babikian, Y. (1971). An empirical investigation to determine the relative effectiveness of discovery, laboratory, and expository methods of teaching science concepts. *Journal of Research in Science Teaching*, 8, 201–209.

Barnett, M., & Moran, J. (2002). Addressing children's alternative frameworks of the Moon's phases and eclipses. *International Journal of Science Education*, 24, 859–879.

Bass, J. E., Contant, T. L., & Carin, A. A. (2009). *Teaching science as inquiry* (11th ed.). New York, NY: Pearson.

Battelle for Kids. (2020, April). *Portrait of a graduate*. Retrieved from https://portraitofagraduate.org/

Beck, I. L., McKeown, M. G., & Kucan, L. (2013). *Bring words to life: Robust vocabulary instruction* (2nd ed.). New York, NY: Guilford Press.

Bell, B. (2005). *Learning in science: The Waikato research*. New York, NY: RoutledgeFalmer.

Bell, R. L. (2008). *Teaching the nature of science through process skills: Activities for grades 3–8*. New York, NY: Allyn & Bacon/Longman.

Berliner, D. C. (1987). Simple views of effective teaching and a simple theory of classroom instruction. In D. Berliner & B. Rosenshine (Eds.), *Talks to teachers*. New York, NY: Random House.

Berliner, D. C. (1990). What's all the fuss about instructional time? In M. Ben-Peretz & R. Bromme (Eds.), *The nature of time in schools: Theoretical concepts, practitioner perceptions* (pp. 3–35). New York, NY: Teachers College Press.

Biggs, J. B., & Collis, K. F. (1982). *Evaluating the quality of learning: The SOLO taxonomy (structure of observed learning outcome)*. New York, NY: Academic Press.

Black, P., & Wiliam, D. (1998). Assessment and classroom learning. *Assessment in Education: Principles, Policy & Practice*, 5(1), 7–74.

Blackburn, B. R. (2018). *Rigor is not a four-letter word*. New York, NY: Routledge.

Boaler, J. (1998). Open and closed mathematics: Student experiences and understandings. *Journal for Research in Mathematics Education*, 29(1), 41–62.

Bosse, S., Jacobs, G., & Anderson, T. L. (2009). Science in the air. *Young Children*, pp. 10–15, reprinted and retrieved at www.naeyc.org/files/yc/file/200911/BosseWeb1109.pdf

Buck Institute for Education. (2020, May). PBLworks. Retrieved from https://www.pblworks.org/research

Bybee, R. (1997). *Achieving scientific literacy: From purposes to practices*. Portsmouth, NH: Heinemann Publications.

Bybee, R., & Landes, N. M. (1990). Science for life and living: An elementary school science program from Biological Sciences Improvement Study (BSCS). *The American Biology Teacher*, 52(2), 92–98.

Bybee, R. W. (2015). *The BSCS 5E instructional model: Creating teachable moments*. Arlington, VA: NSTA Press.

Carey, S. (1985). *Conceptual change in childhood*. Cambridge, MA: The MIT Press.

Carter, G., Jones, G., & Rua, M. (2003). Effects of partners' ability on achievement and conceptual organization of high-achieving fifth-grade students. *Science Education*, 87, 94–111.

Chen, Z., & Klahr, D. (1999). All other things being equal: Children's acquisition of the control of variables strategy. *Child Development*, 70(5), 1098–1120.

Chinn, C. A., & Malhotra, B. A. (2002). Epistemologically authentic inquiry in schools: A theoretical framework for evaluating inquiry tasks. *Science Education*, 86, 175–218.

Darling-Hammond, L., & Youngs, P. (2002). Defining "highly qualified teachers": What does "scientifically-based research" actually tell us? *Educational Researcher*, 31(9), 13–25.

DEC/NAEYC. (2009). *Early childhood inclusion: A summary*. Chapel Hill, NC: The University of North Carolina, FPG Child Development Institute.

Dohrenwend, B. S. (1965). Some effects of open and closed questions on respondents' answers. *Human Organization*, 24(2), 175–184.

Driver, R., Squires, A., Rushworth, P., & Wood-Robinson, V. (1994). *Making sense of secondary science: Research into children's ideas*. London, UK: Routledge.

Duran, L. B., & Duran, E. (2004). The 5E instructional model: A learning cycle approach for inquiry-based science teaching. *The Science Education Review, 3(2)*, 49–58.

Earl, L. (2003). *Assessment as learning: Using classroom assessment to maximise student learning*. Thousand Oaks, CA: Corwin Press.

Erickson, F. (2011). On noticing teacher noticing. In M. G. Sherin, V. R. Jacobs, & R. A. Philipp (Eds.), *Mathematics teacher noticing: Seeing through the teachers' eyes* (pp. 3–13). New York, NY: Routledge.

Estes, T. H., & Mintz, S. L. (2015). *Instruction: A models approach* (7th ed.). New York, NY: Pearson.

Feelings, M., & Feelings, T. (1971). *Moja means one: Swahili counting book*. New York, NY: Puffin Books.

Fisher, D., Frey, N., & Almarode, J. (2021). *Student learning communities: A springboard for academic and social-emotional development*. Alexandria, VA: ASCD.

Fisher, D., Frey, N., Almarode, J., Flores, K., & Nagel, D. (2020). *PLC+. Better decisions and greater impact, by design*. Thousand Oaks, CA: Corwin Press.

Fisher, D., Frey, N., Amador, O., & Assof, J. (2019). *The teacher clarity playbook. A hands-on guide to creating learning intentions & success criteria for organized, effective instruction*. Thousand Oaks, CA: Corwin Press.

Fisher, D., Frey, N., & Hattie, J. (2016). *Visible learning for literacy*. Thousand Oaks, CA: Corwin.

Forness, S. R., Kavale, K. A., Blum, I. M., & Lloyd, J. W. (1997). Mega-analysis of meta-analyses. *Teaching Exceptional Children*, 29(6), 4–9.

Frey, N., Hattie, J., & Fisher, D. (2018). *Developing assessment-capable visible learners*. Thousand Oaks, CA: Corwin.

Gelman, R., & Brenneman, K. (2004). Science learning pathways for young children. *Early Childhood Research Quarterly*, 19, 150–158.

Gelman, R., Brenneman, K., Macdonald, G., & Roman, M. (2010). *Preschool pathways to science: Ways of doing, thinking, communicating and knowing about science*. Baltimore, MD: Brookes Publishing.

Goodrum, D., Hackling, M., & Rennie, L. (2001). *The status and quality of teaching and learning of science in Australian schools*. Canberra, ACT: Commonwealth of Australia.

Graham, S., Kiuhara, S. A., & MacKay, M. (2020). Effects of writing on learning in science, social studies, and mathematics: A meta-analysis. *Review of Educational Research*, 90(2), 179–226.

Guskey, T. R., & McTighe, J. (2016). Pre-assessment: Promises and cautions. *Educational Leadership*, 73(17), 38–43.

Hadden, R. A., & Johnstone, A. H. (1982). Primary school pupils' attitudes to science: The year of formation. *International Journal of Science Education*, 4, 397–407.

Hamilton, L., Stecher, B., & Yuan, K. (2008). *Standards-based reform in the United States, history, research, and future directions*. Santa Monica, CA: RAND Corporation.

Harlen, W. (1997). Primary teachers' understanding in science and its impact in the classroom. *Research in Science Education*, 27, 323–337.

Hattie, J. A. (2012). *Visible learning for teachers: Maximizing impact on learning*. New York, NY: Routledge.

Hattie, J. A. C. (2009). *Visible learning: A synthesis of over 800 meta-analyses relating to achievement*. New York, NY: Routledge.

Hattie, J. A. C., & Donoghue, G. M. (2016). Learning strategies: A synthesis and conceptual model. *NPJ Science of Learning*, 1, 1-13.

Hockett, J. A., & Doubet, K. J. (2014). Turning on the lights: What pre assessments can do. *Educational Leadership*, 71(4), 50–54.

Hook, P., & Mills, J. (2011). *SOLO taxonomy: A guide for schools. Book 1.* Laughton, UK: Essential Resources Educational Publishers Limited.

Hook, P., & Mills, J. (2012). *SOLO taxonomy: A guide for schools. Book 2.* Laughton, UK: Essential Resources Educational Publishers Limited.

Jacobs, V. R., Lamb, L. L. C., Philipp, R. A., & Schappelle, B. P. (2011). Deciding how to respond on the basis of children's understandings. In M. G. Sherin, V. R. Jacobs, & R. A. Philipp (Eds.), *Mathematics teacher noticing: Seeing through the teachers' eyes* (pp. 3-13). New York, NY: Routledge.

Jimenez, B., Browder, D., Spooner, F., & DiBiase, W. (2012). Inclusive inquiry science using peer-mediated embedded instruction for students with moderate intellectual disability. *Exceptional Children*, 78, 301–317.

Johnson, D. W., & Johnson, R. (1999). *Learning together and alone: Cooperative, competitive, and individualistic learning* (5th ed.). Boston, MA: Allyn & Bacon.

Joyce, B., & Weil, M., & Calhoun, E. (2003). *Models of teaching* (7th ed.). Englewood Cliffs, NJ: Prentice Hall.

Katz, L. G., & Chard, S. C. (2000). *Engaging children's minds: The project approach* (2nd ed.). Stamford, CT: Ablex.

Kirby, J., & Biggs, J. (1981). *Cognitive abilities, students' learning processes and academic achievement.* Canberra,ACT: Final Report to Australian Research Grants Committee.

Klahr, D., & Nigam, M. (2004). The equivalence of learning paths in early science instruction: Effects of direct instruction and discovery learning. *Psychological Science*, 15, 661–667.

Krajcik, J. S., & Shin, N. (2014). Project-based learning. In R. K. Sawyer (Ed.), *The Cambridge handbook of the learning sciences* (2nd ed., pp. 275–297). Cambridge, UK: Cambridge University Press.

Leahy, S., Lyon, C., Thompson, M., & Wiliam, D. (2005). Classroom assessment: Minute-by-minute and day-by-day. *Educational Leadership*, 63(3), 18–24.

Lee, H., Chung, H. Q., Zhang, Y., Abedi, J., & Warschauer, M. (2020). The effectiveness and features of formative assessment in US K-12 education: A systematic review. *Applied Measurement in Education*, 33(2), 124–140.

Lin, S., Luo, W., Tong, F., Irby, B. J., Alecio, R. L., Rodriguez, L., & Chapa, S. (2020). Data-based student learning objectives for teacher evaluation. *Cogent Education*, 7(1), 1–19.

Loughran, J. (2013). Pedagogy: Making sense of the complex relationship between teaching and learning. *Curriculum Inquiry*, 43(1), 118–141.

Maltese, A. V., & Tai, R. H. (2010). Eyeballs in the fridge: Sources of early interest in science. *International Journal of Science Education*, 32, 669–685.

Martin, S. (2012). *Using SOLO as a framework for teaching.* Laughton, UK: Essential Resources Educational Publishers Limited.

Marzano, R. J. (2007). *The art and science of teaching: A comprehensive framework for effective instruction.* Alexandria, VA: Association for Supervision and Curriculum Development.

Mastropieri, M. A., & Scruggs, T. E. (1994). Text versus hands-on science curriculum: Implications for students with disabilities. *Remedial and Special Education*, 15, 72–85.

McDevitt, T. M., & Ormrod, J. E. (2013). *Child development and education* (5th ed.). New York, NY: Pearson.

Meador, D. (2020, February 11). *High stakes testing: Overtesting in America's Public Schools.* Retrieved from https://www.thoughtco.com/high-stakes-testing-overtesting-in-americas-public-schools-3194591

Medina, J. (2014). *Brain rules: 12 principles for surviving and thriving at work, home, and school.* Seattle, WA: Pear Press.

Milner, H. R. (2013). Scripted and narrowed curriculum reform in urban schools. *Urban Education*, 49(7), 743–749.

Moursund, D. G. (2003). *Project-based learning in an information technology environment.* Eugene, OR: ISTE.

Murphy, C., & Beggs, J. (2005). *Primary science in the UK: A scoping study. Final report to the Wellcome Trust.* London, UK: Wellcome Trust.

National Association for the Education of Young Children (NAEYC). (2013). *All criteria document*, pp. 17–18. Retrieved from www.naeyc.org/files/academy/file/AllCriteriaDocument.pdf

National Research Council (NRC). (2007). *Taking science to school: Learning and teaching science in grades K-8.* Washington, DC: National Academies Press.

National Research Council (NRC). (2012). *A framework for K-12 science education: Practices, crosscutting concepts, and core ideas*. Washington, DC: National Academies Press.

National Science Teachers Association (NSTA). (2002). *NSTA position statement: Elementary school science*.

National Science Teachers Association (NSTA). (2009). *NSTA position statement: Parent involvement in science learning*.

National Science Teachers Association (NSTA). (2014). *NSTA position statement: Early childhood science education*.

NGSS Lead States. (2013). *Next generation science standards: For states, by states*. Washington, DC: The National Academies Press.

Novak, G., Patterson, E. T., Gavrin, A. D., & Christian, W. (1999). *Just-in-time teaching: Blending active learning with web technology*. Upper Saddle River, NJ: Prentice Hall.

Osborne, J. F. (2008). Engaging young people with science: Does science education need a new vision? *School Science Review*, 89, 67–74.

Osborne, J. F., & Simon, S. (1996). Primary science: Past and future directions. *Studies in Science Education*, 26, 99–147.

Park, V., & Datnow, A. (2009). Co-constructing distributed leadership: District and school connections in data-driven decision making. *School Leadership & Management*, 29(5), 477–494.

Pianta, R. C., Belsky, J., Houts, R., & Morrison, F. (2007). Opportunities to learn in America's elementary classrooms. *Science*, 315, 1795–1796.

Pijanowski, L. (2018). *Architects of deeper learning. Intentional design for high-impact instruction*. Rexford, NY: International Center for Leadership in Education, Inc.

Rahayu, S., & Tytler, R. (1999). Progression in primary school children's conceptions of burning: Toward an understanding of the concept of substance. *Research in Science Education*, 29, 295–312.

Riggs, I., & Knochs, L. (1990). Towards the development of an elementary teacher's science teaching efficacy belief instrument. *Science Education*, 74, 625–637.

Ritchhart, R., Church, M., & Morrison, K. (2011). *Making thinking visible. How to promote engagement, understanding, and independence for all learners*. San Francisco, CA: Josey-Bass.

Robinson, V. (2011). *Student-centered leadership*. San Francisco, CA: Jossey-Bass.

Robinson, V. M. J., Phillips, G., & Timperley, H. (2002). Using achievement data for school-based curriculum review: A bridge too far? *Leadership and Policy in Schools*, 1(1), 3–29.

Rutherford, F. J., & Ahlgren, A. (1990). Science for all Americans [earlier version appeared as: American Association for Advancement of Science (AAAS) (1989)]. Science for all Americans: A Project 2061 report on literacy goals in science, mathematics, and technology. Washington, DC: AAAS.]. New York: Oxford University Press.

Samarapungavan, A. (1992). Children's judgements in theory choice tasks: Scientific rationality in childhood. *Cognition*, 45, 1–32.

Santagata, R. (2011). From teacher noticing to a framework for analyzing and improving classroom lessons. In M. G. Sherin, V. R. Jacobs, & R. Philipp (Eds.), *Mathematics teacher noticing: Seeing through teachers' eyes* (pp. 152–168). New York, NY: Routledge.

Santelises, S., & Dabrowski, J. (2015). *Checking in: Do classroom assignments reflect today's higher standards?* The Education Trust.

Schulz, L. E., & Bonawitz, E. B. (2007). Serious fun: Preschoolers engage in more exploratory play when evidence is confounded. *Developmental Psychology*, 43, 1045–1050.

Scriven, M. (1967). The methodology of evaluation. In R. W. Tyler (Ed.), *Perspectives on curriculum evaluation* (pp. 39–83). Chicago, IL: Rand McNally.

Sherin, M. G., Jacobs, V. R., & Philipp, R. A. (2011). Situating the study of teacher noticing. In M. G. Sherin, V. R. Jacobs, & R. A. Philipp (Eds.), *Mathematics teacher noticing: Seeing through the teachers' eyes* (pp. 3–13). New York, NY: Routledge.

Sodian, B., Zaitchik, D., & Carey, S. (1991). Young children's differentiation of hypothetical beliefs from evidence. *Child Development*, 62, 753–766.

Spooner, F., Knight, V., Browder, D. M., Jimenez, B., & DiBiase, W. (2011). Evaluating evidence-based practice in teaching science content to students with severe developmental disabilities. *Research and Practice for Persons with Severe Disabilities*, 36, 62–75.

Stein, S. J., & McRobbie, C. J. (1997). Students' conceptions of science across the years of schooling. *Research in Science Education*, 27, 611–628.

Strand-Cary, M., & Klahr, D. (2008). Developing elementary science skills: Instructional effectiveness and path difference. *Cognitive Development*, 23, 488–511.

Tai, R. H., Liu, C., Maltese, A. V., & Fan, X. (2006). Planning for early careers in science. *Science*, 312, 1143–1144.

Tomkins, S. P., & Tunnicliffe, S. D. (2001). Looking for ideas: Observation, interpretation and hypothesis-making by 12-year-old pupils undertaking science investigations. *International Journal of Science Education*, 23, 791–813.

Tytler, R., & Peterson, S. (2003). Tracing young children's scientific reasoning. *Research in Science Education*, 33, 433–465.

Virginia Department of Education (VDOE). (2012). *Practices for science investigation: Kindergarten-physics progression*. Richmond, VA: Author.

Visible Learning Meta X. (2020, April). Retrieved from https://www.visiblelearningmetax.com/

Wandersee, J., Mintzes, J., & Novak, J. (1994). Research on alternative conceptions in science. In D. Gabel (Ed.), *Handbook of research on science teaching and learning* (pp. 177–210). New York, NY: Macmillan.

Weizman, A., Shwartz, Y., & Fortus, D. (2008). The driving question board. *The Science Teacher*, 75(8), 33–37.

Wiggins, G., & McTighe, J. (2005). *Understanding by design* (2nd ed.). Alexandria, VA: Association for Supervision and Curriculum Development.

William, D., & Leahy, S. (2015). *Embedding formative assessment. Practical techniques for K-12 classrooms*. West Palm Beach, FL: Learning Sciences International.

Willingham, D. T. (2009). *Why don't students like school? A cognitive scientist answers questions about how the mind works and what it means for the classroom*. San Francisco, CA: Jossey-Bass.

Yin, Y., Tomita, M. K., & Shavelson, R. J. (2008). Diagnosing and dealing with student misconceptions: Floating and sinking. *Science Scope*, 31(8), 34–39.

Zembal-Saul, C., McNeill, K. L., & Hershberger, K. (2012). *What's your evidence?: Engaging K-5 children in constructing explanations in science*. Boston, MA: Pearson.

Zimmerman, C. (2000). The development of scientific reasoning skills. *Developmental Review*, 20, 99–149.

Zimmerman, C. (2007). The development of scientific thinking skills in elementary and middle school. *Developmental Review*, 27, 172–223.

Index

Page numbers in *italic* indicate figures. Page numbers in **bold** indicate tables; *a* refers to appendix.